Organizing
the Presidency

STEPHEN HESS

Organizing the Presidency

THIRD EDITION

with JAMES P. PFIFFNER

BROOKINGS INSTITUTION PRESS
Washington, D.C.

Copyright © 2002

THE BROOKINGS INSTITUTION

1775 Massachusetts Avenue, N.W., Washington, D.C. 20036

www.brookings.edu

Library of Congress Cataloging-in-Publication data

Hess, Stephen.

Organizing the Presidency / Stephen Hess.— 3rd ed.

    p.   cm.

Includes bibliographical references and index.

    ISBN 0-8157-3638-X (cloth : alk. paper) –

    ISBN 0-8157-3637-1 (pbk. : alk. paper)

1. Presidents—United States—Staff.   2. United States—
Politics and government—1933–1945.   3. United States—Politics
and government—1945–1989.   4. United States—Politics and
government—1989–   I. Title.

    JK552 .H47 2002

    352.2'0973—dc21   2002011827

9 8 7 6 5 4 3 2 1

Typeset in Adobe Caslon

Composition by R. Lynn Rivenbark

Macon, Georgia

FOR

Rachel Elizabeth Cody Hess

who will organize her presidency
in 2036, if she chooses to run

Foreword

Steve Hess's *Organizing the Presidency* is not just a book but an institution—one that Brookings is proud to be associated with.

When the first edition appeared in 1976, Gilbert Y. Steiner, acting president of Brookings and a distinguished political scientist, began his foreword: "The presidency has provided a rich field of inquiry for social scientists and historians, but its organization has remained largely unexamined. Partly, one suspects, this is because the inner workings of the White House have been hidden from public scrutiny by some former presidential assistants and mythologized by others. It may also be that scholars have been little attracted to what seemed to be questions of mechanics."

That is no longer true. A quarter of a century later there is a vast literature and vigorous debate in the press and in public policy institutions about the right and wrong ways presidents organize their administrations. That's partly due to Steve Hess. His book played a seminal role in framing the issues at a time when the nation was searching for an antidote to the dark side of Richard Nixon's White House. Written with the broad knowledge gained from Steve's service on the staffs of Presidents Eisenhower and Nixon, it was read by the newly elected Jimmy Carter, who promptly sought Steve's advice on organizing his presidency, a tale told in appendix A of this edition. No wonder the book became the main selection of the Fortune Book Club and an alternate selection of the Book of the Month Club.

By the time the second edition appeared in 1988, Bruce K. Maclaury, then Brookings's president, could assert confidently in the foreword that "the organization of the presidency has become a crucial element in directing the policies of the United States." Studying the presidency in terms of "when organizations succeed and where and why they fail" was no longer "largely unexamined." By that time the nation had lived through the organizational disaster known as the Iran-Contra affair.

As this 25th anniversary edition of *Organizing the Presidency* goes to press, carrying the story through the first year of George W. Bush's administration, the nation's chief executive confronts a new organizational challenge: how to rearrange the government to plan and execute a homeland security strategy, a subject that has deeply engaged the scholars at Brookings.

Among colleagues in the political science community whom Steve thanks for their help are Richard F. Fenno, University of Rochester; Fred I. Greenstein, Princeton University; Phillip G. Henderson, Catholic University of America; Charles O. Jones, University of Wisconsin; Martha Joynt Kumar, Towson State University; Paul C. Light, director of the Brookings Center for Public Service; G. Calvin Mackenzie and L. Sandy Maisel, Colby College; Thomas E. Mann, a mainstay of the Brookings Governance Studies program; Richard E. Neustadt, Harvard University; Norman Ornstein, American Enterprise Institute; James P. Pfiffner, George Mason University; Stephen J. Wayne, Georgetown University; and Kathryn Dunn Tenpas, University of Pennsylvania.

Administrative support was provided by Susan Stewart, Elizabeth McAlpine, Gary Harding, and Daniel Reilly. The book originally was edited by James R. Schneider, and Eileen Hughes edited this edition. Janet Walker was managing editor. Lawrence Converse and Susan Woollen were responsible for production and design. The proofreader was Carlotta Ribar, and Susan Fels prepared the index.

We're confident that this latest iteration of a Brookings classic will provide timely and at the same time enduring insight into the evolving organization and management of the American presidency. I wouldn't be surprised if, in due course, one of my successors introduces the golden jubilee edition.

Strobe Talbott
President, Brookings Institution

Washington, D.C.
August 2002

Contents

PART TWO
Redefining the Presidential Task

Organizing
the Presidency

CHAPTER 1

The Evolving Modern Presidency

 This study examines the ways modern presidents have organized their administrations. Primarily it concerns the White House staff and secondarily those other avenues of advice—the Executive Office, the cabinet, the vice president, outsiders—on which presidents rely. The next chapter describes the context in which presidents work from the vantage point of those who have been president. It provides a frame of reference for the subsequent discussion of presidential administrations from Franklin Roosevelt's to George W. Bush's and why presidents have acted the way they have in handling such common duties as personnel selection, congressional relations, press relations, speechwriting, information gathering, and relations with their cabinets and between their department heads and White House assistants.

Presidents before Franklin Roosevelt did not run or manage the executive branch from the White House, at least not in the sense that a chief executive officer runs or manages a corporation. During Roosevelt's first two terms, the White House staff was structured to serve his personal needs. It was considerably bigger though not significantly different from that of his predecessors. Because Roosevelt, in the manner of his cousin Theodore, conceived of the presidency as a "bully pulpit," his assistants were mostly engaged in helping him try to shape public opinion.

There was no National Security Council or National Economic Council with responsibilities for departmental oversight. There was no congressional relations office in the White House. Presidential assistants were considered utility infielders who were moved from one position to another as needed or as the president's fancy dictated.

While Roosevelt did not seek collective counsel from his cabinet, the cabinet officers still had the major responsibility for running their departments, drafting legislation, and lobbying it through Congress. At the same time, however, Roosevelt created myriad new agencies, reporting directly to him, that impinged on the jurisdiction of the cabinet departments.

During Roosevelt's third term some independent power bases were established on the White House staff. Subtly, the direction of decision-making changed. Certain major policies began to be devised in the White House offices of intimate advisers who frequently assumed the prerogatives of the department heads.

The new Executive Office of the President, created in 1939, vastly expanded Roosevelt's outreach, and he began to see a president's task as being chief manager of the executive branch. This alteration was crucial. Roosevelt lived in the White House for twelve years, during which the United States fought a great depression and a great war. As those events encouraged the growth of the central government, his long tenure meant that to an unusual degree his response to that growth and his distinctive style shaped the concept of the office of president. Thus by the time of his death in 1945, most of the elements of the modern presidency were in place, even if in embryonic form. The president, rather than Congress, had clearly become the center of federal attention.

Under Harry Truman, the atomization of the White House—the separation of staff by function—assumed modest momentum. While most of his assistants, like Roosevelt's, were generalists, some handled such specific assignments as labor-management relations or congressional liaison. Hierarchies also started to take shape as top presidential aides began to take on assistants of their own, precedents for the fiefdoms that later characterized the White House.

The distinction between cabinet officers, who advocated policy, and White House staff, who provided the president with personal services, was further obscured in Truman's administration. Moreover, the success of Clark Clifford, Truman's chief counsel, as the main architect of the Fair Deal, illustrated that proximity to the president was a blessing of no small value. The theoretical line between the institutional and personal presidencies that separated the Executive Office from the White House also became more blurred as the Bureau of the Budget provided staff and services for presidential assistants. At the same time, two major units, the Council of Economic Advisers and the National Security Council, joined the White House complex, each giving the president a capability for overseeing important government activities that was not totally dependent on the departments.

The assimilation of power in the White House continued, if a bit more slowly, under Dwight Eisenhower. Having spent most of his life in the military, Eisenhower organized the White House along stricter lines that he found more familiar and congenial. He surrounded himself with a staff secretariat in charge of the flow of papers to and from the Oval Office and a secretariat in charge of the machinery of cabinet meetings. Experts rather than generalists advised on questions he felt were inadequately handled by the departments. An elaborate apparatus was invented to coordinate national security affairs, and a full-scale congressional relations office was added to the White House. Eisenhower's press secretary devised more sophisticated techniques for controlling the flow of news. A chief of staff was now responsible for the proper functioning of all these new offices, which had increased the size of the White House but not its operational capability. Eisenhower still expected cabinet officers to run their departments with a minimum of second-guessing from his staff.

John Kennedy and Lyndon Johnson scuttled much of the machinery they found in the White House because they were told that it was unsuited to the needs of an activist liberal administration and because it made them uncomfortable. Yet even without the paraphernalia of staff and cabinet secretariats, a chief of staff's office, and an overblown National Security Council, the president's personal staff, Executive Office units, and presidential councils continued to grow. Because both presidents wanted government to do more faster, agencies such as the Office of Economic Opportunity were placed directly under the presidential umbrella.

A consequence of the trend toward more direct White House involvement in department operations was that presidential aides sometimes issued instructions to cabinet officers' subordinates. This reflected Kennedy's lack of interest in organizational maintenance, the energy and impatience of his White House staff, and his conception of the presidential office as the moving force of government. By the time the Johnson administration was fully active, "the White House was no longer an antiseptic shrine where high policy was formulated and promulgated in dignity"; it had become, for the first time, "the operational center" of the executive branch.[1]

The Rooseveltian model as adapted by Kennedy attracted some superior people to Washington, raised the level of debate on such issues as civil rights and disarmament, and produced several government initiatives. But the model seemed to have developed flaws. Kennedy took the nation on a roller coaster ride of failures and successes—the Bay of Pigs invasion and the Cuban missile crisis—and when the presidency was inherited by Johnson, who retained most of his predecessor's advisers and who shared Kennedy's faith in the Rooseveltian model, the result was a string of stunning legislative triumphs and massive involvement in Vietnam.

By Johnson's time, the advantages of the personalized presidency and the centralized presidency had been well documented. Now the liabilities began to come under serious questioning. The personalized presidency largely depends on the president's ability to mobilize public opinion to put pressure on the government to perform as he desires and to support what he believes is right. If the president lacks this skill or if his vision of "right" is flawed, he cannot compensate for long by relying on the inherent strength of the office. The centralized presidency largely depends on the president's ability to keep lines open to those outside his immediate circle and to resist minutiae. If he is suspicious of cabinet members and relies too heavily on overworked assistants, he is apt to lose perspective and even his sense of reality. Such were the problems that would plague the Nixon presidency.

When Richard Nixon succeeded Johnson he became the first activist conservative president. In the White House, party and ideology had changed, but the direction of the personalized and centralized presidency had not. There was, however, an essential difference in style. Even when the Vietnam protest limited his mobility, Johnson had quested for contacts beyond the confines of the White House; Nixon sought isolation. He structured his White House staff to limit his associations to those with whom he felt most comfortable, his most loyal aides over whom he had greatest control. In the end, this Greta Garbo conception of the presidency proved unsuited to democratic leadership. But even putting aside the character of Richard Nixon and the question of how precedents, when pushed beyond the limits of legality, contributed importantly to Watergate and the resignation of a president, Nixon's mode of operating illustrated the difficulties of running the government through an overly personalized, centralized White House command post, a problem that in varying degrees has plagued the presidents who followed him.[2]

The nine chapters on the administrations of Roosevelt II through Bush II trace the development of four characteristics of the modern presidency.

The first is its prodigious growth. By the time Richard Nixon left office the number of people employed by the White House and the Executive Office was nearly twice that under Johnson, just as Johnson's staff was nearly twice that of Roosevelt's. In sixty-seven years the White House staff has grown from thirty-seven to more than one thousand, the Executive Office staff from zero to many thousands.[3] With the bureaucratizing of the presidency, it is hardly surprising that the White House fell heir to all the problems of a bureaucracy, including the distortion of information as it passes through the chain of command and frustrating delays in decisionmaking.

The modern presidency has also been witness to presidents' increasing suspicion of the permanent government. This has led to a proliferation of functional offices within the White House and to a White House that carries out plans because the president does not trust the bureaucracy to do so. Blaming the bureaucracy is an easy way to gloss over the failures of government, yet trying to run a government without its support is like trying to run a train without an engine.

Another characteristic of the modern presidency is the rising influence of White House staff members on the president and the corresponding decline in cabinet influence. This has meant a serious separation of policy formulation from policy implementation. It also may have created more idiosyncratic policy, since White House aides often operate with fewer constraints and less feel for what can be achieved.

The fourth characteristic is that presidential assistants have increasingly become special pleaders. This trend began benignly enough when Truman gave an aide responsibility for minority group affairs, in a sense creating a presidential spokesman for those who were otherwise underrepresented in the councils of government. Each successive president added other representatives, until under Nixon there were White House assistants for the aged, youth, women, blacks, Jews, labor, Hispanic-Americans, the business community, governors and mayors, artists, and citizens of the District of Columbia, as well as such concerns as drug abuse, energy, environment, physical fitness, volunteerism, telecommunications, and national goals.

Where once the White House had been a mediator of interests, it now had become a collection of interests.

Ultimately the modern presidency has moved toward creating all policy at the White House, overseeing the operations of government from the White House, using White House staff to operate programs of high presidential priority, and representing in the White House all interests that are demographically separable. This attempt can never succeed. Even an overblown White House staff is simply too inadequate a fulcrum for moving the weight of the executive branch, which employs nearly 5 million people and spends over 2 trillion dollars annually.

In the final chapters of this study I propose a redefinition of the tasks of presidents, those activities that they must perform and that cannot be performed by others. The corollary is that the many other tasks currently performed badly by presidents must be performed elsewhere. My contention is that, starting with Roosevelt, presidents have made a serious mistake in asserting that they are the chief managers of the federal government. It is hard to find firm support for such an assertion in the Constitution. In fact, except in the case of the secretary of state and in certain emergency legislation, Congress gives the authority to run programs directly to department heads, not to the president to be redelegated to department heads.

Rather than chief manager, the president is chief political officer of the United States. His major responsibility, in my judgment, is each year to make a relatively small number of highly significant political decisions— among them setting national priorities, which he does through the budget and his legislative proposals, and devising policy to ensure the security of the country, with special attention to those situations that could involve the nation in war.[4]

Agreed, this is a considerably more modest definition of the presidency than national leaders and some scholars have led Americans to expect, and it does not guarantee that U.S. leaders will always make wise decisions. It is also a definition that may warrant rethinking at some future time and under different circumstances. For now, however, it is a definition for presidential conduct that is apt to provide more effective government services, fewer unfulfilled promises, and less alienation in our society.

To the extent that presidents undermine confidence in the presidency by burdening the White House staff beyond its capacity to effect change and deliver services, a different set of reciprocal relationships between presidents, presidential staffs, and cabinet members must be devised. The final chapters of this study seek ways to arrive at a more functional presidency. These ideas do not relate to ideology: a liberal or a conservative president could operate equally well within this framework with markedly different results. My task is to make the case that these arrangements are both necessary and feasible.

PART *One*

Evolution

1933–2002

CHAPTER 2

A Composite Presidency

 A presidency is unique, the reflection of a specific person at a particular historical moment. Still, presidencies share patterns as much as they differ in detail. In their beginnings they reflect one another in the problems they confront and their reactions to them. So too in their endings. Beginnings and endings are themselves disparate experiences within each administration, different in pace, attitude, objectives, and response. Such observations would be readily apparent in a detailed year-by-year description of each presidency. For the purposes of this study, however, I have chosen to base my conclusions on relatively short, sometimes impressionistic, accounts of a dozen modern presidencies. This approach tends to stress differences—how twelve different men chose to organize their different presidencies. Yet because there is also sameness—the similarity of beginnings and endings, for example—this chapter constructs a composite presidency.

What follows, then, is a portrait of the presidency as it appears to a president during his years in office. At times the portrait may seem strange, given that much literature focuses on the powerfulness of the office. The president may seem instead a hapless giant, surrounded by enemies, hemmed in by competing power centers, responding to events that he did not create and cannot control. Yet my conclusion is not that the office is unpowerful. But that is how the presidency increasingly looks to the person

11

who is president. The vantage point may help to explain why presidents act the way they do.

Every second even-numbered year, on a Tuesday between the second and eighth of November, a president is elected. If he is not the incumbent, he has a period of grace until the twentieth of January during which he can organize his administration without having to assume the responsibilities of office. He brings to this task a certain knowledge and experience, and certain obligations and commitments.

If he is like most of his predecessors, he probably has a background as a legislator or a governor. If the nation has recently fought a popular war, he may be a military man. It is possible that he has served as vice president. The odds, however, are great that he has not held an executive position in the federal government.[1] He may, in fact, never have been an executive. Some of his experience will be of considerable value: Lyndon Johnson's years in the Senate gave him an understanding of the workings of Congress and Dwight Eisenhower's military career an understanding of the workings of the Pentagon. By the act of running for the presidency, all elected presidents should have gained some useful understanding of public opinion. But no matter what his experience or how much he may have thought and read about the presidency, a new president is deeply ignorant about the *job* to which he has just been elected. Thus each new president will face a period of orientation and learning, which may take as long as eighteen months.[2] One consequence is that a new president will make some of his most important decisions at a time when he is least capable of deciding wisely.

The White House staff will consist largely of those who surrounded the president during his campaign and who have his trust. They bring to their jobs an understanding of the president-elect, loyalty, and in some cases a set of skills that are transferable from the campaign, such as press relations and scheduling. Their primary interest, however, will usually have been the art of politics, not governance. But while they are apt to begin their White House duties in a personal services relationship with the president, they will eventually acquire more and more governmental responsibilities, for presidents have a habit of giving the jobs at hand to the persons at hand. Some may be qualified to assume operational assignments, but not because they have been campaign workers. One need only look at why they were in the campaign. Often their chief qualification—and an important one in a campaign—was availability; their chief motivations may have been the expectation of excitement, an excess of zeal, or hero worship.

The policy commitments of a new president are found in his campaign speeches, in the party platform, and to a lesser degree in the promises of other members of his party. But these commitments are usually vague, given the tendencies of elective politics to blur the sharp edges of policy disputes. In no sense can they be considered a presidential program—a program has a price tag and relates to available resources. One consequence is that at the time Congress is inclined to be most responsive to the wishes of a president, he is least able to make his wishes known in concrete terms.

On the morning after his victory a president-elect is consumed with thoughts of choosing his cabinet and other matters of the transition. No shadow cabinet waits in the wings, and he suddenly discovers how few people he knows who are qualified to assume major posts in government. "People, people, people!" John Kennedy exclaimed three weeks after his election. "I don't know any people. I only know voters."[3] A president-elect has political debts and obligations, but they are not necessarily to those with the backgrounds he now needs. Thus he sometimes picks incompetents. Often he turns to strangers. With each appointment, he makes a contract to share his responsibilities. If it turns out that the appointee and the president disagree, the appointee can quit or the president can fire the appointee. Either action is a tacit admission of failure on the part of the nation's leader. More commonly, the president and the appointee split their differences and the president loses some part of the direction of his administration.

The presidential transition may be made more difficult by animosities between the incoming and outgoing presidents and by tensions between the incoming president and the civil service. If the newly elected president is from the party out of power, he may have campaigned against bureaucracy, red tape, and the failures of government programs. And almost all presidents-to-be ascribe an alien political coloration to the permanent government. Franklin Roosevelt considered it too conservative; Richard Nixon considered it too liberal. Nor is the new president necessarily paranoid. He is committed to change and perhaps even to reductions in programs and personnel; the permanent government may well see its interests as threatened.

The new president is exhausted from the campaign. He will undoubtedly devote some of his precious transition days to recuperating, and if he holds another position, such as governor, he will also have to wind up that business. Other chores must be attended to—planning for the inauguration, writing an inaugural address, making budget revisions, and getting ready for the opening of Congress. Government has a way of treading water during presidential campaigns as it waits to see who will be its next leader. And decisions postponed build pressure for resolution. This means that on taking office, the new president will be confronted with a backlog of decisions that need to be made. Thus is he presented with great opportunities and great dangers.

The dangers are compounded by the arrogance of an incoming administration. For two years or more the candidate and his closest advisers have been working toward a single goal, one that is incredibly difficult to achieve. Gaining it comes to few, and they have a right to believe that they have succeeded because of their skill, intelligence, political understanding, and hard work. It is not surprising that some of the greatest presidential mistakes—even those of second-term presidents—and some resulting disasters for the nation have come in the immediate afterglow of election victories.[4] Indeed, the bigger the victory, it would seem, the greater the opportunity for disaster.

The new president also finds he has inherited various organizational arrangements that were created to deal with his predecessor's problems. Each administration comes to invent offices that reflect the special talents or deficiencies of appointees, rivalries between advisers, pet projects of the president, and constituent pressures. Sometimes new presidents will overreact to this legacy, as when John Kennedy jettisoned the National Security Council machinery of the Eisenhower administration and was left without an appropriate way for the White House to evaluate foreign policy when the decision on whether to invade Cuba had to be made.

Each president soon comes to agree with Woodrow Wilson: "Governments grow piecemeal, both in their tasks and in the means by which those tasks are to be performed, and very few governments are organized as wise and experienced men would organize them if they had a clean sheet of paper to write upon."[5] Yet no matter how inefficiently or illogically the government is organized, there are those who like it that way. Congress, special-interest groups, and bureaucrats have grown comfortable with existing arrangements and have a vested interest in their continuation. And because the public is not usually much concerned about such bloodless matters as structural change, it is hard to mobilize. Presidents fret a lot about the ill-fitting shape of government, but generally they conclude that serious attempts at restructuring are not worth the political capital they would have to invest. Not even the annals of history reward them for such efforts. So (with the exception of Roosevelt, Nixon, and Carter) they propose only marginal reforms. They add boxes to the organizational chart as needs arise, rarely erase existing offices unless they are glaringly obsolete, and leave government even more cumbersome than they found it.

Other elements of a president's inheritance also come into focus soon after he takes office. He finds that not until his third year will he be able to operate under a budget that his appointees have initiated. Even then much federal spending will be in so-called uncontrollable categories, such as Social Security, and not subject to his influence. He finds that his power to appoint extends to only some 3,000 people out of a government civilian work force of nearly 2 million, and because some of those 3,000 have term appointments, they cannot be removed before their time is up. The new president must also abide by laws and treaties that are not of his making. And there are traditions that he cannot ignore except at great risk, such as senators' prerogatives in choosing judges in their states. His ability to act, he finds, is also limited by the size of his electoral mandate, the composition of Congress and the Supreme Court, the rate of inflation, the balance of payments, the state of the world economy, and whether the nation is at war.

Yet a new administration begins in a state of euphoria. Reporters choose to be kind. Congress is as docile as the president will probably ever see it. There is not yet a record to defend. The president, for the only time, can take a broad-gauged look at existing policies. His popularity ratings in the polls will never again be as high.[6] An adviser to presidents summed up this situation:

> Everything depends on what you do in program formulation during the first six or seven months. I have watched three presidencies and I am increasingly convinced of that. Time goes by so fast. During the first six months or so, the White House staff is not hated by the cabinet, there is a period of friendship and cooperation and excitement. There is some animal energy going for you in those first six to eight months, especially if people perceive things in the same light. If that exists and so long as that exists you can get a lot done. You only have a year at the most for new initiatives, a time when you can establish some programs as your own, in contrast to what has gone on before.[7]

Then the administration has its first foreign crisis and its first domestic scandal. Weaknesses in personnel begin to appear. The novelty of new personalities wears off for the press. The president introduces his legislative program. The process known as the coalition of minorities takes hold: every presidential action will alienate someone; the longer a president is in office, the more actions he must take and the larger the number of those alienated will be. Groups that would not attack him when his popularity was high now become vocal. His poll ratings start to drop.

By the end of his first year the president should have learned two important lessons: that the unexpected is likely to happen and that his plans are unlikely to work out as he had hoped. A U-2 spy plane is shot down over the Soviet Union. Iran takes U.S. citizens hostage. There is a riot in Watts, an uprising in Hungary, an invasion of South Korea. U.S. missiles that he thought had been removed from Turkey were not removed. The Chinese explode a nuclear device earlier than his intelligence forecasts had predicted. Terrorists attack the twin towers of the World Trade Center and the Pentagon. The president finds that much of his time is spent reacting to events over which he has no control or trying to correct the errors of others.

As a result a president starts to turn inward, the quickness of the reaction depending on his personality and his ratio of successes to failures. Reading the morning newspapers becomes less satisfying. They bring bad news. They never seem to get their stories straight. Editorials and columns note only the things that go wrong. The president holds fewer news conferences. He looks for ways to go over the heads of the press corps, such as televised speeches. He grants exclusive interviews to friendly reporters.

Some members of his cabinet, he feels, have gone native, badgering him on behalf of their departments' clients. Others he finds long-winded or not very bright. There are now longer intervals between cabinet meetings. He tells his appointments secretary to make it difficult for certain department heads to get in to see him alone.

Time is running out on his first term. Things are not getting done, or not fast enough. He begins to feel that if he wants action he will have to initiate it himself—meaning through his White House staff. His staff grows bigger, despite his early promises to reduce its size. Types of decisions that used to be made in the departments now need White House clearance. Bottlenecks develop as decisions for too many agencies are funneled through too few presidential assistants. Programs that the president wishes to give high priority to are placed directly within the Executive Office.

The midterm congressional elections approach, and the president tries to restore his luster at the polls. He always fails.[8] His party loses seats. The new Congress is less receptive to his wishes. As Lyndon Johnson summed it up late in his administration:

> You've got to give it all you can that first year. Doesn't matter what kind of majority you come in with. You've got just one year when they treat you right, and before they start worrying about themselves. The third year, you lose votes. . . . The fourth year's all politics. You can't put anything through when half of the Congress is thinking how to beat you. So you've got one year. That's why I tried. Well, we gave it a hell of a lick, didn't we?[9]

The president now devotes a larger part of his time to foreign policy, perhaps as much as two-thirds. This is true even if his interests had been mainly in domestic issues. He takes trips abroad, attends summit meetings, hosts heads of state at the White House. Like Kennedy, he believes that the big difference between domestic and foreign policy concerns "is that between a bill being defeated and the country [being] wiped out."[10] But he also turns to foreign policy because it is the area in which he has the most authority to act and, until recently, the least public and congressional restraint on his actions. Moreover, history usually rewards the foreign policy president, and the longer a president stays in office, the larger his place in history looms before him.

In a president's third year the exodus of his appointees from government begins. Many who were attracted to the glitter of a new administration find that they cannot spare any more time away from their "real" careers, especially if they come from the highly competitive corporate world. Others find that their government experience has created job offers from the private sector that they cannot refuse. Some realize they have made a mistake in coming to Washington, or their families are urging them to return home. Then too, "fatigue becomes a factor," as Henry Kissinger noted.[11] Replacing these people takes on more importance than it once had. And it is more difficult: the lure of a waning administration is not great. The president now often turns to careerists, promoting from within.

By this time, too, personal alliances and rivalries have had full opportunity to develop within the administration. Remembering his experiences on the Truman staff, Clark Clifford recalled how "you develop areas of resistance. You come up with an idea, and you could guarantee in advance those men in government who would take the opposite position, just because you favored something."[12] The president's needs also change. Milton Eisenhower noted that Roosevelt, in the beginning of his presidency, needed ideas (and turned to Raymond Moley, Rexford Tugwell, and A. A. Berle); later he needed legislative and political skills (Thomas Corcoran); and finally his "greatest need was for administrative trouble shooters" (Harry Hopkins and Samuel Rosenman).[13] Rarely can the same person serve all three needs.

The president may have taken office with only the most limited notions of what he wanted to do, but by the second half of his term he has accumulated a long list of his positions, which must be promoted and defended and which will determine whether he is reelected. He now has strong feelings about what is in the national interest and what must be done—regardless of the popularity of his actions. He has come to see the national interest as uniquely his to uphold. When announcing the decision to send troops into Cambodia in the spring of 1970, President Nixon told the American people, "I would rather be a one-term President and do what I believe is right than to be a two-term President at the cost of seeing America become a second-rate power and to see this Nation accept the first defeat in its proud 190-year history."[14] There may have been some posturing in his statement, yet it is a posture eventually assumed by all presidents. The lines harden.

As the administration enters its fourth year, the president's attention snaps back to domestic matters.[15] The political quotient that enters into each presidential act becomes more determining. Appointments are made with an eye to mending fences in his party. High-risk decisions to alter or end programs may be deferred. "Wait until next year, Henry," Roosevelt told Treasury Secretary Morgenthau in May 1936. "I am going to be really radical."[16] Some members of the administration join the campaign staff. Those who stay in government must consider the electoral consequences of their actions. The president finds excuses to make ostensibly nonpolitical speeches around the country. By summer he is nominated for a second term and begins active campaigning.

If the president is reelected, it is largely on the basis of the past—the state of the nation during his incumbency—rather than his promises for the future. What is unspoken is that his next four years will be less productive than the first four. There are some exceptions: Wilson in 1917 and Roosevelt in 1941 had opportunities to preside over "just" wars. Generally, however, at least since Jefferson, the second term is downhill.[17]

But first the newly reelected president will make an effort to recast his administration by bringing in new people or by giving new assignments, as Nixon did in 1973 and Reagan did in 1985. He will take advantage of his renewed popularity by pushing his legislative program, as Johnson did in 1965. He will unveil pet schemes that he had previously kept to himself, as Roosevelt did in 1937 when he proposed to increase the number of Supreme Court justices. In the president's fifth and sixth years, as in his third, there is considerable maneuvering room to shape events. (Deaths and a resignation, of course, have meant that some presidents have not had their full allotment of years in office.)

Then, as Harold Laski observed more than sixty years ago, the two-term tradition (now the two-term limitation) "operates decisively to weaken his influence in the last two years of his reign. Few Presidents have had substantial results to show during that period."[18] The president's party again loses seats in the midterm election—a signal for potential presidential candidates to start increasing their visibility. One way to make news is to attack the incumbent. The attention of the press gradually shifts to these new contenders. Some of the president's executives resign to enter the embryonic campaigns. The personnel pattern of the first term repeats itself, but it is now even more difficult to recruit from outside government. The president will continue to hold the nation's attention if there is an international crisis; otherwise, he must try to manufacture interest through summit meetings, foreign travel (the more exotic the better), and by attaching himself to major events—space exploits, disaster relief, even the Olympic games. Foreign powers may prefer to stall various negotiations until a new president takes office. The last year of his administration is also an election year for the House of Representatives and a third of the Senate, with predictable consequences for the president's legislative program.

In the final July or August the national presidential convention nominates someone else. The president will campaign for the party's nominee, but it is not his battle.

After the election in November there is no longer any vital force in the administration. There is some rush to tidy loose ends. Most appointees are looking forward to new jobs or retirement. The president collects his papers and ships his files home to be able to get a quick start on his memoirs. There are farewell parties and a farewell address. The incoming people arrive for routine briefings, but except for mechanical advice, they are not really interested in the wisdom of those they will succeed.

At noon on January 20 the president watches his successor being sworn in. He is an instant elder statesman.

This account stresses the institutional forces that press in upon a president. But, of course, being president need not be a grim experience. Depending on his personality, a president may have a very good time. Social scientists are beginning to become more aware of the important effect of personality on presidential performance. In a heroic stab at identifying a healthy presidential character, James David Barber used "positive-negative effect" as one measurement. The positive character "gives forth the feeling that he has fun in political life."[19] Roosevelt, Kennedy, Reagan, and Clinton come to mind as men who displayed a special enjoyment in being president.

And being president need not be an unproductive experience. Each president does realize some of his legislative goals and prevents by veto the enactment of legislation he feels is not in the nation's best interests. His authority in the conduct of war and peace is substantial. Because of his position, the doctrines he espouses have a better chance of penetrating the public consciousness than the competing ideas of other politicians. His power and influence may be limited, but they are greater than those of any other individual.

Still, the experience of being president was different from what he thought it would be or from what he learned in his civics textbooks. Four years or eight years seemed like a very long time from the outside, a very short time when he was in office. It is never long enough to do any real planning—to think about where the country ought to be, even in the next decade, and to design programs to get from here to there. His time was consumed by crises and the demands of others, bargaining with legislators, waging feuds, performing small symbolic acts, worrying about getting reelected, finding people for jobs and getting rid of them (often by kicking them upstairs), approving budgets that he could only change around the edges. He never really "ran" the government, as he had expected. Rather, he found that his job was to try to keep the social fabric intact; to keep the peace if possible; to defend the nation from aggressors; to maintain the nation's place in the world, even by force; to attempt to balance economic growth and stability; and at best to make some new initiatives that the history books would record as his.

CHAPTER 3

Franklin D. Roosevelt
1933–1945

 When Franklin Delano Roosevelt assumed the
presidency in March 1933, the White House staff
consisted of thirty-seven people, nine of profes-
sional rank. Those in the three key positions, known as secretaries to the
president, were assigned to handle appointments, press, and correspondence. The executive branch also included a career executive clerk in charge
of presidential mail and files; the Bureau of the Budget, located in the
Treasury Department but otherwise an arm of the presidency, employing
thirty-five persons; and ten cabinet departments.[1] A number of commissions, although within the executive establishment, were beyond the range
of presidential control, except for the power to appoint members for fixed
terms.

In all there were 578,231 executive branch employees, of whom 467,161
were in the classified civil service. "A considerable proportion of them," in
the opinion of a Roosevelt adviser, "had been appointed during the preceding twelve years of Republican rule. . . . What we called the Civil Service
was, in the main, merely a mass of Republican political appointees frozen
into office by act of Congress."[2]

It was a familiar arrangement, and other administrations had found it
workable. But the election year just past had seen the Great Depression
spread inexorably. The agricultural heartland was devastated by years of
drought and mismanagement of the land. Banks were failing at a rate of a

hundred a month. More than a quarter-million families had been evicted from their homes. The government Roosevelt inherited had neither the structure nor the personnel to deal with the most serious economic crisis in the nation's history.

The new president would change that forever, not simply by enlarging the government but by fundamentally redefining its goals and the way it achieved them. He would, in effect, be the first person to be the presiding officer of the modern presidency. But he certainly had no coherent plan. Despite having been governor of the most populous state, he was not much interested in the traditional forms of administration. "The Presidency is not merely an administrative office," he told Anne O'Hare McCormick in 1932. "That's the least of it. It is more than an engineering job, efficient or inefficient. It is pre-eminently a place of moral leadership."[3] He was to stay in office long enough to give special weight to his view. His administrative predilections were to be flexible, to work informally, often outside the normal chain of command, to give competing assignments, to keep shifting the composition of his inner circle, to marshal support through adroit appeals to the public, and to maintain himself at the center of the action. A generation of political scientists would make of this style a virtue by which to measure subsequent presidents.

In staffing the administration Roosevelt generally relied on five (often overlapping) sources of talent:

—The friends and colleagues of his young years, contemporaries in Washington such as Daniel Roper, William Phillips, Breckinridge Long, and William Bullitt when Roosevelt was assistant secretary of the navy under Woodrow Wilson, and more important, a small band of supporters (Louis McHenry Howe, Stephen Early, Marvin McIntyre) who had recognized his political potential, in some cases as early as during his pre-World War I tenure in the New York state legislature.

—Those who had been in his state administration (Frances Perkins, Henry Morgenthau Jr., Harry Hopkins, Samuel Rosenman).

—The 1932 campaigners, particularly those who supported him before the Democratic convention in Chicago: professional politicians (James Farley); financial backers (Joseph Kennedy); and the Brain Trust, mostly Columbia University professors (Raymond Moley, Rexford Tugwell, Adolf Berle) who had provided position papers and otherwise sought to educate the candidate on policy.

—The old boy networks, people who knew people who knew Roosevelt, the most fertile being united through a connection with Professor Felix Frankfurter and the Harvard Law School.

—The rank and file of the Democratic party, the foot troops of politics whose just rewards would be the more lowly jobs in Washington and around the country.

Roosevelt's staffing choices were a haphazard blend of chance, friendship, obligation, and pressure, as were those of the presidents who followed him. He was luckier than most, and his network of acquaintances was larger than most. It was not until much later that presidents began to make tentative efforts to systematically assess the qualities needed in appointive office, and even now staffing remains an underdeveloped responsibility of public administration.

When selecting the cabinet, Roosevelt seemed guided, according to Raymond Moley, by "neither a well-defined purpose nor an underlying principle."[4] He picked Frances Perkins as secretary of labor in part because he wanted a woman in the cabinet, although she was only tolerated by the unions. Harold Ickes at the Interior Department was a Bull Mooser and not personally known to the president-elect. The choice of Claude Swanson for secretary of the navy may have been made for no better reason than to create a place in the Senate for Governor Harry Byrd of Virginia, and anyway, as an old navy man Roosevelt would have wanted to make key decisions himself. Henry Wallace, the new secretary of agriculture, while a distinguished agricultural economist, was, like Ickes, a nominal Republican. Daniel Roper added no weight of any sort, but Commerce was no longer to be treated as a first-line department. Homer Cummings at the Justice Department was a last-minute substitution, again like Ickes, reflecting the fact that four senators had declined to enter the cabinet. The practice of appointing the national committee chairman of the president's party to the position of postmaster general was continued: Farley was also put in charge of routine patronage, and by July 1934 he had located jobs for about 100,000 deserving Democrats, mostly in the new emergency agencies.

The only appointee of national stature was the secretary of state, Senator Cordell Hull of Tennessee, "the one man in public life," according to Samuel Rosenman, "who could give the President substantial concern by threatening . . . to resign."[5] Other men of distinction, such as Republicans Henry Stimson and Frank Knox, would join the cabinet on the eve of

World War II, when Roosevelt wished to give a bipartisan cast to national defense. And still others, of course, would acquire distinction in office. But Rosenman's comment hinted at an underlying principle: Roosevelt sought cabinet subordinates who would neither overshadow him nor prove politically threatening. His administration was designed to be distinctly Rooseveltian.

A second underlying principle, although it is hazardous to attribute too much theorizing to Roosevelt, who operated largely on instinct, was to balance opposites. William Woodin, the first secretary of the treasury, was a conservative financier, as was Lewis Douglas, the budget director; others such as Hopkins, the federal emergency relief administrator and later secretary of commerce, were clearly spenders. "A little rivalry is stimulating, you know," the president was to explain to Perkins. "It keeps everybody going to prove he is a better fellow than the next man. It keeps them honest too."[6] In practice, the balancing of opposites sharpened internal policy debates, but the price paid was that frictions often carried over into program implementation.

Appointments to the subcabinet—under secretaries, assistant secretaries, general counsels—were of superior quality. Dean Acheson, Jerome Frank, Charles Wyzanski, James Landis, and many others were generally in their late thirties and early forties, which was younger than the cabinet members, and they were more ideological. They also were technicians and academicians who, in the opinion of Vice President John Nance Garner, had never worked a precinct. As the supreme mixmaster of his administration, Roosevelt made the secondary selections himself. His cabinet members acquiesced with forbearance or veiled distaste. Observing the blend of disparate ingredients from within the Agriculture Department, Russell Lord reported "national figures using the same washroom, shoulder to shoulder, and pretending not to see each other."[7]

The presidential staff, those on the White House payroll, were noted primarily for their dedication to Roosevelt. "Those who were closest to him for the longest time," thought Rexford Tugwell, "were kept there because they did not probe or try to understand but rather because they gave an unquestioning service."[8] McIntyre, Early, military aide Edwin (Pa) Watson, and Roosevelt's personal secretaries, Missy LeHand and Grace Tully, provided the president with a comfortable, good-humored core around which the New Deal revolved. That the core did not become a cocoon was due mostly to Roosevelt's insatiable appetite for information and his immediate staff's recognition of its own role and limitations. Primus inter pares of this original group was Louis Howe, who, like the other members of the inner circle, was little interested in policy questions other than for their political ramifications. He was more hair shirt than comforter to the president, however. "Howe was the only one who dared to talk to him frankly and fearlessly," Ickes remembered. "He not only could tell him what he believed to be the truth, but he could hang on like a pup to the root until he got results."[9] After Howe's death, there was never to be another intimate with the same willingness to tell the president to go to hell, as Howe was known to have done.

Roosevelt placed other personal aides in the departments. When they also had departmental duties—as did assistant secretary of state Moley and assistant secretary of agriculture Tugwell—they were eventually drawn into conflicts with the cabinet officers to whom they supposedly reported. But others, such as Thomas Corcoran and Benjamin Cohen, were more like detailees, essentially presidential assistants who were carried on payrolls other than the White House's, a duplicitous though harmless budgeting arrangement.

The president also relied heavily on volunteers outside government to perform duties that would later become regular White House operations. This was often true of speechwriting. But outsiders were not always available when needed. Rosenman, for instance, was a justice of the New York Supreme Court and could be in Washington only on weekends and during summer recesses. The physical strain finally led to his resignation from the court in 1943, at which time he was given the title counsel to the president.

Dividing the Roosevelt staff into those on the White House payroll, department officials with special presidential assignments, those in the departments who were on loan to the White House, and outside volunteers still leaves out one important member of the president's establishment. Eleanor Roosevelt was "essentially a presidential aide."[10] Her special responsibilities were twofold: she was an experienced fact finder who traveled widely and reported to her husband, and she was an in-house advocate for liberal causes, social welfare programs, minority groups, and youth. In tracing the organization of the modern presidency, it is apparent that those chief executives who can rely on members of their families (usually wives or brothers) for advice and even for carrying out formal assignments are uniquely blessed.

Although there was never anyone resembling a chief of staff to the president, Roosevelt played favorites at least to the degree that the press was constantly bestowing the title of assistant president on someone or other. Over the course of three terms those who received this appellation included Moley, Donald Richberg, Tugwell, Corcoran, Hopkins, and James Byrnes. All except Byrnes worked on presidential speeches, although none did so exclusively. Tugwell and Moley were involved in different aspects of economics; Corcoran, more than the others, drafted bills and handled congressional relations; Richberg and Byrnes were coordinators; and Hopkins was given a broad but fairly random variety of assignments, including diplomatic missions. None performed duties similar to those later given to Sherman Adams by Dwight Eisenhower or to H. R. Haldeman by Richard Nixon.

The White House staff's relations with Roosevelt were informal. There were no staff meetings with the president. Staff members, singly or in combination, would appear while the president was having breakfast to discuss the day's work. They could then see him in his office if necessary—if not by going through the office of appointments secretary McIntyre, then through the more accessible door of Missy LeHand. Roosevelt also was usually available during the daily cocktail hour. And the evenings were reserved for drafting sessions with his speechwriters.

The official members of his administration formed only the first line of the president's information network. Unlike some presidents whose careers have been on a single track, often legislative or military, Roosevelt's earlier years in national politics and state and federal government and simply as a Roosevelt had given him broad and diverse acquaintances throughout the country whose opinions and observations he now used to supplement or challenge the advice he received from his subordinates. He also sought ancillary information by expanding the device known as the presidential commission. One study covering the Roosevelt years through 1940 mentions more than one hundred advisory bodies.[11]

What the president chose to do, and where he needed assistance, is reflected in the pattern of his week. Although always subject to change, the schedule revolved around three events: sessions with the congressional leadership on Mondays or Tuesdays, press conferences on Tuesday afternoons and Friday mornings, and cabinet meetings on Friday afternoons.

There was no organized congressional liaison office in the White House. Roosevelt handled this chore himself with the assistance of ad hoc troubleshooters such as Corcoran. The president's dealings with Capitol Hill were conducted almost exclusively with the House Speaker, majority leaders, and committee chairmen, a system that created some dissatisfaction among the less privileged legislators. "There is a group of aggressive progressive Democrats who have stuck by you through thick and thin, about seventy-five in number, as well as a number of other progressives, not classed as Democrats," wrote Representative Kent Keller of Illinois in 1938, "and I do not believe that you have ever called in a single one of this group in consultation as to administration policies."[12] Still, in an era of ironbound congressional seniority, this was a grumble more than a problem.

The press conferences were held in the Oval Office with the reporters crowded around the president's desk. The frequency of these sessions meant that Roosevelt, rather than his press secretary, was the chief White House spokesman. The president prided himself on his detailed mastery of government operations and needed little advance preparation; as a rule, press secretary Steve Early merely reminded him of topics on which inquiries were expected. Roosevelt broke with tradition by abolishing written questions, but he established three ground rules: no reporters could quote him directly unless granted permission; his answers could be given for background, meaning that the reporters must not identify their source; and he could speak off the record, that is, strictly for information. Nearly half the meetings began with a statement by the president, ensuring in these cases that he controlled at least part of the session's substance. On occasion, moreover, the press secretary planted questions with friendly reporters.

Thus Roosevelt tailored the format of the press conference into an instrument of considerable utility. The flexibility of responding without quotation or sometimes even without attribution allowed him to meet the press with hardly any fear of error—political, substantive, or grammatical—a luxury that rules out comparisons with later presidents.

But it was also Roosevelt's keen knowledge of the mechanics of journalism and the elements of newsworthiness that ensured proper attention would be paid to what he wanted emphasized. The White House press corps liked him (Leo Rosten found that 64 percent of its members favored his reelection in 1936)[13] because he was good copy and they were sympathetic to his programs. And he liked the reporters, who were often invited to Sunday suppers at which Eleanor Roosevelt scrambled eggs. Then, too, he was a masterful performer. After observing a Roosevelt press conference, John Gunther wrote, "In twenty minutes Mr. Roosevelt's features had expressed amazement, curiosity, mock alarm, genuine interest, worry, rhetorical playing for suspense, decision, playfulness, dignity, and surpassing charm. Yet he said almost nothing. Questions were deflected, diverted, diluted. Answers—when they did come—were concise and clear."[14] These relations could not, of course, have continued at their initial level of mutual admiration, the interests of press and president often being contradictory. The enthusiasm of the press corps was based on "a will-to-believe which, because it ignored future possibilities and past experiences, would end by tearing down the myth it was creating."[15] While the situation never reached that point, Roosevelt's press relations did deteriorate in his second and subsequent terms.

Speeches were the other primary way in which the president reached the public. As governor, Roosevelt had grasped the potential of radio as a way to break through "the paper curtain of the publishers and appeal directly to the voters."[16] His calm and reassuring voice was ideally suited to the medium. Yet his celebrated fireside chats averaged only two or three a year; as he explained, "individual psychology cannot . . . be attuned for long periods of time to a constant repetition of the highest note in the scale."[17]

Given the consistent style of Roosevelt's rhetoric, it is startling that so many hands were involved in crafting the speeches. Drafts were prepared by teams or by one writer gathering submissions from a number of sources. During 1933 Moley was chief gatherer; drafts were prepared in 1933 and 1934 by Richberg, Howe, Bullitt, Frankfurter, Hugh Johnson, Tugwell, Cohen, and Corcoran. The team of Cohen and Corcoran played a more important role after Moley broke with the administration. Rosenman, who had been Roosevelt's draftsman in Albany, again emerged as chief speechwriter in 1936; Stanley High was active in the second presidential campaign; and Roosevelt's last team, from 1940 until his death, consisted of Rosenman, Hopkins, and Robert Sherwood, with occasional help from Archibald MacLeish. Roosevelt's distinct style of speaking seemed to be made to order for speechwriters, but that phrases from so many sources could have taken on a unitary character can be explained only by his involvement in the process. In the end, as Sherwood wrote of FDR's martinis, the president "mixed the ingredients with the deliberation of an alchemist."[18]

The speechwriting operation often also served as a mechanism for forcing decisions. Rosenman explained, for example, that in preparing a 1942 congressional message on economic stabilization he first arranged a conference of the vice president, secretary of the treasury, chairman of the Federal Reserve Board, director of the budget, and the price administrator, whose suggestions and disagreements were presented to the president in a memorandum, then fought out in various forums, and eventually resolved by Roosevelt under deadline pressure."[19]

Despite their regular appearance on the president's weekly agenda, cabinet meetings were not an important administrative mechanism. Roosevelt did not consider his department secretaries a collegial body whose collective wisdom should be applied to making high government policy. "Our Cabinet meetings are pleasant affairs," Ickes wrote in his diary, "but we only skim the surface of routine affairs." The chief value of the Friday sessions, Stimson felt, was their usefulness "as a way in which to get into the White House to have a word with the President in private after the meetings were over."[20]

In relating to the cabinet members as individuals, Roosevelt had little respect for jurisdictional boundaries. Secretary of the Treasury Morgenthau was given assignments that rightly belonged to Secretary of State Hull and Secretary of War Harry Woodring. Cabinet members survived as best they could in this laissez-faire atmosphere, if not by implicit contract with their fellow department heads, then by conquest. At Interior, Ickes was tenacious in his quest for additional responsibilities, as when he attempted to snatch the Forest Service from the Department of Agriculture. Hull, however, drew a narrow line around the State Department, even allowing himself to be excluded from wartime summit meetings on the grounds that they dealt with military planning and were not of diplomatic concern.

The president tried to stay above the interdepartmental battles. Typical of this approach was a memorandum he sent to Rosenman: "Get [budget director] Harold Smith, usually known as 'Battling Smith,' into a room with the Secretary of the Treasury, usually known as 'Sailor Morgenthau,' lock them in and let the survivor out."[21] Yet despite the president's seemingly cold-blooded practice of management by combat, he was almost incapable of firing anyone for incompetence or even disloyalty. Rather, he devised ways to go around them, as when he chose to conduct War Department business with assistant secretary Louis Johnson instead of Woodring, who was too isolationist for the president.

When Roosevelt believed most strongly that a job was important, however, he often simply ignored the departments and created a new agency. Topsy was the patron saint of his administrative theory. As a deliberate policy, this implied one or more of the following: that a new function was to be undertaken for which there was no niche in the existing structure, that the costs of giving new duties to an ongoing agency were too high in terms of disrupting existing programs or disturbing the delicate relationship between departments, that a new agency symbolized a higher level of concern, that existing agencies either lacked capable personnel or were unable to move quickly enough, or that a new agency could circumvent existing regulations. James Rowe, a Roosevelt aide, thought that one reason the president frequently employed this device was that it was the best way to deliver on his patronage obligations.[22] The result was an administrative monstrosity, proliferating the number of executives who had the right and obligation to report directly to the president.

Roosevelt made a short-lived attempt to coordinate the work of the new agencies with that of the old-line departments through the creation of the Emergency Council in 1934. At one time the coordinating involved 124 interdepartmental committees and 224 subcommittees. The enterprise ultimately collapsed under the weight of its apparatus, the unwieldy size of its meetings, the pro forma reading of mimeographed reports, and the president's disenchantment with its director, Donald Richberg. General confusion may have been somewhat lessened, however, by government's ability to attract experienced managers because of decreased employment opportunities in the private sector during the Depression.

By the time Roosevelt stood for reelection in 1936 his methods of running the government had become as controversial in some quarters as his goals. He therefore set up the Committee on Administrative Management, with Louis Brownlow as chairman and Charles Merriam and Luther Gulick as the other members. Their report, which he enthusiastically forwarded to Congress in January 1937, accepted as its premise that "the American Executive must be regarded as one of the very greatest contributions by our Nation to the development of modern democracy." The need for reorganization was not based on potential savings to the taxpayers, as in past reports, but because "the President needs help."[23] The committee's solution, as George Graham put it, was "a plan of salvation by staff."[24] The report recommended that the White House Office should be augmented by six administrative assistants, "possessed of high competence, great physical vigor, and a passion for anonymity."[25] In addition, there should be an Executive Office of the President consisting of "managerial arms" for personnel, fiscal affairs, and planning.

The reorganization bill became entwined in Roosevelt's attempt to alter the composition of the Supreme Court and did not become law until 1939.

But eventually he got what he asked for, with the exception of having the functions of the Civil Service Commission transferred to the White House. The Executive Office was physically located next door to the White House.[26] Into it was placed the Bureau of the Budget and the National Resources Committee, renamed the National Resources Planning Board. Thus the president controlled two of the recommended three managerial arms, fiscal affairs and planning.[27]

The reorganization act did not measurably increase the size of Roosevelt's White House staff; the more significant expansion had taken place in 1933–34 as the president borrowed personnel from the departments. Although authorized to have six administrative assistants, Roosevelt chose to appoint only three in 1939. While the new aides—William McReynolds, James Rowe, and Lauchlin Currie—were largely generalists standing ready for whatever assignments were uppermost on the president's mind, they also developed areas of special interest. McReynolds became liaison officer for personnel management, Rowe's particular involvements were in politics and patronage, and Currie was concerned with economics. The importance of the Brownlow report was in legitimating what Roosevelt had been doing all long. It was a ringing manifesto for presidential supremacy, which had not been an accepted fact before the New Deal.

The National Resources Planning Board, charged with preparing long-range plans for public works, helping state and local planning bodies, and informing the president of trends in the economy, did not fare well and was abolished by a 1943 action of Congress, which further stipulated that its functions could not be transferred to any other agency. Sherwood claimed that "the N.R.P.B. was dear to Roosevelt's heart, but to the conservative majority on Capitol Hill the very word 'plan' was considered a Communist invention and any planning must be part of a plot to disrupt the capitalist system of free enterprise."[28] At least one academic observer, however, could find no evidence "to support a claim that the research product of the Board ever influenced vital decisions of the President."[29] The legislators feared a long-term planning operation in the White House as an assault on their prerogatives; they were perfectly happy to create a planning operation of their own, as when the Senate set up the Special Committee on Post-War Planning shortly after cutting off funds to the NRPB. The collapse of the NRPB was the first of a series of unsuccessful attempts to graft long-range planning capacity onto the White House. Ultimately they have failed because of the character of presidents and the demands of the presidential office. The politicians who generally become presidents have had little experience with and patience for extended planning, and once in the White House they find it increasingly difficult to focus on projections beyond their terms of office.

The Bureau of the Budget, however, blossomed in the Executive Office, and under the directorship of Harold Smith (1939–45) it rapidly expanded from a staff of forty to one of more than 500. It retained its position as the primary agency for reviewing the budget and vastly increased its other powers. For instance, while the departments had previously had to clear legislative requests with the bureau only if they cost money, now all proposed legislation went through its clearance process. A similar system was instituted for the preparation of executive orders and proclamations, and recommendations for presidential vetoes also were funneled through the Budget Bureau. It became the coordinator of statistical services and drafted reorganization plans. Survey teams recommended management improvements in the departments, and as particularly competent young professionals were attracted to the bureau in the early 1940s, the president relied on it more and more to represent him on interdepartmental committees and to perform other odd jobs. In short, the augmented Bureau of the Budget provided a significant presidential presence throughout the executive branch.

So now Roosevelt had two types of staffs: the one in the White House whose services were to the president and were of a personal, public relations, and political nature; and the one in the Executive Office whose responsibilities were to the presidency and were institutional in nature. But policy and program initiatives still flowed up to the president through the departments and agencies. The president's men were not involved in operations; as the Brownlow report recommended, they issued no orders.

The pressures of World War II, however, brought measurable changes to this system. Except for sporadic periods, presidents had in the past spent most of their time concerned with domestic matters. The ushering in of world responsibility meant that from the 1940s forward they would become more and more consumed by international affairs.

During the war, Harry Hopkins, who lived at the White House, often acted as a direct link between Roosevelt and allied governments; the State Department was informed of arrangements after they had been concluded. Admiral William Leahy, also operating out of the White House, presided over meetings of the Joint Chiefs of Staff as Roosevelt's representative and daily briefed the president on military matters. Rosenman, now a full-time drafter of presidential messages and public documents, assumed responsibility for creating domestic policy. The addition of these three White House advisers markedly altered the direction of decisionmaking. In particular, Rosenman's domestic duties expanded to fill the void left by the president's preoccupation with the war. Policies of the utmost importance were devised in his office at the White House and moved out from there, thus reversing the traditional flow. Moreover, as Roosevelt's health declined, all his aides assumed added responsibilities.

The president mobilized the civilian side of the government for war in much the same manner he had earlier organized for the economic emergency, through the creation of numerous ad hoc agencies in response to problems as they arose or were called to his attention. But while he had been given to picking the leadership of the New Deal agencies from a free-floating body of lawyers, professors, social workers, and state and local administrators, he chose representatives of economic groups (corporate executives, union leaders, and farm organization officials) to head the new war agencies. The Office of Production Management, for example, was placed under the joint direction of William Knudsen of General Motors and Sidney Hillman of the Amalgamated Clothing Workers Union. Scientists, recruited by Vannevar Bush, for the first time began to play an important role in government, developing an atom bomb being only the most obvious example.

Roosevelt also became the first president to give major executive responsibilities to the vice president. Henry Wallace was made chairman of the Economic Defense Board, the Supply Priorities and Allocation Board, and the Board of Economic Warfare. This was in sharp contrast to the job description for the vice presidency under John Nance Garner, whose primary assistance to Roosevelt had been as a bridge to Congress, at least until the ideological gulf between the president and the vice president became unbridgeable. The liabilities of giving a vice president responsibility for implementing policies became apparent, however, when Wallace and Commerce Secretary Jesse Jones clashed over policy and jurisdictional questions, exchanged public insults, and had to be relieved of their assignments. Less controversial was Roosevelt's novel use of the vice president as an envoy extraordinary on missions to South America, China, and the Soviet Union.

Roosevelt's war government has been described as a collection of action agencies—dealing with such matters as the allocation of rubber, drafting men into the armed forces, and price controls—and coordinating agencies "to keep the action agencies from getting in each other's way."[30] Coordination was arranged in a series of layers with first-step coordinators such as the National Housing Agency, regional coordinators like the Plant Site Board, second-step coordinators such as the Office of War Information and, at the White House, the supercoordinator of them all, the Office of War Mobilization (OWM).[31]

To head the OWM, the president lured James Byrnes from the Supreme Court. It was undoubtedly a difficult decision for Roosevelt to give one person so much authority to act in his name, but in picking Byrnes there was little cause for concern. A cautious southern politician long comfortable in the folkways of Washington, Byrnes was not about to handle hot coals if he could help it. He deliberately was not an empire builder; he worked out of tiny cluttered offices in the east wing of the White House, with a staff never exceeding ten and with the unassuming Ben Cohen as his chief deputy. The OWM chose to deal with issues only if they could not be resolved at lower levels and interpreted its role narrowly as one of adjudicating controversies rather than planning and commanding the home front from its elevated perch.

But Roosevelt's management techniques were better suited to the needs of the Depression than the wartime 1940s. When the New Deal groped its way toward economic solutions that had never before been considered within government's province, the heady clash of ideas and the heavy emphasis on experimentation proved highly productive. The needs of massive warfare were not as well served by improvisation and redundancy. The president's administrative juggling sometime caused vital military messages to be delayed for days or weeks, and there were even times when the Pentagon first learned about a White House decision from the British.[32]

Franklin Roosevelt's methods of organizing the presidency illustrate the intensely personal nature of the office. Even before the 1939 Reorganization Act gave him congressional sanction, he had reshaped his staff to suit his style and needs. Despite his domination of the government, the White House staff during Roosevelt's first two terms was primarily a personal services unit, considerably bigger but not essentially different from that of past presidents. His strong desire to mold public opinion called especially for aides who could assist in such symbolic and informational duties as speechwriting and press relations.

Only during Roosevelt's last years did new powers begin to shift to the staff. This coincided with the war and the president's failing health. A vigorous Roosevelt, one suspects, would have been much more hesitant to delegate duties that he considered presidential. And what delegation did take place would have been more carefully limited. As it was, Hopkins's diplomacy impinged on the prerogatives of the secretary of state, and Rosenman's initiation of domestic policies invaded what had been the exclusive domain of the departments and agencies.

The accretion of White House staff functions was not part of a deliberate plan. The creation of the Executive Office of the President, however, had a theoretical base in the Brownlow report and in effect produced a quantum jump in staff available to a president. Although Roosevelt was relatively meticulous, for instance, in using the Bureau of the Budget for institutional purposes, there were signs by the end of the administration that it was slipping into a more personal role. Late in the war Harold Smith reportedly told a friend, "Roger, I am afraid I am becoming Mr. Fixit for the President, and this is bad for the Bureau of the Budget."[33]

While the cabinet failed to serve Roosevelt as a mechanism for gathering collective advice—as it had failed previous presidents—cabinet officers continued to be responsible for running their departments and proposing legislation. However, Roosevelt's habit of creating agencies outside the departmental framework diffused power throughout the executive branch, diminished the standing of some department heads, and increased the number of officials reporting directly to the president. Within limits, this served the purpose of keeping subordinates dependent on the president, but the practice held the inherent danger of spiraling beyond one person's span of control.

The Rooseveltian legacy was that the reach of the presidency had been expanded and that the people's expectations of what government could and should do had been forever altered. Whether the growth of government would outstrip a president's ability to oversee its activities was a challenge Roosevelt left to his successors.

CHAPTER 4

Harry S. Truman
1945–1953

Harry S. Truman, a tidy man himself, was offended by Roosevelt's freewheeling style as an administrator. He believed that government should be orderly, that promoting rivalries between members of an administration was disruptive, and that loyalty was the most important unifying principle for an administration. Truman's background was also a clear contrast to Roosevelt's. He had spent most of his adult life in Missouri organization politics and in the U.S. Senate, which limited his circle of acquaintances and his knowledge of bureaucracy.[1]

It was his sense of order and loyalty, and his background in the Senate, that determined the way he would conduct the business of the presidency. In the words of Richard Neustadt, who was there, "Truman's White House rather resembled a senatorial establishment writ large."[2] Just as Truman came between Roosevelt and Eisenhower, so his vision of running the government lay halfway between the designed chaos of his predecessor and the structural purity of his successor.

On assuming office after Roosevelt's death in 1945, Truman invited the members of his inherited cabinet to remain in their posts, but it did not take long for the new president to realize that he must have his own team. Within three months he had replaced six of the ten department heads. Ultimately, twenty-four men would serve as his cabinet officers. Four of the first half-dozen appointees were or had been members of Congress (only

three had been during Roosevelt's three-plus terms). Treasury Secretary
Fred Vinson, a former congressman from Kentucky, proved to be a person
of exceptional perception. But Truman's eye for talent was not always so
sure. When Vinson was moved to the Supreme Court in 1946, the president replaced him with John Snyder, an orthodox banker without Vinson's
breadth, who, like Postmaster General Robert Hannegan, was an old friend
from Missouri. Continuing the tradition, Hannegan doubled as chairman
of the Democratic National Committee.[3] Secretary of State James Byrnes
and a holdover, Secretary of Commerce Henry Wallace, had been Truman's
rivals for the vice presidential nomination in 1944. Both proved disloyal
according to Truman's definition of loyalty and were eventually asked to
resign. For his second- and third-wave cabinet appointments, Truman generally sought people with long experience in the departments and even
chose a career bureaucrat to supervise the Post Office. Under secretaries
and assistant secretaries such as Oscar Chapman at Interior and Charles
Brannan at Agriculture were promoted to the cabinet. By and large the
later appointees were an improvement in quality.[4]

Overall Truman's appointments were a blend of stunningly capable
patricians, unimaginative professionals, and incompetent cronies. He generally picked superb people for the important jobs, however, and ordinary or
even unqualified people for the less important ones. There were exceptions,
of course. Truman never had a topflight attorney general, and Louis
Johnson was one of the least successful secretaries of defense. But the key
posts in foreign policy and national security went to such luminaries as
George Marshall, Dean Acheson, James Forrestal, Robert Patterson,
Robert Lovett, Will Clayton, Paul Hoffman, David Lilienthal, and Averell
Harriman. Many of these appointees were part of the American aristocracy,
products of élite schools and long-held wealth, who had been brought into
government by the Hyde Park Roosevelt and had little in common socially
with the former haberdasher from Independence. Their relations with
Truman were highly formal, but it was clear that they held him in affection
and were deeply devoted. The contrast with the performance of some
Truman friends in the administration, those with whom he shared a comfortable intimacy, was striking. Secretary of State Marshall won the Nobel
Peace Prize; White House appointments secretary Connelly went to jail
for conspiring to fix a tax case.

At first Truman believed that the cabinet should be analogous to a board
of directors, "the principal medium through which the president controls

his administration."⁵ Cabinet meetings dealt with more substantive questions than they had during the Roosevelt era, and he sometimes even asked members to vote on major issues. Yet even then collective advice proved useful primarily on matters of tactics and political strategy. For example, when he announced to the cabinet that he planned to send aid to Greece, he requested their opinion not on his decision but "on the best method to apprise the American people of the issues involved." (They suggested a presidential address to a joint session of Congress.)⁶ Gradually he drew back from the board of directors concept: powers delegated could be powers lost, and Truman, while modest about himself as president, was zealous in protecting those prerogatives that he felt were inherent in the presidency. Moreover, after the outbreak of the Korean War he began to hold weekly meetings of the new National Security Council, in effect a cabinet subcommittee, thus further lessening the utility of full cabinet sessions.

At first Truman intended to return the White House staff to its prewar size—secretaries for press, correspondence, and appointments, plus a handful of general assistants. But under the pressures of an increasing workload, he reversed himself. Within a year the White House, in addition to the three traditional secretaries, took on the following configuration:

Assistant to the president (John R. Steelman). The appointment of the former head of the Federal Mediation and Conciliation Service reflected the seriousness with which the president viewed labor-management relations as a national problem (116 million days of work were lost because of strikes in 1945) and the ineffectuality of his secretary of labor, Lewis Schwellenbach. Negotiations in major disputes such as those in the railroad and steel industries were conducted in Steelman's White House office. Steelman also acted as coordinator of federal agency programs and policies, which meant that he concerned himself with those cabinet-level problems that were beneath presidential attention, and he served as the route to the president for the minor agencies that were without direct access to the Oval Office.

Special counsel (Clark Clifford). The office remained as defined by Samuel Rosenman: the most important position on the White House staff for domestic policy formulation. It also controlled the speechwriting process and was responsible for reviewing congressional bills and executive orders. In addition to his other duties, Clifford, who first joined the Truman White House as a naval officer, handled liaison with the Pentagon and the State Department.

Administrative assistant (Charles Murphy). Unlike Roosevelt, who used troubleshooters to deal with Congress on an ad hoc basis, Truman gradually looked to Murphy as his coordinator of congressional messages. When Murphy replaced Clifford as special counsel in 1950, he continued his congressional liaison work but did not assume Clifford's responsibility for coordinating national security. Some duties were a function of the office and others a function of the officeholder.

Administrative assistant (Donald S. Dawson). As staff coordinator for personnel and patronage, Dawson maintained the files from which Truman made appointments, except for those in the customs houses and the federal courts system. He also handled the arrangements for the president's trips and political appearances.

Administrative assistant (David Niles). A holdover from Roosevelt's staff, Niles had special responsibility for liaison with minority groups.

Other administrative assistants had more generalized assignments and usually served as aides to Steelman, Clifford, or Murphy. The presence on the White House staff of such men as David Lloyd, David Bell, George Elsey, Richard Neustadt, and David Stowe was in itself a development of some note, the beginning of a cadre of supporting staff for senior presidential aides.

Categorizing the duties of key staff members somewhat underestimates the extent to which Truman parceled out assignments "on the basis of who was available" (as Lloyd recalled the system.)[7] Nevertheless, functional divisions in the presidential office were now emerging in sharper form. No one on Roosevelt's staff had had either labor-management responsibilities similar to Steelman's or such a continuing involvement in congressional relations as Murphy.

Equally important, a simple description of White House assignments veils what Clifford called "two forces fighting for the mind of the president," a dynamic that was to have significant consequences for the balance of power in the Truman administration. The fight over what was to become known as the Fair Deal developed along classic liberal-conservative lines. The chief conservative advocates were Steelman and Treasury Secretary Snyder. The liberals, led by Clifford, included Murphy, Leon Keyserling of the Council of Economic Advisers, and several members of the subcabinet, such as Oscar (Jack) Ewing, director of the Federal Security Agency; Oscar Chapman, under secretary of the interior; and David Morse, assistant secretary of labor.

As Clifford remembered,

> I think it was Jack Ewing who first suggested the idea that a few of us get together from time to time to try to plot a coherent political course for the administration. Our interest was to be exclusively on domestic affairs, not foreign. . . . We wanted to create a set of goals that truly met the deepest and greatest needs of the people, and we wanted to build a liberal, forward-moving program around those goals that could be recognized as a *Truman* program.
>
> The idea was that the six or eight of us [meeting each Monday evening in Ewing's apartment] would try to come to an understanding among ourselves on what direction we would like the president to take on any given issue. And then, quietly and unobtrusively each in his own way, we would try to steer the president in that direction.
>
> Naturally, we were up against tough competition. Most of the cabinet and the congressional leaders were urging Mr. Truman to go slow, to veer a little closer to the conservative line. . . .
>
> Well, it was two forces fighting for the mind of the president, that's really what it was. It was completely unpublicized, and I don't think Mr. Truman ever realized it was going on. But it was an unceasing struggle during those two years [1946–48], and it got to the point where no quarter was asked and none was given.[8]

Of his own role, Clifford said, "If I rendered any service to President Truman . . . it was as the representative of the liberal forces. I think our forces were generally successful. We had something of an advantage in the liberal-conservative fight because I was there all the time. I saw the president often, and if he wanted to discuss an issue, I was at hand."[9]

The liberal forces prevailed. For example, Truman vetoed a bill to extend the life of the wartime Office of Price Administration, which liberals felt was too weak, and the Taft-Hartley bill, which curbed union activities, both actions urged by Clifford and opposed by almost the entire cabinet. Clifford's skills—vastly greater than his opponents'—well may have been a factor. But he also was pushing the president in a direction that was clearly in keeping with the president's instincts.

There is nothing unusual, of course, about struggles within an administration. They are inherent in a structure of government built on the separation of the departments along interest-group lines, and Roosevelt had designed his whole theory of management on conflict. Yet as a rule of thumb, there had always been a distinction between cabinet officers (policy advocates and managers) and White House aides (facilitators, mediators, and performers of personal and political services). This changed somewhat in the closing years of the Roosevelt administration when the president, preoccupied with the war and in ill health, allowed Rosenman and others greater leeway in shaping domestic programs. But Clifford's performance during five years under Truman was of a different magnitude: since he acted primarily as a presidential adviser on policies and programs rather than on ways and means, the theoretical line between cabinet and White House staff began to blur. And as Clifford's experiences illustrate, in any conflict between the two the law of propinquity is apt to govern.[10]

Besides Steelman, Clifford, and their assistants, there were others, distinctly different characters, who shared administrative duties at the Truman White House. Ithiel de Sola Pool would later write, "Every president has felt the need to surround himself with a small group of mediocre men whose main qualification is loyalty. . . . In every administration they have gotten the president into trouble by their lack of moral perspective. . . . The president needs loyal personal assistants, yet they are dangerous."[11] Truman's mediocre men included military aide Harry Vaughan, appointments secretary Matthew Connelly, Donald Dawson and George Schoeneman of the patronage operation, and Dr. Wallace Graham, the president's physician. They were people Truman liked to have around. They were comfortable. They were fun. Some of them also were accepters of petty graft, mink coats, freezers, and free hotel rooms and were friends of fixers. Collectively their activities became known as "the mess in Washington" during the 1952 presidential election campaign.[12] That Harry Truman, of unexcelled personal integrity, could have tolerated their presence says something about his background in machine politics, about his sentimentality and sense of loyalty, and about his deep-seated need for companionship. A president, even more than most, needs friends. The post of court jester has a long history. Indeed, the persistence with which court jesters have been found in the company of presidents seems to attest to some useful service that they perform—"yet they are dangerous." Recent presidents have protected themselves by keeping their court jesters out of government or by making sure that their governmental duties were not substantial. Truman's problems resulted from giving assignments of state to his court jesters.

There were definite patterns to the way Truman spent his days.[13] Mornings were devoted to what he called customers—often legislators.

Afternoons were spent on the more serious business of government—meetings of the cabinet and National Security Council and sessions with the budget director. Time was measured out sparingly; meetings rarely lasted more than a half hour, individual appointments often less than ten minutes. The only times the president was alone were early in the morning and late at night, when he could study or merely catch up with the bureaucratic conveyor belt that constantly deposited papers on his desk. Almost everyone who came into his office wanted something. His days were predetermined by other people—VIPs who asked for time with the president, officials who needed decisions—or by the cycles of government (in January he saw a great deal of the budget director because the budget cycle was reaching its climax). Private meetings were scheduled twice a week with the secretary of state and once a week with the secretary of defense, but none was scheduled on a regular basis with any member of the domestic departments. All cabinet members may have been equal, but some were more equal than others.

In addition to his own accessibility to members of Congress, after the 1948 election Truman assigned two low-level White House aides, one for the Senate and one for the House, to handle Capitol Hill requests for favors. They served under appointments secretary Connelly and did not deal with important legislation. The operation was rated "relatively ineffectual" by other Truman staff members.[14]

Press conferences were held about once a week, only half the frequency that they were in Roosevelt's administration. Truman lacked his predecessor's skill in dealing with reporters; his maladroit handling of some questions, such as at one point leaving the impression that he was considering the use of the atomic bomb in Korea, created special problems for his press secretaries. (It is probably only coincidence that two of them died in office.) In time Truman came to regard the press as often unfair to him and his administration. When a reporter prefaced a question by saying that he was puzzled, Truman snapped, "You're easily puzzled. You're always speculating about something you don't know anything about."[15] As self-protection, he was briefed by the White House staff before each press conference. Toward the end of his presidency the briefing included a notebook containing possible questions and answers, a practice continued by subsequent presidents. Press conferences were no longer an informal give-and-take around the president's desk, in part because the press corps had grown too big. Conferences were now held in the Indian Treaty Room of the Executive Office Building. For the first time, too, they were recorded and portions released for radio use.

Truman seemed always to have time for budget business, however, and the period from 1947 through 1949 is considered by some as a golden age when the Bureau of the Budget took on enormous importance in the White House organization. The close involvement of the bureau in shaping and directing administration policy was a product of Truman's interests and budget director James E. Webb's notion of his agency's role. The president later wrote, "The federal budget was one of my most serious hobbies, but it was also much more than that. In fact, I regarded it as one of the most serious of the responsibilities of the president—a responsibility that never failed to prove thoroughly fascinating." He claimed that he spent "twice as much time on the preparation of the budget as any former president ever did."[16] Most presidents soon become bored with the tedious juggling of figures that Truman found so fascinating and delegate these responsibilities for fine-tuning policy priorities. It is beyond coincidence that the two presidents who had served on congressional appropriations committees, Truman and Ford, have had the greatest personal involvement in preparing the budgets during recent years.

As relations between Truman and his budget director became more intimate, Webb emerged as a principal adviser to the president, as distinct from adviser to the presidency, the prime role assumed by past directors. Neustadt reported that Webb "broke precedent by making his subordinates freely available to White House aides, on their terms, for their purpose." The Clifford-Murphy axis in particular used Budget Bureau people as its personal backup staff. The interchange of personnel was such that, according to Neustadt, "in 1953 fully a third of the outgoing Truman assistants had come to the White House staff from the career service in the Budget Bureau." Starting in 1948 the bureau's legislative clearance operation moved from "negative protection of president and agencies to positive development and drafting of Administration measures."[17] Policy often was formulated by working teams, with the bureau's Legislative Reference Office functioning as secretariat. Only the advent of the Korean War and the usual loss of energy that afflicts an administration whose days in office are numbered caused some diminution of the Budget Bureau's influence.

While Truman was in the White House, Congress sought for the first time to shape the institutional presidency. The Employment Act of 1946 added the Council of Economic Advisers to the Executive Office and the National Security Act of 1947 added the National Security Council.[18] Both were attempts to structure in statute the president's information systems.

But although Congress could mandate advice, could a president be forced to listen?

At least one economist has called Harry Truman "indifferent to the complexities of economics."[19] In this regard he was no different from his predecessor, or for that matter from most of the presidents who have come after him. No professional economist has ever been a major party candidate for president. Rexford Tugwell had proposed that Roosevelt create a federal economic council attached to the executive.[20] Roosevelt instead chose to gather economic advice from his constantly shifting inner circle, some of whose members were economists. His several changes in economic policy may be attributed to changes in advisers. As a posthumous reaction to his ways of conducting the affairs of state, Congress decreed in 1946 that, starting with Truman, presidents would have to have a pride of professional economists in the Executive Office. A president's economic advice would come from a council, not a solitary adviser, and its three members would be confirmed by the Senate, a provision that had never before been attached to presidential aides. A new joint committee of Congress would monitor the council's recommendations. Senator Joseph C. O'Mahoney, a principal supporter of the measure, made his intention clear: "This . . . is a bill to restore the functions of Congress."[21]

For the first chairman of the Council of Economic Advisers, Truman chose Edwin G. Nourse, vice president of the Brookings Institution and generally regarded as a moderate conservative. The other two members, John D. Clark and Leon Keyserling, were liberals. Nourse reported,

> After the lapse of a little more than a year, it can be said that there has been no single case when [Truman] has called upon us in any specific situation for counsel in his study of any matter of national economic policy. While he has accepted the material which we have presented to him for use in the Economic Report and passed it on without material change and with only minor omissions, there is no clear evidence that at any juncture we had any tangible influence on the formation of policy or the adoption of any course of action or feature of a program.[22]

This situation had at least three causes. Nourse was not in sympathy with the policy tendencies of the administration. At the same time, he believed presidential economic advisers could and should be "scientifically objective," somehow outside the political implications of their data. And there was an unfortunate chemistry between chairman and president. Keyserling would later contend that "Dr. Nourse was simply unable to adjust himself to the nature and the problems of the Presidency. He could never understand that the president of the United States has too many things to do to engage in long bull sessions on economics of the kind that take place at The Brookings Institution."[23] Viewing the relationship from the president's perspective, Gerhard Colm, a member of the initial CEA staff, thought that perhaps Truman kept his distance because "he did not feel equal to discussing economics with a man whom he respected as a great scholar and authority."[24]

After Nourse resigned in 1949 and the chairmanship was assumed by Keyserling, whose views of the White House operation were more realistic and whose views of policy were more in tune with the president's, the council became a serious contending force in devising administration policy. Unlike the Budget Bureau, which had a monopoly in its primary area of concern, the CEA still had to negotiate with the Treasury, Commerce, and Labor departments and the other elements of government that took strong stands on the direction of the economy. However, freed of operating responsibility (with the exception of preparing the economic report) and located in proximity to the president, it had ample opportunity to develop and to expound its judgments within the higher reaches of the administration. Moreover, the council was given a small but competent staff, eight professionals at first, most drawn from the ranks of government economists. Their networks of friendships were invaluable in keeping the CEA in touch with the agencies and in avoiding the type of insensitivity that could have hampered a new entry in a crowded field. Harold Smith, for example, expected bad blood to develop between his Budget Bureau and the new council; that did not happen, and it was not insignificant that two of the early CEA staff members came from the bureau.

Congress was wrong in its belief that it could direct the president to accept economic advice; the experience with Nourse graphically proved that. But it was right in believing that the presence of professional economists in the White House could result in additional sources of information and analysis, which the president absorbed, often through his personal staff, sometimes by osmosis. The lesson of the CEA was that a president could be aided in policymaking by this type of expertise if his experts were congenial enough to gain his attention—this could not be taken for granted—and if they could provide him with information that was immediately and politically useful. Ironically, it was Nourse who correctly summed up the CEA's proper role: "The success of the Council as an institution, the importance of the place it occupies and the value of its work will be just what the president makes them."[25]

The National Security Act of 1947 and its 1949 amendments were meant to unify the military and to create a new system for advising the president—the National Security Council. The original members of the NSC were the president (chairman), the secretary of state, the secretary of defense, the three military service secretaries (who were at the same time removed from the cabinet), the chairman of the new National Security Resources Board (a standby mobilization body that was later merged into the Office of Defense Mobilization), and such other department or agency heads as the president might choose to give membership. The 1949 amendments dropped the service secretaries and added the vice president. The Central Intelligence Agency was placed under the NSC, but it has never really been regarded as part of the Executive Office. In theory, the NSC would help the president define broad national policy. The State Department would then know what policy to implement in its conduct of foreign relations, the military would know the policy for which it must devise strategic and logistic plans, and the National Security Resources Board would know the policy for which it must prepare mobilization plans for industry, labor, and raw materials.

Truman at first viewed the NSC with appropriate suspicion. There were some, particularly in the Pentagon, who hoped to use it as a vehicle for committing the president to their department's positions. Truman had to make sure that the council would be limited to giving advice. He chose to accomplish this in part by not attending council meetings: if he was not there, he could make no instant commitments, although he justified his absence by contending that council members would speak more freely if he was not in the room. He rejected a proposal to give the executive secretary the authority to see that NSC decisions were carried out. The staff, he felt, should not be insinuated between him and his principal advisers, the secretary of state and the secretary of defense. His momentous decision to intervene in Korea was made without formally consulting with the NSC. (He did, of course, meet with his key officials, some of whom were council members.)

The war, however, convinced him that the NSC could be used to greater advantage. The council began to meet weekly, with the president in the chair. A senior staff of eight persons drawn from the departments was assembled—a precursor of Eisenhower's Planning Board. The first executive secretary had been primarily a briefing officer; the second now became a staff director as well. NSC papers began to be developed in the Executive Office, rather than in the departments. Although Truman was not prepared to turn the NSC into a comprehensive policymaking system, he did discover that when molded to his terms it could serve him as a convenient way to get staff work done. Without fulfilling its congressional backers' original expectation of defining broad national policy, it nonetheless had its uses. It provided the excuse for Truman to regroup his advisers into a sort of war cabinet with its own secretariat. Thus again Congress failed to bind a president to its intent; again a president chose to use or not use a body that Congress had unilaterally imposed on the institution of the presidency; and again, perhaps serendipitously, a president found functions for a staff to perform after it had been given to him.

The shape of the modern presidential organization that was beginning to be defined at the end of the Roosevelt administration started to come into sharper focus under Truman: the greater differentiation of staff functions; the building of staff to support chief presidential assistants; the moving of policy advocacy into the White House; a blurring of the distinction between the Executive Office and the White House Office in the use of Budget Bureau personnel by White House aides; and the grafting onto the White House of the CEA and the NSC. Most important was the public's acceptance of the president as the locus of federal government responsibility.

In 1947 a Republican Congress, looking forward to the election of a Republican president the next year, approved a bill to set up the Commission on the Organization of the Executive Branch of the Government. One of its stated objectives was "defining and limiting executive functions."[26] While Truman might have viewed himself as the commission's target, he was enthusiastic about the undertaking and promised and delivered the full cooperation of his administration to the commission's chairman, Herbert Hoover. Hoover threw his prodigious energy into the assignment, serving as his own staff director and placing his personal imprint on all the commission's work. The first of the nineteen reports of the Hoover Commission appeared in 1949, and its first recommendation was to give the president continuing powers to reorganize federal agencies unrestricted by limitations or exemptions. It also recommended that the Executive Office of the President should be strengthened, that the president should have stronger staff services, and that he should have complete discretion over how the augmented White House staff should be used.[27] Newspapers such as the *New York Herald Tribune* and the *Chicago Daily News,* which had greeted Roosevelt's efforts to implement the Brownlow report as a "dictator bill" and an "aggrandizement of the president's constitutional powers," now hailed the Hoover Commission's recommendations and wrote of a strong, unified executive as "a prime requisite of republican institutions."[28] Herbert Hoover, the last president before the modern era, had come out of retirement to legitimate the Rooseveltian concept of the presidency. It was symbolism of some potency.

CHAPTER 5

Dwight D. Eisenhower
1953–1961

 If a new administration appears to be a tabula rasa, it is not because the tablet is blank but because the writing is invisible. It is there. But it is best discerned after the fact, when those traits and experiences in a president's background that are casual can be distinguished from those that are causal in that they determined the shape and the organization of his presidency.

Dwight D. Eisenhower, elected president in 1952, was a genial, shrewd, optimistic, confident, successful small-town American of sixty-two years. He had devoted his life to government service in the military, and although he was a newcomer to partisan politics, he was skilled at bureaucratic politics. He had spent much time abroad, which gave a somewhat anomalous internationalist cast to his otherwise conventional beliefs. His aspirations as president were limited to two overriding objectives: peace abroad and a balanced budget at home. In keeping with those aspirations, his view of the presidential role was circumscribed.

Eisenhower followed the pattern characteristic of the modern presidency by reacting to the style of the president who preceded him. As Roosevelt, the disorganization man, was followed by the tidy Harry Truman, so Eisenhower saw the purpose of his presidency as trying "to create an atmosphere of greater serenity and mutual confidence" in the wake of the cocky controversialist whose legacy, he felt, was "an unhappy state . . . bitterness

. . . quarreling."[1] (Truman, of course, would have argued that presidential prestige is meant to be used to force desirable actions.) Later, the youthful Kennedy would react to the aging Eisenhower, and so on, back and forth in the whipsaw fashion that almost defines a principle of contrariness in presidential succession.

Confronted with the immediate problem of putting together a government—the first controlled by the Republican party in twenty years—Eisenhower turned not to his party's leaders, whom he did not know well, but to an old friend, former General Lucius Clay, chairman of the board of Continental Can Company, and a new one, New York attorney Herbert Brownell. To them was left the initial screening of the cabinet. The job was made easier because no one declined the invitation to join Eisenhower's cabinet, a statistic unique in the modern presidency. The cabinet then made the initial selection of the subcabinet. Other matters of personnel were handled by Eisenhower's chief of staff, Sherman Adams. An assistant to Adams estimated that the Governor, as Adams was called inside the administration, made 75 percent of the final decisions on personnel; the rest were made by the president from lists of candidates prepared by Adams.[2] Eisenhower's noninvolvement was partly a deliberate delegation of responsibilities, partly an expression of his distaste for the process of patronage, and partly a reflection of his limited circle of acquaintances outside the military, coupled with his strong belief in not appointing military people to civilian jobs if equally capable civilians were available.

The result was that Eisenhower picked a cabinet of strangers. Not one member could have been considered an old friend; most were barely known to him or not known at all. Only two of the ten initial department heads, Attorney General Brownell and Postmaster General Arthur Summerfield, had played major roles in the campaign. (Some others had more minor parts, and several had been opposed to Eisenhower's nomination.)

The construction of the cabinet was not totally without attempts at balance. Following tradition, the position of Interior secretary went to a westerner, Douglas McKay, the retiring governor of Oregon. Eisenhower wanted a woman in the cabinet, and Oveta Culp Hobby was made director of the Federal Security Agency with the promise that the agency would be quickly transformed into a Department of Health, Education, and Welfare (Hobby's appointment also gave the cabinet a southerner and a registered Democrat).

In the president's only eyebrow-raising selection, he named a trade unionist as secretary of labor. Picking Martin Durkin, head of the AFL

Plumbers and Pipe Fitters Union, had two justifications. First, Eisenhower was trying to rectify what he felt was Truman's unwise practice of allowing the presidency to be drawn into labor-management relations. If the unions had their own person at the Labor Department, presumably they would not go over his head to the White House.[3] More conventionally, Eisenhower was seeking to broaden the perspective of the cabinet—"to help round out any debate," as he put it. In choosing Durkin he unrealistically believed that he could get "an impartial adviser," not a "special pleader for labor."[4] He did not, however, look upon his secretary of commerce, businessman Sinclair Weeks, as potentially being a special pleader for business. Durkin resigned after nine months. Eisenhower then got the type of secretary he wanted by going outside union ranks. In replacing Durkin with James Mitchell, a respected specialist in industrial relations, he was able to keep labor disputes away from the White House and add a more liberal voice to his cabinet. Mitchell remained in the post until the administration left office in 1961.

More than any other president, Eisenhower was looking for types rather than merely weighing the competing merits of individuals. "Eight millionaires and one plumber" was how the *New Republic* described the cabinet.[5] But Eisenhower was not impressed by money per se—Truman's administration had more men of wealth. What impressed Eisenhower was the ability to succeed (money was simply the unit in which success was measured). He believed that a successful person, someone who had already proved he could run something big, would be best able to tame a government department. It was a view shaped by his conception of what a government department does (namely manage something) and honed by campaign promises and the business-oriented philosophy of his party. The only two members of the cabinet (except of course for Durkin) who did not have backgrounds in management, attorneys John Foster Dulles and Brownell, were put in charge of the State and Justice departments, which from a presidential perspective can be considered more analytical than operational. Moreover, Eisenhower wrote in his diary on January 5, 1953, that to seek a government position is "clear evidence of unsuitability. I feel that anyone who can, without great personal sacrifice, come to Washington to accept an important government post, is not fit to hold that post."[6] He would hire people who were above chiseling, or not in need of it. As the representative of a party that placed its faith in the private enterprise system, who better than a business executive could ferret out waste and recognize reckless spending?

This proclivity for bringing in the successful outsider also held true in the selection of under secretaries (later renamed deputy secretaries). Before Eisenhower the standard practice had been to divide the work in a department between the two top political appointees along "outside" and "inside" lines—with the secretary being the spokesman to the outer world, the under secretary managing the bureaucracy. Yet most of the Republican under secretaries were carbon copies of their superiors.

Eisenhower's business executives joined the government in the same spirit that one contributes to the United Way, not joyously but because it is what civic-minded citizens ought to do. What was remarkable was that they stayed, held by the magnetism of Ike's personality more than by any other force. Seven of his original cabinet members were still in place at the end of the first term; most stayed much longer. One died in office, one left because he failed of Senate confirmation, and two lasted the full eight years. With only one exception, replacements came from the ranks of the subcabinet or the White House staff.

The kind of person the president chose was the kind of person he was. Dwight D. Eisenhower of Denison, Texas, and Abilene, Kansas, born October 14, 1890, surrounded himself with people of similar background. Only Dulles was older—by two years. George Humphrey, secretary of the treasury, and Charles E. Wilson, secretary of defense, were born in 1890. Thirteen of the twenty-one cabinet officers were within a decade or so of the president's age. Their places of birth read like a gazetteer of small-town America—Killeen and Burleson, Texas; McRae, Georgia; Whitney, Idaho; Minerva and Berea, Ohio; Pinconning and Grand Rapids, Michigan; Charleston, West Virginia; Kingston, New York. Their personalities also matched the president's. Cheerful and confident, they were not the dour conservatives buried in the stuffed chairs of the Union League Club. While Dulles or Agriculture Secretary Ezra Taft Benson could not be mistaken for the life of the party, they were the exceptions that Eisenhower made in the name of expertise. "Foster has been in training for this job all his life," he often said.[7]

They were decidedly not politicians. The three cabinet members who had been in the U.S. Senate—Dulles, Weeks, and Eisenhower's second secretary of the interior, Fred Seaton—had held interim appointments. The only elected senator to whom the president gave cabinet status was UN Ambassador Henry Cabot Lodge, his earliest supporter. Legislator-politicians were difficult for Eisenhower to fathom. They seemed consumed with concerns such as headlines and patronage that did not concern him. He was much more comfortable with executive-politicians, and five former governors were to serve on his White House staff.

Under the Eisenhower system the cabinet officers were expected to run the daily operations of their departments without presidential interference. They had the right to come to Eisenhower when their problems were big enough, which was left for them to decide. But the president was impatient if they sought his counsel too often on matters that he felt were strictly operational. Defense Secretary Wilson infuriated him by constantly wanting to discuss the internal workings of the Pentagon, problems that the president considered unpresidential. Cabinet officers also were to come to the White House—meaning Sherman Adams—when they disagreed among themselves. Adams "spent many hours," for example, with Commerce Secretary Weeks and Labor Secretary Mitchell "sitting across the table from each other while they ironed out their differences."[8] It was hard for the press to accept the fact that someone as powerful as Adams was not making policy, but he saw his role otherwise and largely resisted the temptation to overrule the department heads, although he was equally willing to take the blame for doing so when the decision really had been made by the president.[9]

Of course, basic differences within the cabinet were minimal, at least by the standards of the preceding administrations. The like-mindedness of the department heads ensured it. Nevertheless, the Eisenhower cabinet was composed of very strong personalities. A body that included John Foster Dulles, Charles E. Wilson, George Humphrey, Ezra Taft Benson, and Harold Stassen must rate high for sheer tenacity. The feuds smoldered, but they rarely surfaced, and the president effectively used his weekly cabinet meetings to give what historian Stephen Ambrose called "his standard pitch for teamwork."[10]

Eisenhower's conception of the cabinet differed markedly from the conceptions of the other White House occupants during the modern era. In an effort to convert the cabinet into a major deliberative mechanism, he expanded meetings to include such key aides as the UN ambassador, the budget director, the director of defense mobilization, the mutual security administrator, and the White House chief of staff. He thought it useful to gather the views of all cabinet members even if their departments were not directly involved. This practice did not, however, mean that all members were equal. George Humphrey and his successor, Robert B. Anderson, were more-than-equal voices in domestic affairs, the predictable role of Treasury in a conservative government; and Dulles jealously guarded his position as chief adviser on foreign policy.

Eisenhower got his information from listening; he formed his opinions by talking with others. This preference, perhaps more than theory, accounted for the heightened role of the cabinet and the National Security Council. He concentrated on discussion around the table, and then if he had reached a conclusion he would announce it on the spot, thus making sure that all his subordinates heard what he had decided. This was not collective government, any more than it had been with other presidents; Eisenhower accepted the fact that the decisions were his alone to make. The job of the White House was to ensure that important matters were placed on the cabinet agenda, that department heads were prepared to state their positions, and that they were periodically reminded of their responsibilities in implementing decisions the president had made.

That department heads, competing as they must for scarce resources and answerable to constituents beyond the administration, would freely put their most cherished proposals up for grabs was not an entirely workable notion. Despite the prodding of the cabinet secretariat in the White House, the trivial often substituted for the controversial. Douglas Dillon, the under secretary of state, later recalled that at one meeting "We sat around looking at the plans for Dulles Airport. They had a model and everything, and we would say why don't you put a door there, and they would explain why they didn't."[11]

Eisenhower's doctrine of delegation had a number of consequences. It may have helped to keep his appointees on the job longer than they planned. It contributed to their comfort (some said complacency), for they knew the outer limits of their assignments and had no fear of poachers. It removed burdens from the president, which added to an impression that he was not on top of his job. (He would have argued that no presidential decisions were made by anyone except the president and as few as possible non-presidential decisions were made by the president.) And according to the power equations by which presidents are often measured, Eisenhower gave himself considerable freedom of action by giving his subordinates considerable latitude to act.

What Eisenhower artfully constructed was an elaborate system of buffer zones.[12] Press secretary James Hagerty later recalled, "President Eisenhower would say, 'Do it this way,' I would say, 'If I go to that press conference and say what you want me to say, I would get hell.' With that, he would smile, get up and walk around the desk, pat me on the back and say, 'My boy, better you than me.'"[13] These buffers meant, for one thing, that the Republican loss in the 1954 midterm elections was blamed on Benson, not Eisenhower. In one poll, 33 percent of farmers gave Benson a poor rating, while only 8 percent considered Eisenhower's performance inadequate.[14] It was as if the president and the secretary of agriculture worked for different administrations. In foreign relations (especially with the British), the secretary of state was as unpopular as the president was popular. If a cabinet officer could not get to see the president, he blamed Adams, not Eisenhower.

In one important instance, however, Eisenhower chose not to employ a buffer. When the Soviet Union shot down a spy plane over its territory in 1960 and threatened to cancel the Paris summit meeting, Allen Dulles, director of the Central Intelligence Agency, volunteered to take full responsibility for ordering the mission and to resign. Premier Khrushchev seemed to invite this approach when he stated he was "quite willing to grant that the president knew nothing."[15] But Eisenhower felt that to have denied knowledge of the U-2 would have been an unconscionable admission that he did not control the country's national security apparatus. He took the blame and the summit collapsed.

Another part of Eisenhower's buffer system was to use Vice President Richard Nixon as his political surrogate, an arrangement that also reflected the president's strong distaste for party politics. The vice president assumed the burdens of campaigning during the midterm elections of 1954 and 1958. This was Eisenhower's contribution to resolving the apparent conflict between the presidential roles of chief magistrate and chief party leader.

Because Eisenhower came from a career outside politics and often expressed his aversion to partisanship, some were led to conclude that he lacked the political moxie to direct the machinery of government to his ends. Marquis Childs presented the conventional wisdom when he noted in 1958 that the president "brought to the office so little preparation."[16] Yet a cogent case can be made for reassessing Eisenhower, as a highly skilled bureaucratic politician.[17] The contemporary portrait of him as the forthright old soldier beyond his depth in a world of high government machinations was a caricature; he had, after all, spent a lifetime in the Byzantium of military politics and come out supreme Allied commander. It should be noted, however, that the portrait was also a self-caricature drawn by Eisenhower for his own reasons. (Once when asked about a newspaper column at a press conference, he replied that he could not answer because he never read the columns. The statement was patently false; he began each day with a heavy dose of newspaper reading.)[18]

Eisenhower brought with him to the White House very definite ideas of how a staff should be constructed and should work. They were based on the military model, but as only a professional soldier fully understood, they were adaptable to the vicissitudes of circumstance. The ideas worked for him; later they would not work for Nixon, who did not understand their subtleties. "The use of staff is a kind of art," David Lilienthal once mused in his diary, and another New Dealer, Rexford G. Tugwell, wrote of Eisenhower that he "was more skilled in using staff and more willing to delegate than any of his predecessors."[19] Although Tugwell profoundly disagreed with the aims of the Eisenhower administration, there was no sense in confusing Eisenhower's constricted aspirations for his government with his means of achieving them. Tugwell was simply stating what he knew to be a fact.

Eisenhower's staff was an entirely different sort of entity from his cabinet, with different functions and a different kind of personnel. Because they were personal assistants, staff members were better known to the president. Of the original thirty-two professional members, excluding military aides, twenty-two had worked in the presidential election, often on board the campaign train, five had served under Eisenhower in the army, and two had been with him at Columbia University. Twelve stayed in the administration for the full eight years.[20]

Members of the staff, much more than of the cabinet, were likely to have had previous employment in the federal government. Five had worked in congressional offices, one had served in Congress, and seven had held appointments in the executive branch. As in all administrations, top White House aides generally were younger than cabinet officers, although this did not create the friction it has in other presidencies. Thus while the Eisenhower cabinet was unique in its pervasive business background and in its lack of Washington experience, the presidential staff was more in the traditional mold. It did have more members from the corporate world than would have been found in a Democratic administration, but the business executives on Eisenhower's staff seemed to have a more contemplative cast of mind than those in the Eisenhower cabinet.[21]

Whereas the talents of the staffs under Roosevelt and Truman were to be found largely in their possession of highly sensitive political antennae, their overarching loyalty, or their creativity, the top echelon of Eisenhower's staff was noted for its functional professionalism. James Hagerty was a professional press secretary; that had been his occupation since 1942. He had also been a reporter, which may have given him certain insights, but that was not his chief qualification: Truman chose his press secretaries directly from the ranks of working journalists, without notable success. Former General Wilton (Jerry) Persons, who headed Eisenhower's congressional relations office, was a professional congressional lobbyist. That had been his role for the army during World War II. Special counsel Bernard Shanley was hired as a lawyer, not as a ghostwriter in mufti. The writing was to be done by Emmet Hughes of *Time* and *Life* magazines, in a sharp break with the past, when the distinction between policymaking and word production was left deliberately fuzzy. Besides relying on the statutory Council of Economic Advisers, Eisenhower added a personal economist, Gabriel Hauge, to the staff. Robert Montgomery, the actor-producer, was on call to advise the president on the use of television. The chairman of the Civil Service Commission was given the additional duty of advising the president on personnel management. And experts were eventually added in science, foreign economic policy, aviation policy, public works planning, agricultural surplus disposal, disarmament, and psychological warfare.

A review of the organization of the White House under Eisenhower must begin with the assistant to the president, Sherman Adams. Eisenhower's recollection of his chief aide differs in no respect from the way Adams appeared to those who served under him:

> From our first meeting in 1952 Sherman Adams seemed to me best described as laconic, businesslike, and puritanically honest. Never did he attempt to introduce humor into an official meeting. On the many occasions during our White House years when I called him on the telephone to ask a question, he never added a word to his "yes" or "no" if such an answer sufficed. It never occurred to him to say "Hello" when advised by his secretary that I wanted him on the phone or to add a "Good-bye" at the end of the call. For Sherman Adams this was neither bad manners nor pretense; he was busy. Absorbed in his work, he had no time to waste.[22]

Eisenhower saw the function of his assistant, called the White House chief of staff in subsequent administrations, as that of being his personal "son of a bitch," a role ably played for him by General Walter Bedell Smith during World War II, and he deliberately sought a person with the same talents to head his White House operation. After Adams was forced out in late 1958, having been accused of accepting favors from a Boston industrialist, his place was taken by Jerry Persons. A gentle, humorous southerner, Persons had chosen a career as conciliator, and he was not overly concerned with running a tight ship. He allowed more staff members direct access to the president and was less interested in scrutinizing the matters that were to be put before his boss. This change did not, however, notably affect the operations of the government. By this time staff members were proficient in their assignments, comfortable in their relations with each other, and part of a waning administration. It was the Adams style that set the tone of the Eisenhower White House.

All activities except those relating to foreign relations came under Adams's eye. These included appointments and scheduling, patronage and personnel, press, speechwriting, cabinet liaison, congressional relations, and special projects. A newly created staff secretariat (proposed in the Hoover Commission report, a well-thumbed document during the 1952–53 transition) kept track of all pending presidential business and ensured the proper clearances on all papers that reached the Oval Office. A two-man operation within the secretariat prepared daily staff notes for the president, giving him advance notice of actions to be taken by the departments and agencies. Adams coordinated White House work through early morning staff meetings, generally three times a week. These sessions also were used for briefings by the CIA and preparation of suggested answers to questions that might be asked at presidential press conferences.

Although there had been some formalized responsibility for lobbying Congress in the Truman White House, it had been essentially a closet operation. Lobbying without acknowledging that it was being done presumably was least offensive to the legislature's sensibilities as a coequal branch of government. From Eisenhower's point of view, however, the best reason to end this fiction was that he wanted staff positioned between himself and all those nattering members of Congress. Like many professional military men, he had a high regard for Congress, but not for its members.[23] The six aides who served at some point in the White House congressional relations office had had considerable experience on Capitol Hill; one had been a member of the House of Representatives, and three had more substantial ties to the Democratic party than to the GOP. Given that the Democrats controlled Congress for three-fourths of the time Eisenhower was in office, these relationships were not without significance. The Republican congressional leadership was wooed through weekly meetings with the president for which the staff prepared detailed agendas. Eisenhower confessed that "these Legislative meetings were sometimes tiresome."[24] But in general the program fared well because of the president's great popularity, his personal friendships with Democratic leaders Sam Rayburn and Lyndon Johnson, the skill of his staff, and mostly because he did not ask for a great deal. The White House conducted a major assault on Congress for a legislative objective only once or twice a year; the rest of the time the departments were on their own.

Eisenhower regarded meetings with the White House press corps, like those with members of Congress, as a necessary though less than pleasant aspect of being president. He could not and would not manipulate them in the manner of Roosevelt, but they did not irritate him to the degree that they had Truman. If he could not point to his meetings with the reporters as a positive accomplishment, he did take some pride in having survived: "I was able to avoid causing the nation a serious setback through anything I said in many hours, over eight years, of intensive questioning. . . . It is far better to stumble or speak guardedly than to move ahead smoothly and risk imperiling the country."[25]

His press conferences averaged one every other week, down from once a week during the Truman presidency, although illness accounted for some of the decline.[26] Hagerty's press briefings doubled, however, with sessions each morning and afternoon. The press secretary also managed to coax greater mileage out of fewer presidential press conferences by releasing full transcripts within hours and by allowing them to be taped for radio and filmed for later use on television. Since Eisenhower did not grant personal interviews and since staff members generally referred reporters' inquiries to Hagerty, the press secretary emerged for the first time as the principal spokesman for the government.

The reputation for efficiency that the White House staff had under Adams's direction was well earned, but the reputation for organizational rigidity was overstated by contemporary observers. There was a box on the chart for speechwriter, but other staff members, notably Gabriel Hauge and Bryce Harlow, were pressed into service from time to time. Maxwell Rabb, the cabinet secretary, also handled relations with Jewish and other minority groups. Frederic Morrow was the administrative officer for special projects as well as being deeply involved in civil rights (he was the first black professional on a White House staff). Paul Carroll and Andrew Goodpaster, both military officers, successively headed the staff secretariat while also being responsible for the day-to-day liaison on national security affairs. Although such mixed assignments were exceptions, there was some flexibility in the system to take advantage of special talents.

There was more organizational rigidity in the redesign of the White House foreign policy machinery. By 1956 the National Security Council staff consisted of twenty-eight members, of whom eleven were considered "think people." Eisenhower was the first president to appoint a special assistant for national security affairs with responsibility for long-range planning. Day-to-day liaison with State and Defense, as has been noted, was handled by the staff secretary. Neither were operational, so that even together their duties did not add up to those later assumed by Henry Kissinger. The first assistant for national security affairs, Robert Cutler, described his domain as "the top of Policy Hill."[27] On the upside of the hill was the Planning Board (basically Truman's NSC senior staff renamed). It was made up of departmental representatives at the assistant secretary level, with the presidential assistant as its chairman. The Planning Board developed position papers, which the presidential assistant carried up to the crest, the National Security Council. Assuming that decisions were made by the president at the summit, the decisions then went down the hill to be implemented by the departments. On the downside, Eisenhower placed a new mechanism, the Operations Coordinating Board, consisting of officers at the under secretary level, whose job was to expedite decisions and follow them up.[28]

The NSC Planning Board met Tuesday and Friday afternoons for three hours. It normally took three or four meetings before a paper was ready to be sent forward. Gordon Gray, special assistant for national security affairs, cited one paper that consumed all or part of twenty-seven meetings and on which twenty-three consultants worked. After reviewing a paper the Planning Board would return it to a group of assistants, who met for four to eight hours on each redraft. This laborious process was designed to force agreement, but despite the best efforts of the chairman of the Planning Board that was not always possible, and Gray mentioned one policy paper that was finally forwarded to the NSC with nineteen "splits."[29]

The president presided over 329 of the 366 weekly NSC meetings during his two terms. These meetings were particularly useful during the first two years of the administration, when the work of the council was largely taken up with examining all the policies of the Truman administration. But the machinery kept getting more cumbersome. Meetings were attended by the five statutory members (president, vice president, secretary of state, secretary of defense, and director of the Office of Civil and Defense Mobilization); the two statutory advisers (chairman of the Joint Chiefs of Staff and director of the CIA); three officers that the president added to the NSC (secretary of the treasury, budget director, and chairman of the Atomic Energy Commission); and enough regular invitees to add up to twenty persons around the cabinet table.[30] In addition there were others, such as the attorney general or the administrator of the National Aeronautics and Space Administration, whose presence was requested for specific agenda items. As Cutler early warned, at some point a group turns into a town meeting, and "once this invisible line is passed, people do not discuss and debate; they remain silent or talk for the record."[31]

When Eisenhower met with President-elect Kennedy on December 6, 1960, he reported that "the National Security Council had become the most important weekly meeting of the government." Yet in one of the afterthoughts in his memoirs, he suggested that part of the committee structure could be usefully replaced "by a highly competent and trusted official with a small staff . . . who might have a title such as Secretary for International Coordination."[32] Still, as tedious as some of Eisenhower's NSC procedures were, there is no evidence that they caused unreasonable delay when prompt action was necessary. The decision to dispatch U.S. troops to Lebanon in 1958 did not emanate from an NSC discussion; it was considered by a smaller gathering in the president's office after an NSC meeting. The more urgent the stakes, the less likely a decision will be the result of large, formal sessions. Indeed, as Douglas Kinnard concluded in his study of Eisenhower's national security planning: "I saw few instances where the key decisions on strategic policy were not made by the president in small informal meetings."[33] By the end of the administration, however, the NSC apparatus was coming under heavy attack from Senator Henry Jackson's Subcommittee on National Policy Machinery, whose reports would influence Senator John Kennedy.

Much of the growth in the White House staff came in the area of foreign relations. Besides the elaborate NSC operation, the presidential establishment included new offices for psychological warfare, disarmament, foreign economic policy, food aid abroad, and the international aspects of science and atomic energy. Eisenhower also relied on his brother Milton, president of Johns Hopkins University and an expert on Latin America, who has been called his "closest and most versatile adviser."[34] John Foster Dulles viewed these offices and specialists with suspicion and, when possible, cut their ranks down to what he thought was an appropriate size. Neither Nelson Rockefeller, special assistant for cold war strategy, nor Harold Stassen, special assistant on disarmament, could long survive the secretary's enmity.

To explain the apparent paradox of the giving and taking of Dulles's power, it is necessary to consider the role of Eisenhower's growing staff. Grow it did. There were thirty-two presidentially appointed professionals in the White House at the beginning of his first term; forty-seven at the beginning of his second term; and fifty when he left office. The new aides fitted into four categories, each a perceived need of the president. What initially caused the expansion was Eisenhower's desire for efficiency. "Organization cannot make a genius out of an incompetent," he wrote. "On the other hand, disorganization can scarcely fail to result in inefficiency."[35] That was the reason for the creation of the staff secretary system. Eisenhower's second need was for coordination, which brought about the cabinet secretariat and the NSC machinery. In certain areas, such as science and economics, Eisenhower also felt the need for his own experts. In paying tribute to the science adviser, a post he established in 1957 after the Soviets launched Sputnik, he wrote, "Without such distinguished help, any president in our time would be, to a certain extent, disabled."[36] And what was probably behind the increase in foreign policy advisers was Eisenhower's quest to fill gaps in the regular advice system of the government, to make up for what he felt were deficiencies in his cabinet members. As Adams put it, "Granted that Dulles was a man of great moral force and conviction, he was not endowed with the creative genius that produces bold, new ideas."[37] Therefore Eisenhower turned to such special assistants as C. D. Jackson and Rockefeller to provide what he was not getting from his secretary of state. Eisenhower's two "bold, new ideas," the Atoms for Peace (1953) and Open Skies (1955) proposals, did not come from the State Department and were met with skepticism by Dulles. All presidents have shared Eisenhower's need for coordination and expertise, but the desire for staff efficiency—until Jimmy Carter's presidency—has been a uniquely Republican motivation, perhaps related to differences in philosophy and personnel of the two parties.

Within the Executive Office, Eisenhower had an opportunity to kill off the Council of Economic Advisers in 1953. The Republican Congress, disenchanted with the politics and economics of Leon Keyserling, had drastically cut the CEA budget. But Gabriel Hauge convinced the president to keep the council and to hire Arthur Burns as its chairman. Under the 1946 enabling act, the three members of the council were to be coequal, but Eisenhower quickly won approval of a reorganization plan giving operating responsibility to the chairman, a variation of a Hoover Commission proposal. Burns chose his staff mostly from the academy rather than from government service. Although Adams feared that Eisenhower and Burns would not get along, his worry proved groundless. When the 1954 economic downturn began, Burns introduced regular briefings, often lasting thirty minutes, at the cabinet meetings, and according to Adams, "Eisenhower listened to him with fascination."[38] The CEA survived its first crucial transition in administrations because of the increased stake of the president in the behavior of the economy, because the council members and their staff were congenial to the president, and because they provided him with information he considered immediately useful.

The Bureau of the Budget, so important in the Truman administration, did not fare as well. Two of Eisenhower's four budget directors were bankers and two were accountants, whereas their predecessors had had backgrounds in public administration.[39] For instruction in management reorganization the president was more apt to look to the second Hoover Commission and to his Committee on Government Organization (Nelson Rockefeller, Arthur Flemming, and Milton Eisenhower). Otherwise the Budget Bureau continued to do about what it had always done, but it was not as central to the making of policy. This was caused less by suspicion of the career bureaucrat than by a simple law of physics: everyone could not occupy the same space. Eisenhower's system of an expanded White House staff and a more powerful cabinet left less room at the center for the Budget Bureau to occupy.

The testing of Eisenhower's staff-and-cabinet system came during his extended illnesses. The illnesses happened to coincide with periods of considerable calm in the nation and the world, for which the White House–cabinet arrangement could hardly take credit. But from Eisenhower's viewpoint these periods proved that his organizational design would work as intended—efficiently, without friction, confidently. And this was his objective for his government and his country.

Dwight Eisenhower chose a way of organizing the presidency that was very different from that of his predecessors. His structured staff system increased the size of the White House, yet the White House was to continue to grow even when it returned to more fluid designs. However, as a result of his having asked for and received substantially increased appropriations from Congress for staff purposes, a new floor was established.

The emphasis on creating new staff mechanisms did not have an adverse effect on the efficiency of domestic operations but did become burdensome for conducting foreign relations. Eisenhower's White House showed that a large staff need not be operational, at least if it is balanced with tenacious cabinet officials. Still, as future presidents would prove, the larger the staff, the greater the temptation to try to run the departments from the White House.

The use of the cabinet for collective advice was particularly suited to Eisenhower's preferences for receiving information and was relatively frictionless because of the homogeneity of the members. The rudimentary cabinet secretariat, however, was less successful in forcing the most important decisions through the system.

The combination of an efficient and orderly White House staff and unusual reliance on the cabinet fit the president's personal needs and limited objectives. The liabilities of the administration—the absence of a steady stream of creative proposals and the failure to recognize the boiling point of the civil rights issue and certain other domestic conditions—have been blamed on Eisenhower's techniques of management. Could the same system that worked for an intrinsically conservative and nonactivist president be adapted to the needs of a liberal, activist one?

The proposition was not tested by Kennedy and Johnson, who simply assumed that it could not. Nixon was an activist, but while he favored a highly structured White House staff, he quickly rejected a collegial use of the cabinet, and, lacking Eisenhower's skill in the art of using staff, his methods turned out to be more a perversion than an extension of the Eisenhower system.

In the wake of Eisenhower, conservative results and a structured staff system were often equated by social scientists who may have been personally uncomfortable with such systems and unfamiliar with how they operate. It is hardly surprising that they would propose methods of organization that seemed more congenial to them. Yet there is no evidence to prove that Eisenhower's system was ineffective. Certainly imaginative people prefer to work within systems of least constraint. It is unlikely, however, that a liberal president with liberal personnel would produce a conservative administration even if the presidency were organized along more structured lines.

CHAPTER 6

John F. Kennedy
1961–1963

When John F. Kennedy became president, he promptly dismantled Eisenhower's Operations Coordinating Board of the National Security Council and abolished scores of interdepartmental committees. He determined that there would be few cabinet meetings and that those few would be primarily for symbolic purposes, because "public confidence [is] inspired by order and regularity."[1] He also redesigned the White House organizational chart, eliminating the staff secretariat. There would be no chief of staff; top aides would be generalists and would have roughly equivalent titles, usually special assistant. The pyramid was to be replaced by the wheel, with the president at the hub.

Kennedy proceeded on the assumption, later articulated by Roger Hilsman, that the way Eisenhower organized the government produced "the basically conservative policies that . . . the Eisenhower administration desired." Eisenhower's operation discouraged "new and innovating policies," forced agreement on "the lowest common denominator," and supported the status quo.[2] To change policies, the new administration had to change mechanisms.

The new president would have been thoroughly uncomfortable with the Eisenhower machinery even if he had wished to make use of it. Like Roosevelt, "Kennedy evinced little interest in organization structure and

administration."³ Whereas Eisenhower was a product of the rigidly structured military organization that had planned and coordinated the invasion
of Europe, Kennedy had been a backbencher in the legislature, operating as
a sort of free lance in the competition for public attention. His career, made
possible by family wealth, had been decidedly individualistic, an occurrence
relatively uncommon in a society in which most people's status is determined by position in an organization. Kennedy could be expected to produce a singularly personal presidency.

For this kind of chief executive there of course existed an operating
model other than Eisenhower's. As Richard Neustadt wrote the Democratic candidate in 1960, "if you follow my advice you will commit yourself
not to each detail of Rooseveltian practice—some details are out of date,
others were unfortunate—but to the *spirit* of his presidential operation."⁴
That was congenial advice. Franklin Roosevelt's style was attractive to one
who was fascinated by the techniques of wielding power, at which Roosevelt was a master. And Roosevelt had created the modern activist presidency, which was partly a product of his techniques and which Kennedy
also found attractive. As he told the National Press Club early in 1960, the
presidency must be "the vital center of action in our whole scheme of government . . . the President [must] place himself in the very thick of the
fight."⁵ Young, restless, highly intelligent, pragmatic, with a strong sense of
history, John Kennedy knew what kind of president he wanted to be even
before he knew what he wanted his presidency to do.

Like Eisenhower, however, Kennedy surrounded himself with men
whose age and background was similar to his own. Kennedy was forty-three
years old when he took office. The three original members of his Council
of Economic Advisers were forty-five, forty-four, and forty-two. Other staff
members were equally young. When William Manchester accused him of
being "a generational chauvinist," Kennedy agreed, saying he "felt more
comfortable with people with a common experience."⁶ Among those common experiences were military service in World War II, often in intelligence or guerilla warfare at the line officer level, an excellent education
(there were fifteen Rhodes scholars in the administration), and participation in one of the longest presidential campaigns in history (Kennedy's
active quest for the nomination had begun in 1956). With the exception of
McGeorge Bundy, his top White House aides had been his top campaign
aides. Quoting Shakespeare's *Henry V,* they spoke approvingly of themselves as "we band of brothers." This was not a phrase that would have

quickly come to mind among Roosevelt's helpers (until much later, when sentimentality had set in). Yet it was not an inexact characterization of the Kennedy White House. There was little friction. Kennedy was not one to create conflict among his subordinates, and when he inadvertently gave competing assignments, his assistants were apt to sort them out among themselves.

There also were no factions as there had been at the Truman White House. The press expected a power struggle between the so-called Irish Mafia—Kenneth O'Donnell, appointments secretary, and Lawrence O'Brien, who was in charge of congressional relations—and the so-called eggheads, such as special counsel Theodore Sorensen and Arthur Schlesinger Jr. But the fight never came off. First, the intellectuals in residence did not place politics lower in the scheme of things than did the politicians. In fact, under secretary of state George Ball later complained that the academics drawn to "the yeasty air of the Potomac" had been "so seduced by the challenge of operational problems as to renounce any attempt at conceptual thinking as 'theology.'"[7] Second, the press underestimated the strength of the centripetal forces—not only the personality of the president and the staff's loyalty to him but also the length of time he and his staff had been together.

Thus the informal arrangements at the Kennedy White House were more than a result of the informality of the staff; they reflected a division of labor and the trust that had developed in the pre–White House period. Eisenhower's organizational design was a working plan for a group of relative strangers, a substitution of procedures for group instinct and experience. Kennedy could do without procedures as long as other arrangements kept his aides from tripping over themselves. If he had served a second term and there had been a high personnel turnover, it is possible that his White House also would have become more procedurally oriented.

In contrast to the White House staff, the Kennedy cabinet reflected traditional political balances. Kennedy may have felt that because he had been elected with little more than 100,000 votes to spare, the appointment of department secretaries was an opportunity to reassure uneasy factions in his party and important constituent groups around the country whose acquiescence was needed to govern. So a Republican investment banker, C. Douglas Dillon, became secretary of the treasury, and Luther Hodges, a southern governor and former businessman, was named secretary of commerce. A New England governor, Abraham Ribicoff, was picked for the

Department of Health, Education, and Welfare; a midwestern governor, Orville Freeman, for Agriculture; and a western congressman, Stewart Udall, for Interior. The general counsel for the industrial union department of the AFL-CIO, Arthur Goldberg, was made secretary of labor. Incumbent directors J. Edgar Hoover and Allan Dulles were retained at the Federal Bureau of Investigation and the Central Intelligence Agency.

There were, however, three surprising choices: Attorney General Robert Kennedy, Secretary of Defense Robert McNamara, and Secretary of State Dean Rusk. For a president to select his younger brother and campaign manager, a person with limited experience as a practicing attorney, to be his chief legal officer was an audacious decision. McNamara and Rusk, on the other hand, were unknown to Kennedy and were the products of an informal network of talent hunters that generally produces the same types of people regardless of party—certain corporate executives, foundation officials, members of major law firms, and university administrators—with interesting subcategories, such as Republicans who turn up consistently in Democratic administrations. McNamara, the president of Ford Motors and a nonpolitical Republican, delighted Kennedy from the start. He was self-confident, articulate, energetic, and comfortable at the helm of a large organization. Kennedy would not have to concern himself with running the Pentagon, which was no small recommendation to a president who had no background or interest in management. But Rusk was of another nature, a nonassertive southerner, guarded in speech, with an infinite patience for the folkways of the State Department, where he had served as an assistant secretary during the Truman administration. In effect McNamara functioned as a member of Kennedy's inner circle; Rusk seemed more a member of the bureaucracy.

Although foreign affairs had always interested Kennedy far more than domestic issues, he initially expected to move foreign policy formulation from the White House to the State Department, which was one reason he cut the staff and mechanisms of the National Security Council. Yet the hierarchy he created at the State Department left him "discouraged . . . almost as soon as he took office. . . . It was never clear to the President who was in charge."⁸ The selection of Rusk was one of those risks that confront all presidents. "I must make the appointments now," Kennedy had told John Kenneth Galbraith in December 1960. "A year hence I will know who I really want to appoint."⁹ But lack of forethought, not time, was at the root of Kennedy's frustration. In constructing a national security triumvirate of

Rusk, McNamara, and McGeorge Bundy, the special assistant for national security, the president put the most diffident person in the post that required the most assertive. This decision was to have profound consequences as events in Vietnam became more pressing. A McNamara in the State Department, where he would have represented the institutional interests of diplomacy rather than national security, would have shifted the balance of advocacy.

The problem of who was in charge at the State Department was compounded when Kennedy personally chose many of the key secondary personnel, even announcing some of these appointments before Rusk's. Reflecting on government in 1968, Bundy thought it "nonsense" to prevent a department head from picking his own subordinates. "The historical record is full of examples of the trouble and frustration for all concerned that can come from the oh-so-skillful insertion of a President's man into the second or third level of a department."[10] But although Kennedy soon lost interest in the tedious chore of personnel selection, in the beginning he found it fascinating, and in staffing the State Department he filled at least three secondary positions with men who were more highly qualified than Rusk (Adlai Stevenson, Chester Bowles, and Averell Harriman). A number of others, such as G. Mennen Williams, had strong constituencies of their own. It was a design calculated to promote intrigue, and ultimately both Stevenson and Bowles were trapped by power plays that were not of their making.

This hiring pattern contrasted sharply with that at the Defense Department. McNamara took his job with a guarantee that he could select or veto the selection of subordinates. The White House seemed to care most about picking the secretaries of the military services, but even here McNamara eventually inserted his own people.

Although length of time in office is not always a fair measurement of how well an appointee performs, usually there is a relationship. By this rough standard, Kennedy's appointments were highly satisfactory at Defense and equally unsatisfactory at State. Eleven of the sixteen key State Department people served an average of fourteen months, a much shorter record of service than that of the Pentagon personnel.[11] In filling the top echelons of the State Department, Kennedy was influenced by the strong presumptive claims in foreign policy experience of the Stevensonian wing of his party. The appointment of so many liberals at State and in the ambassadorial ranks in turn heightened the pressures on the president to tilt in the other direction—what Schlesinger repeatedly called a "strategy of reassurance."

Kennedy picked each of his conservatives for slightly different reasons, although the overall strategy was to diminish partisan divisions or, if things went wrong, to help redistribute the blame. McNamara's Republicanism was irrelevant, just as Henry Wallace's had been in 1933; they were chosen for their special abilities. And Douglas Dillon, the Republican at Treasury, was the person most congenial to the president who would still be acceptable to Wall Street. In choosing John McCloy, William Foster, and Arthur Dean as disarmament advisers, Kennedy was, according to Schlesinger, "following the customary practice of seeking a conservative to execute a liberal policy." And he sent Henry Cabot Lodge to Saigon as U.S. ambassador because "the thought of implicating a leading Republican in the Vietnam mess appealed to his instinct for politics."[12] Generally these appointees served the purposes of the president's choosing, despite the inherent risks—as when former general Lucius Clay's blue-ribbon commission produced a report that was considerably less supportive of maintaining foreign aid than Kennedy expected.

Unlike Eisenhower, Kennedy had cabinet meetings as seldom as possible. He dealt with his department heads individually, allotting time according to the degree of his interest in a department's activities, but he listened to them as a group "with thinly disguised impatience," in the opinion of his postmaster general, J. Edward Day.[13] "Cabinet meetings are simply useless," Kennedy said. "Why should the Postmaster General sit there and listen to a discussion of the problems of Laos?"[14] Many of the departments, however, had broad concerns—Interior with the environment, Agriculture with food, Labor with manpower, and so forth—and the perspectives of some cabinet members were hardly parochial, as evidenced by Labor Secretary Arthur Goldberg's subsequent service on the Supreme Court and at the United Nations. But germaneness was not really the issue; the National Security Council, whose members all shared involvement in common questions, met only sixteen times in the first six months of the administration. Rather, Kennedy was too restless to sit for long periods, too impatient with long-winded speakers, and too mentally agile to accept repetitious, circuitous cabinet and NSC discussions as a tolerable method of receiving information. It is possible that he scrapped the concept of collective advice because he hated meetings, just as Eisenhower may have accepted it because of his high tolerance for them. If so, both made theories about the proper way to run a government that were ultimately founded on the rates of their respective metabolisms.

The first test of Kennedy's decisionmaking came in mid-April 1961, when a brigade of guerrillas, trained and supported by the United States, invaded Cuba and was easily repulsed. The plans for a possible invasion had been initiated by the Central Intelligence Agency during the Eisenhower administration, and they were reviewed at many sessions with Kennedy. In opposition to the CIA were Arthur Schlesinger Jr., of the White House staff; William Fulbright, chairman of the Senate Foreign Relations Committee; and under secretary of state Chester Bowles, whose views did not filter through Rusk to the president. Kennedy made a number of modifications and gave his approval. When the operation failed he took full responsibility.

"The lessons of the Bay of Pigs," according to Sorensen, "altered Kennedy's entire approach" to executive management.[15] He seemed to have learned to turn first to those he trusted most and, conversely, to trust little in those he knew least. He subsequently treated the advice of the permanent government with suspicion and inserted his own people into the system whenever possible—General Maxwell Taylor as chairman of the Joint Chiefs, for example. Bundy's NSC staff became a little State Department at the White House, with its own area specialists, such as Michael Forrestal (Far Eastern affairs), Robert Komer (Near East), and Carl Kaysen (Europe). The Foreign Intelligence Advisory Board was reactivated to keep an eye on the CIA. The president's two closest associates, his brother Robert and Theodore Sorensen, previously involved only in domestic matters, were given a broad mandate to concern themselves with foreign policy as well. The president also created ad hoc task forces to make foreign policy recommendations, thus superseding the regular channels of the State Department. The first two task forces, on Laos and Cuba, formed in the spring of 1961, were presided over by deputy secretary of defense Roswell Gilpatric and assistant secretary of defense Paul Nitze, respectively. One result of these changes was that when confronted with the second Cuban crisis—the installation of Soviet missiles in the fall of 1962—and the choice between ordering air strikes against missile bases or setting up a naval blockade, Kennedy accepted the advice of those he trusted most (his brother, Sorensen, McNamara) and rejected the advice of those he trusted least (the Joint Chiefs of Staff, the CIA, Rusk).[16]

Yet except for the addition of Sorensen and Robert Kennedy, the makeup of the advisory groups during the two crises was not markedly different. Irving Janis presented a convincing case that the participants approached the crises in entirely different deliberative manners. The sense of U.S. invulnerability, the suppression of personal doubts in favor of a forced unanimity, the stereotyping of the enemy—all present in the meetings leading to the Bay of Pigs decision—were replaced by a vigilant appraisal of the options during the missile crisis.[17] But one suspects that the underlying reason Kennedy's advisers were able to engage in such successful decisionmaking in the Cuban missile crisis is that they had earlier produced "a perfect failure" at the Bay of Pigs. The decision to invade had all the hallmarks of a determination made in the glow of election victory, just as Roosevelt's attempt to pack the Supreme Court and Johnson's escalation in Vietnam had. A naval blockade, a low-level response, proved to be the right choice during the missile crisis, but it was also the decision of men who had previously risked greatly and lost. Thus the most lasting lesson of the Bay of Pigs may be that the early period of an administration, when arrogance and the illusion of invincibility hangs over the White House, is a time of potential high risk for a president.

Kennedy had a firmer grasp of the importance of subcabinet appointments than did previous presidents. Under the direction of his brother-in-law, Sargent Shriver, an informal network of talent scouts was positioned around the country. There was nothing systematic about this search, but it did manage to cast the net widely and reach out for recruits rather than merely respond to the entreaties of office seekers. As a rule of thumb, Shriver sought persons who could be described as "action intellectuals," business executives who had written books or professors who had run businesses. People on transition task forces also represented potential appointees that the incoming government had an easy opportunity to assess; at least twenty-four of these participants were given positions during the initial hiring period.[18]

The president and his advisers also viewed the civil service personnel with a low quotient of paranoia. They did not look upon the bureaucracy as a hotbed of covert political oppositionists. Yet before long they began to think of the rest of government not so much as a political resistance movement but as an institutional resistance movement, "a bulwark against change" and "a force against innovation with an inexhaustible capacity to dilute, delay and obstruct presidential purpose."[19] This frustration was deepened by generational differences. Careerists work their way up a hier-archical ladder; political appointees short-circuit the system—their rise to the top is quick, if the stay is brief. When the two intersect they are at dif-ferent ages, with different metabolisms, different types of rewards, a differ-ent sense of time.

The friction between the staffs of the permanent government and the Kennedy White House was also a product of contrasting styles. The Schles-ingers and the Salingers were the antithesis of the Brownlow report's vision of presidential assistants with "a passion for anonymity."[20] Not only did they have a personal flair that attracted attention, but their sense of the necessity for action meant they could not wait for problems to work themselves up through the bureaucracy. And waiting would also have been a violation of their instructions: their activist president expected them to seek out incipi-ent crises. At times the White House staff may have confused the pace of the permanent government with its intent; the bureaucracy moved slowly, but it did not necessarily move in the opposite direction, nor was it totally immune to political leadership. The staff's suspicions of the civil service, however, steadily increased in the Kennedy White House. They were to increase even more quickly under Johnson and to become pathological under Nixon.

Consequently, the White House staff continued to expand. While the underlying reason for growth under Eisenhower had been the president's faith in management (a staff secretariat, a cabinet secretariat, and so forth), the growth of the Kennedy White House was based on the president's belief that if a task was important enough, it was necessary to have some-one at the White House with responsibility for prodding the bureaucracy. Roosevelt's favored technique was to spawn new agencies; Kennedy more often chose to add White House expediters.

Kennedy's expansion of the White House–Executive Office complex had various causes: to comply with congressional legislation (Office of Special Representative for Trade Negotiations); to save face for an official discharged from another position (Chester Bowles); to provide a good address from which to run for office (placing Food for Peace director George McGovern in the White House); to find a useful activity for the vice president (chairing the National Aeronautics and Space Council); to lobby a bill through Congress (Howard Petersen's operation in support of the Reciprocal Trade Act); to respond to the personal interest of the presi-dent's wife (the arts); and because no one else in government cared (the

District of Columbia). There was no resistance to growth. Indeed, creating another White House office was often the easiest way to solve a personnel or constituent problem, a way to confer high status with little effort. The White House was also the one place in government where the president had total control over expenditures and was free to move personnel and establish units at will.

In addition to the random growth of the Kennedy White House, there was also renewed attention to the public aspects of the presidency. Speeches, press conferences, symbolic activities were in keeping with Kennedy's conception of the office, what Roosevelt called "moral leadership." Under the direction of press secretary Pierre Salinger, more elaborate preparations than ever before were made for briefing the president before press conferences, which now were carried on live television.[21] Kennedy held these meetings slightly less often than Eisenhower had, but he was infinitely more effective in answering reporters' questions. The production of speeches again became a major White House activity. Instead of isolating this function on the organizational chart, as Eisenhower had, Kennedy returned to Roosevelt's practice and to the title that had been invented for Rosenman and had been continued through the Truman administration: as chief draftsman, Sorensen was special counsel and primary White House adviser on domestic policy.

Using the powers of the public presidency did not uniquely improve Kennedy's success rate with Congress. His Congressional Relations Office, headed by Larry O'Brien, remained about the same size as the Persons-Harlow operation under Eisenhower. But O'Brien greatly expanded his outreach through the placement and coordination of legislative liaison officers in the departments and agencies. These operatives sent him weekly reports and projections, which were analyzed for the president and formed the basis of his meetings with congressional leaders. Periodically O'Brien would also call together his network, which numbered approximately forty.[22] So the Kennedy innovation in congressional relations was to build more systematic links with the rest of the executive agencies.

The Council of Economic Advisers also took on special primacy under Kennedy. The president discontinued Eisenhower's practice of employing a White House economist in addition to the CEA. And although the council still competed with other sources in providing advice to the president on the economy, the creation of an economic troika that met regularly had the effect of elevating the CEA chairman to the level of the budget director and the treasury secretary, despite their major operational roles and extensive staffs.

The three members of Kennedy's CEA—chairman Walter Heller, James Tobin, and Kermit Gordon—fit the personality profile that the president found most arresting. As Herbert Stein wrote, "They were, for one thing, extremely self-confident."²³ Truman's CEA was drawn from government service and Eisenhower's from the academy; Kennedy's was drawn from both—all three members were professors with experience in Washington. They were, in short, action intellectuals. They knew the proper way to lecture the president, and a CEA memorandum reached Kennedy's desk on the average of once every third day. Before long, council members were taking on the sort of assignments that had been unknown to previous economic advisers, such as developing legislative proposals to reduce poverty and improve transportation. Heller concluded that "the forces of both law and practice make it increasingly natural that the major focus of presidential economic advice should be in the Council."²⁴ The question is not as settled as Heller suggested, since both law and practice have a way of being disregarded when it suits a president's purposes. But what is most convincing is that foreign policy and the economy have become of overriding presidential concern. In this context the temptations are great for a president to have his chief advisers close at hand.

The CEA, with its staff of only nineteen full-time professionals, was able to relate quickly and comfortably to the president—indeed, to move effectively across the invisible line that separates the Executive Office of the President from the White House staff. The same could not be said of the Bureau of the Budget, with its 500 employees. Kennedy preferred to deal with individuals, not institutions. Moreover, two other forces worked to diminish the traditional role of the bureau as an extension of the presidency. The first was Kennedy's lack of interest in questions of management, an important element in the bureau's portfolio. The second was the tendency for the legislation that was most important to the president to be designed by Sorensen's office after direct negotiations with the departments and renegotiations on Capitol Hill by O'Brien's staff. This still left a great deal of work for the Budget Bureau's legislative reference unit, but it was mostly the clearance of the more minor bills.²⁵ The irony is that as the bureau became less influential, budget directors David Bell and Kermit Gordon gained influence, in effect becoming personal and powerful special assistants to the president. Kennedy sought persons with the expertise that he found most helpful. Roosevelt and Truman had picked budget directors from the field of public administration; Eisenhower's directors were bankers and accountants; Kennedy's men had backgrounds in program analysis and economic policy.

By the sudden end of John Kennedy's life, virtually every aspect of White House staffing had been altered to conform with the habits and priorities of the president. Only personal services, such as scheduling and appointments, continued to be handled in a way that Herbert Hoover would have recognized as familiar. Even where boxes remained on the organizational chart, the apparent continuity was deceptive. The roles of the budget director and the CEA chairman, to name just two, were significantly different under Kennedy than they had been under Eisenhower.

As Kennedy found, a new president has full power to appoint his own staff, to make assignments, to create or abolish White House offices, to give or withhold his time and attention, and to seek advice from any source and measure the consequences of rejecting it. That realization should not be startling, yet students of the White House have tended to view each president's flexibility as circumscribed by the precedents of his predecessors, which cling to the office like barnacles. Even though the very idea of an institutional presidency implies that a president accepts and uses what is in place when he arrives at the White House, Kennedy, like Eisenhower before him, discovered that each president is remarkably free to make his own mistakes.

If Eisenhower's mistakes were thought by some to relate to too much structure, Kennedy's were certainly otherwise. He had little interest in the organization of executive branch operations and developed a disdain for its routines. His impatience, the generational chauvinism of his staff, and his administration's emphasis on crisis management also led him to denigrate organization. This disregard meant that Kennedy often depended on advisers he trusted and who were loyal to him rather than advisers whose responsibilities were born of an organizational chart. Cabinet officers, especially in the lesser departments, had a difficult time in engaging his attention. Chains of command were sometimes scrambled. The boundless energy of presidential assistants worked like a magnet, drawing departmental issues into the White House.

Kennedy's organization of the administration conformed to his sense of the presidency as the focal point of the national government. His ability to personalize the office was aided by a stunning capacity to draw attention to himself and his family and by the skill of those assistants who helped him in his symbolic duties, such as speechwriter Sorensen and press secretary Salinger. This was in the spirit of the Rooseveltian model. What had changed since Roosevelt's time, however, was the size and complexity of the federal establishment. It could no longer be assumed that a personalized presidency was sufficient to discharge the responsibilities that were expected of central government.

CHAPTER 7

Lyndon B. Johnson
1963–1969

 On November 27, 1963, Lyndon Baines Johnson, president for five days, declared before a joint session of Congress that the theme of his administration would be continuity. John F. Kennedy had been assassinated. The nation was in mourning. All appointees of the slain leader were being asked to continue to serve the new president. Unlike Truman, who moved quickly to put in his own people, Johnson made no changes in the cabinet for thirteen months. And at the White House he combined his staff with Kennedy's staff, producing what an assistant called Noah's ark: "There's two of everybody."[1] Much later Johnson regretted retaining Kennedy's appointees, but at the time he felt that he had no choice.[2] The nation's paramount need was for stability and reassurance.

When Johnson became president, some friction with his inherited staff was inevitable. Kennedy himself had treated his vice president with civility and respect—Johnson had, after all, helped carry enough southern states to enable Kennedy to win in 1960 and had then relinquished the substantial powers of Senate majority leader for the isolation and the superficial responsibilities of a constitutional appendix. But many of Kennedy's aides looked upon Johnson, when they thought of him at all, as some obscure blood relation whose table manners left room for improvement. He was a southerner in a Northeastern regime; nouveau riche, uncultured, and middle-aged in a patriciate that celebrated youth; a Protestant fundamentalist in the government of the first Catholic president. He was, for them, "a usurper, and an ignoble one at that," as Eric Goldman observed. And so the Kennedy holdovers "snickered and sniped, half performed their tasks, and engaged in petty sabotage."[3]

But those willing to transfer their loyalty to the new president were to have their effectiveness enhanced. McGeorge Bundy, Lawrence O'Brien, Kermit Gordon, and Walter Heller continued their duties without loss of energy. O'Brien eventually was promoted to the cabinet; Gordon was offered and declined a cabinet post. Especially in foreign policy Johnson relied on the people he had inherited from Kennedy. There was a special irony in the case of Secretary of State Dean Rusk. Whereas Rusk and Kennedy dealt with each other formally and warily across cultural and generational chasms, Rusk and Johnson shared a common background of the rural South and were only six months apart in age. Ultimately the president reported that "Rusk had the best understanding of the way I wished to move."[4] Thus the secretary of state, a peripheral figure under Kennedy, again emerged in actuality, as he was in protocol, the first member of the cabinet.

It took six months for the Kennedy incorrigibles to drift back to private life and be replaced by people who sounded more like the president. The most obvious characteristic of the resulting Johnson White House was that it contained so many Texans. Over the years the staff included Walter Jenkins, Bill Moyers, Jack Valenti, Horace Busby, Marvin Watson, Harry McPherson, George Christian, Liz Carpenter, H. Barefoot Sanders, Price Daniel, Jake Jacobsen, and Larry Temple.[5] That was not, however, a distinction that defined ideology. Watson was considered a conservative; Moyers and McPherson were known as liberals. Many of the others, as on all White House staffs, were technicians of no known convictions.

By and large Johnson's aides were younger even than Kennedy's, most of whom were near contemporaries of their president. And since Johnson was a decade older than Kennedy, the age gap between president and staff was considerable. The relationship between president and staff is not, of course, meant to be one of equals; still, the greater the age difference the more inherently unequal the relationship is apt to be. Johnson's young men (there were hardly any women on the professional staff), and later Nixon's, were less able to dispute the decisions of their president than the older, self-made men of Eisenhower's staff. This is not meant to imply that Eisenhower's staff often disputed him, only that they were in a better position to do so.

And while some young people challenge authority more than their elders, they are not the ones who are attracted to the White House. While some of Johnson's aides—notably Moyers and McPherson—persisted in presenting an opposing view of the war in Vietnam, if they were not the exceptions that proved the rule, certainly they were uncommon.[6]

The average age of the White House staffs steadily and markedly decreased from the time of Eisenhower through the Nixon administration, not because succeeding presidents desired less back talk from their assistants but because they wanted more activities to originate in the White House and wanted them done faster. Older persons might not have long been able to sustain the pace nor handle the steady increase in routine functions assumed by the Kennedy, Johnson, and Nixon staffs.

"I'll get my action from the younger men and my advice from the older men," Johnson used to say.[7] The president's older men were contemporaries who had been drawn to the heady atmosphere of the New Deal and had stayed on to get rich in Washington in the practice of law. In his initial reliance on outside advice, Johnson was hardly unique. While the notion of a Kitchen Cabinet—that Jacksonian phrase for a group of outsiders to whom a president regularly turns for advice—has difficulty surviving in this age of the modern presidency (one suspects it always was an exaggeration and that presidential friends were more often close listeners than close advisers), a new president, particularly a president by accident, will turn at first to old friends from outside the government. Some will eventually enter his administration; the influence of the others will begin to fade as the president takes the measure of officials within his chain of command. Moreover, the usefulness of the outsider declines in direct proportion to the increase in information a president needs to make a decision, the speed with which it must be made, and the degree of agreement among insiders necessary to make it stick. Johnson was unusual, however, in that he continued throughout his presidency to have extensive outside advice, especially from Abe Fortas, who counseled the president even after he became a Supreme Court Justice, and Clark Clifford, who became secretary of defense for the last eleven months of the administration. In foreign policy, Johnson regularly met with eleven nongovernmental advisers, who became known as the Wise Men.[8]

For other outside advice Johnson held a steady procession of meetings with representatives of special interests, such as George Meany of the AFL-CIO, for he loved meetings as much as Kennedy hated them. There were constant sessions with congressional leaders, although the president frequently sought their opinions after he had reached a decision.[9] And there were the former presidents: Johnson called on the elderly Truman out of courtesy, but he was anxious to solicit Eisenhower's opinions, especially when they proved supportive.

Although the war in Vietnam led to the repeated accusation that Johnson walled himself off from outsiders, he was in fact the most accessible president since Roosevelt. Yet his outside advisers were not unlike his inside advisers. The Wise Men had been officials in the White House or in the State and Defense departments. Their former association with decisionmaking at the highest level ensured that they would provide advice that took account of constraints and realities in Washington. They might be expected to provide a greater degree of skepticism and detachment than those with daily responsibilities, but by choosing outsiders who had been insiders, the president was not calling for advice that could be expected to be different in kind.

Johnson may indeed have gotten his advice from older men and action from younger ones, but the pace of his administration was so fierce that even many young men could not keep up. He worked a two-shift day, 7:00 A.M. to 2:00 P.M. and 4:00 P.M. to 9:00 P.M. Between 2:00 P.M. and 4:00 P.M. he took a walk, swam, ate lunch, napped, showered, and changed clothes. Then, returning to his office, he was known to say, "It's like starting a new day." Top assistants were expected to be available at all times, for both shifts.[10]

This relentless determination to do more of everything for as long as he would be in office inevitably took its toll on those around him. For example, in 1964, an election year, when he made 424 speeches, almost everyone on the staff was pressed into service as a presidential scribe, and everyone joined the constant talent search for speechwriters.[11] The length of the day, the intensity of the work, and Johnson's reputation for verbally abusing those close to him also meant a ceaseless turnover of presidential assistants, which gave the executive mansion "the appearance of a well-slept rooming house."[12]

Under such circumstances and because of other Johnson characteristics it became difficult to attract people to cabinet and subcabinet positions as well.[13] Some, of course, may have declined because they did not agree with the president's policies; others, especially after he announced that he would not run for reelection, may have viewed the administration as a poor job risk. Johnson turned for help to John Macy, chairman of the Civil Service

Commission, whom he appointed the new White House talent hunter. Macy attempted to bring some scientific management to the task of political recruitment, and one of his innovations was to design a computer system, the White House Executive Biographic Index, which eventually provided the president with prompt information about 16,000 people.[14] The operation was particularly useful in putting together presidential commissions for which demographic considerations played a key role. In previous presidencies the process of finding political appointees was known as BOGSAT—"a bunch of guys sitting around a table."

The fact remains, however, that from the outset the administration relied heavily on promotions from the career service to fill important second-echelon slots. Careerists received nearly half the 265 major appointments Johnson made in his first eighteen months as president.[15] While this was undoubtedly a tribute to the quality of some of them, "Johnson complained privately that too many of his policy positions went by default to career civil servants who were willing, available, and technically competent but had no 'fire in their bellies.'"[16] Nor, compared with previous presidencies, was this White House less suspicious of the bureaucracy.

The most prominent "careerist" on the president's staff was Walter Jenkins, who had served Johnson since 1939 and who functioned loosely, if not in title, as chief of staff. That Jenkins's age was closer to the president's fortified his claim to authority over the younger assistants. As long as he remained there was a semblance of hierarchy at the White House. But his resignation during the 1964 campaign marked the beginning of the staff's disintegration. What had been a successful team became "a shifting band of individuals and groups moving in mutual suspicion around the commanding, demanding figure of Lyndon Johnson."[17] They were, however, welded together by adversity. As the administration's Vietnam policy left them feeling increasingly beleaguered, they turned more and more to each other for reassurance and support.

"President Johnson tended to build his staff around people in a very unstructured way," recalled one assistant. "There was no domestic policy council, very little in the way of formalized staff interaction, meetings, and the like."[18] Despite a gradual trend of nearly twenty years toward sharper definition of White House assignments, Johnson, like Roosevelt, expected his top people to be general handymen. George Reedy was press secretary but also liaison with labor; Marvin Watson was appointments secretary as well as liaison with business. In addition to their other duties, Jack Valenti, a Catholic, and Lee White, a Jew, maintained contact with their organized coreligionists. At lunch in the White House mess, the staff joked among themselves that the president had dealt each of them a resident assignment: resident Italian, resident youth, resident hawk, resident dove.[19] Bill Moyers came closest to being generalist in chief, meaning, as in the earlier case of Harry Hopkins under Roosevelt, that he was more directly concerned with more matters that the president cared about than any other assistant. His amazing string of responsibilities included speechwriter, designer of the media campaign during the 1964 election, press secretary (following Reedy's departure in 1965), domestic policy adviser, conduit to the bureaucracy, and foreign policy gadfly. Johnson also followed Roosevelt's practice of expecting his assistants to remain anonymous. Too much favorable publicity was sure to put a staffer in the president's doghouse.

How deliberately did Johnson try to emulate Roosevelt's system? Having been elected to the House of Representatives in 1937 as a staunch New Dealer, he often said, "FDR was a second daddy to me." He thought of Roosevelt as "a book to be studied, restudied, and reread."[20] Yet such statements should not be taken too literally. Johnson was not a student; rather, like Roosevelt, he was a politician of great energy and ego who instinctively chose systems that kept all components dependent on him, that depended largely on personal loyalty (of which, of course, he was the sole judge), and that were adjustable to his idiosyncratic work habits.

Johnson and Roosevelt arrived at superficially similar staff arrangements out of conceptions of the presidential role that were profoundly different. Roosevelt was a public president who moved in a mysterious symbiotic relationship with public opinion, nudging it forward, retreating when he was too far ahead. Public opinion was the reference point around which his actions were planned. He measured his success in terms of "moral leadership," which placed heavy emphasis on mass communication. Johnson was a congressional president. He saw his reference point as Congress, with whom he shared an equally mysterious and symbiotic relationship on domestic matters. He measured his production in terms of legislative proposals; his success, in enactments. Roosevelt and Johnson were, in their focuses, unlike Eisenhower, whose special relationship with the permanent government required a staff system that emphasized order and routine and that was geared to responding to the departments. Instead they needed creativity and flexibility. They needed aides capable of producing words or proposals quickly and of maneuvering legislators rather than reassuring civil servants.

Thus Johnson sought a staff organization capable of mass-producing legislative initiatives. He demanded proposals that would be labeled "bold and innovative," in the Rooseveltian manner. He also wanted proposals that would prove he was better than Kennedy. These driving forces meant that the traditional path traveled by proposed legislation in the executive branch—from departments and agencies through the Bureau of Budget to the president—was not for him. It was ponderous, when what he wanted was speed. It excluded him until the final decision, when what he wanted was a system that instantly and continuously responded to his wishes. And it often produced the same ideas year after year, when what he wanted were fresh ideas that could carry his brand.

To achieve all this, Johnson supplemented the existing department-centered system for proposing legislation with one that was White House–centered and that, he believed, operated "almost as a separate arm of the government."[21] Under the direction of Joseph Califano, who took over Moyers's job as chief of the White House domestic office, a series of task forces functioned on an annual cycle:

March–April: Compile idea book. (In 1968, for example, this contained more than a hundred possible topics for task force investigation.)

May–June: Select task force subjects (fifty in 1967); gather names of potential members.

July–August: Select task force members; assign staffs from Bureau of Budget and Califano's office.

September–October: Task forces in session. All meetings and reports secret.

November–December: Agencies comment on task force reports; Budget Bureau reviews budget implications; Johnson decides which recommendations to accept.

January–February: Preparation of messages to Congress; introduction of bills. And the cycle begins again.[22]

The president was proud of this innovation. Harnessing the energy of 300 business people, labor leaders, and educators, the task forces originated much of the Great Society, including titles III and IV of the Elementary and Secondary Education Act of 1965, the rent supplement and Model Cities programs of 1966, and the Head Start program. By also including key agency people on the task forces, receiving help from the Budget Bureau staff, and maintaining total secrecy, Johnson felt he had avoided the problems that he associated with Kennedy's preinaugauration task forces—unrealistic recommendations, opposition by those inside government, and the embarrassment of publicizing proposals that the president would not accept. Looking back on the Johnson process, Califano said in 1973, "Programs might originate at the department level in routine areas. In new areas . . . a lot of stuff we just did and handed it to the department concerned."[23]

Nor did White House involvement end with making policy: Johnson wanted to take charge of all aspects of the government. Truman may have brought labor-management relations into the White House when he wanted to settle a rail strike, but he had left the negotiating to an assistant. When Johnson tried to avert a rail strike he did the negotiating himself. And the White House staff conducted itself in a like manner, partly because a staff always takes on the likeness of its president and partly because the coordination of policy was becoming more crucial and complicated as Great Society programs proliferated. Some entity had to be in control. As Califano observed, "The President can't pick up the phone any longer and call the Secretary of Labor and assume that the Secretary of Labor can tell him what is happening in manpower training."[24] Now there were manpower training programs in the Departments of Defense, Labor, Commerce, and Health, Education, and Welfare; in the Veterans Administration; and in the new Office of Economic Opportunity. When the president wanted action—with one phone call—he called Califano, not Labor Secretary Willard Wirtz.

Observing this scene from across the street in the Bureau of the Budget, assistant director William Carey saw Califano's office become a "command post, an operational center within the White House itself, the locus for marathon coffee-consuming sessions dedicated to knocking heads together and untangling jurisdictional and philosophical squabbles."[25] Robert Wood, under secretary of the Department of Housing and Urban Development, who did not like what was happening, later warned:

> Confusion is created when men try to do too much at the top. In order to know what decisions are being made elsewhere in government, the White House tends either to spend time reviewing programs or to take more and more decisions on itself. The separate responsibilities of the White House, the Executive Office, and the agencies are fudged, and the demarcations of who does what become

uncertain. The result is a blurring of the distinction between staff and line, between program and policy.[26]

The blurring and even an inversion of the responsibilities of White House staff and domestic cabinet was illustrated when Johnson secretly moved Labor Secretary Wirtz into the Executive Office Building as his chief speechwriter during the 1964 campaign.[27]

The freewheeling staff assignments, the inversion of duties, and the increasing centralization of operations meant that nothing was simple to chart in the Johnson White House. While Califano and his staff (never exceeding seven professionals) were the primary domestic policy advisers, they were not the only ones. The Council of Economic Advisers—Walter Heller, Gardner Ackley, and Arthur Okun—gained influence as the Vietnam involvement affected the economy. Budget directors Kermit Gordon, Charles Schultze, and Charles Zwick gained influence as federal spending increased, as deficits mounted, and as new programs cut across agency lines. The Office of Consumer Affairs, directed first by Esther Peterson and then by Betty Furness, was placed in the Executive Office as the power and cohesiveness of the consumer movement grew. The Office of Economic Opportunity, the Johnson-created operating arm of the War on Poverty, was also given preferred position in the Executive Office, a sign of the importance the president placed on this effort. There was now a White House aide to oversee health and education policy (Douglass Cater), the arts (Roger Stevens), and civil rights (Clifford Alexander). Johnson even hired Princeton historian Eric Goldman in an effort to treat intellectuals as an interest group and because someone in the White House should know "the kind of thing a President should do"—such as invite Lincoln scholars to lunch on Lincoln's birthday.[28]

By the mid-1960s the White House was clearly more operational, more deeply involved with initiating and carrying out policy. The causes were not hard to find. There was a president who was impatient with the pace of government and distrustful of those beyond his immediate reach. The programs that Johnson had pushed through Congress, grander in scale and more complex than ever to carry out, threatened to overwhelm the traditional machinery of government. And the prevailing view of public administration—nurtured by scholars who had come of age during the New Deal—approved centralizing the management of the executive branch in the Office of the President. The impetus to expand the executive role was reflected in the report (never made public) of the President's Task Force on Government Organization. On June 15, 1967, the task force proposed that Johnson create an Office of Program Coordination within his Executive Office but outside the Budget Bureau, which would be different from what existed in two ways. First, the director of coordination would be empowered to impose settlements when department heads disagreed.[29] Second, senior presidential assistants would be located throughout the country, serving "as the President's eyes and ears in the field" to "overcome the serious gap that has opened between planning in Washington and making the programs work back home." Although Johnson did not implement this recommendation, it was probably less because he disagreed with it than because Vietnam had begun to consume his attention and limit his ability to engage in other controversial activities.

Despite the White House expansion, Johnson had not set out to diminish the importance of the cabinet as Kennedy had. Initially, George Reedy recalled, "Cabinet meetings were held with considerable regularity, with fully predetermined agendas and fully prewritten statements. In general, they consisted of briefings by cabinet members followed by a later release of the statements to the press. It was regarded by all participants except the President as a painful experience."[30] The influence of the domestic cabinet members was, however, individual rather than collective. Some, such as John Gardner, the president held in high regard; others, such as Wirtz and Stewart Udall, were ignored and were in nearly open rebellion by the end of the administration.[31]

With the plethora of new programs, the administration added two new cabinet departments, Housing and Urban Development in 1965 and Transportation in 1966. Johnson also made an unsuccessful attempt to merge Commerce and Labor, and he rejected until he was about to leave office a commission recommendation to remove the Post Office from cabinet status. Twenty-five men served in Johnson's cabinet. Ten he inherited from Kennedy.[32] Of the other fifteen appointees, only four were recruited from outside government—Washington lawyer Clark Clifford at Defense; foundation executive John Gardner at HEW; and two businessmen, John Connor and C. R. Smith, who headed Commerce. The other eleven were internal promotions, such as Wilbur Cohen, Johnson's last secretary of health, education and welfare, who had spent most of his career in the Social Security Administration. The people that Johnson picked rather than retained were competent and well regarded by the clients of their agencies but were usually not household names of independent political reputation. The decline in the importance of the cabinet under Johnson, then, was not directly related to the quality of his appointees.

Just as the cabinet had grown larger but become less important, so had the National Security Council. The council continued to meet regularly, but it dealt with matters other than Vietnam, and its deliberations took on a symbolic quality: "It was impossible to escape the feeling that everything was scripted."[33] Several iron laws of presidential behavior were at work: as a group grows in size, its value to a president becomes more symbolic and less advisory, the chance of leaks increases, and members speak for the record or not at all. Thus the more important the issue, the smaller the group that a president turns to for advice. In issues of utmost importance, a president may confer only with himself. Truman had shunned the NSC until the outbreak of the Korean War, when it replaced the larger and less differentiated cabinet as his chief forum for policy discussion. Similarly, as the Vietnam War became the major issue of the Johnson administration, the president turned from the National Security Council to a smaller group that Henry Graff has called the Tuesday Cabinet. Every Tuesday Johnson had lunch with the secretary of state (Dean Rusk), the secretary of defense (Robert McNamara, Clark Clifford), his special assistant for national security affairs (McGeorge Bundy, Walt W. Rostow), the director of the Central Intelligence Agency (Richard Helms), the chairman of the Joint Chiefs of Staff (General Earle Wheeler), and his press secretary (Bill Moyers, George Christian). In effect, six officials became the war cabinet.

Johnson's Vietnam decisions are often viewed as a product of a malfunctioning advisory system, specifically that alternatives to increased intervention were not available or not allowed a hearing. Alexander George has argued that "multiple advocacy" is crucial in making foreign policy, that a president must listen "in a structured setting to different, well-prepared advocates making the best cases for alternative options."[34] Was Johnson closed off from alternative opinion?

Certainly there was no shortage of key advisers who favored increased involvement in Vietnam, notably the Joint Chiefs of Staff, White House assistant Rostow, and the U.S. ambassadors in Saigon. On the other hand, Johnson declared that "there was no shortage of information at any time"—presumably meaning information both supporting and opposing various options.[35] As a man with three TV sets in his office, he was hardly unaware of opposition to his actions. Moreover, he claimed proudly that he had institutionalized opposition within the government, and in a sense he had. "Under Secretary of State George Ball had been less than enthusiastic about some aspects of our involvement in Southeast Asia," Johnson wrote. "Often in our meetings he spoke in opposition to one proposal or another. Especially from 1965 onward he played the role of devil's advocate frequently."[36] Nor was Ball the only internal critic. Moyers and later McPherson had the same function at the White House. Llewellyn Thompson, the State Department's Soviet specialist, whom Johnson frequently consulted, was known to caution restraint. And Johnson's friend and successor as Senate majority leader, Mike Mansfield, also carried the case against the president's policies to the president. Even the CIA, as the Pentagon Papers disclosed, consistently reported that the war was not going well. The so-called Wise Men were almost evenly divided on the question of disengagement.[37]

"Simply stated," wrote James Thomson, who served in the White House and the State Department, "dissent, when recognized, was made to feel at home." The president and his allies "felt good (they had given a full hearing to the dovish option)."[38] The internal opponents were neither unimportant nor inarticulate. Indeed they were among the best people in government. But they were ultimately ineffective because Johnson disagreed with them. "I am not going to lose Vietnam," he said. "I am not going to be the President who saw Southeast Asia go the way China went."[39]

It would have taken a president with an unconventional cast of mind to have reversed the direction of U.S. policy in Vietnam or a president schooled in military tactics, such as Eisenhower, who understood the hazards of becoming involved in a massive land war on the Asian continent. The involvement in Vietnam, however, accorded with the cold war thinking that Johnson inherited, and once he was committed to fighting there, the idea of reversing policy became increasingly difficult to consider. The U.S. system is not one that makes it easy for a president to admit he is wrong, nor was Johnson a man whose psychological stakes in his actions were insignificant. So the root causes for the Vietnam escalation are not to be found in the theory that the president was a captive of hawkish advice. Johnson was not a captive of his advisers. He was a captive of what he was and what he believed.

Lyndon Johnson's methods of organizing the presidency suggest that presidents can be too idiosyncratic. The continuing needs of large organizations demand a certain degree of predictability in leaders. Johnson's habits may have made good news copy—when they were printable—but they created high personnel turnover on the White House staff, an unhealthy sense of insecurity and dependence on the part of those around him, and constant strain in his relations with some members of his cabinet. A president's right to do things his way, so long a tenet of liberal advocates of a strong presidency, suddenly appeared to be a double-edged sword.

Johnson's skills as a legislative leader and his attention to congressional lobbying did result in an extraordinary record of major enactments. His technique of using task forces with carefully selected memberships and clear schedules to develop legislative packages was innovative. Many of his assistants were talented and all were hardworking. But when applied to grave questions of world security, his legislator's cast of mind produced disaster. He had grown successful by manipulating men in small numbers, a practice based on broad knowledge and careful assessment of politicians whose motivations he understood. But this personalizing of whatever entered his field of vision was not successful and not even applicable to relations between nations, a point he never grasped.

Johnson's need to become directly involved in all aspects of the presidency that he cared about brought a more than normal quotient of minutiae into the White House and engaged his staff in more operational and policymaking matters than ever before. Responsibility gravitated to those closest at hand. Personal loyalty to him became an overriding concern, and he increasingly treated some cabinet members with suspicion.

Adversity fed on itself, producing an us-against-them mentality and further isolating him from the rest of the country. In the end, Lyndon Johnson had turned the presidency into a bunker. Then he handed it over to Richard Nixon.

CHAPTER 8

Richard M. Nixon
1969–1974
Gerald R. Ford
1974–1977

 If the U.S. government were to choose presidents on the basis of a written test, Richard M. Nixon in 1968 would have appeared near the top of the list. Besides having been in the House of Representatives and the Senate, he had served as vice president for eight years, and no other vice president had been given so many duties. Then too, having been out of office since his defeat by John Kennedy in 1960, presumably he had also had eight years to contemplate the nature of the office that had first eluded him.

That with all his experience Nixon became the first president to be forced to resign may say much about the qualities most necessary in an American president, qualities that are beyond the scope of this study. It may say something about how little anyone can know about being president before taking office, a point made by Nixon in a television interview on January 4, 1971, and made earlier, under similar circumstances, by John Kennedy.[1] It may also say something about the way Nixon organized his presidency and the people he picked to assist him—at least that is an assumption made by some in the wake of Watergate.

Nixon was clearly a management-conscious president who was seriously concerned with the way the White House would be organized. Theodore White believed that basic to an understanding of the man was an appreciation of his "fascination with How Things Work." John Osborne of the *New Republic*, a skilled observer of the Nixon White House, stressed the

president's "continuing struggle for neatness," a constant quest for "disciplined order and precision."[2]

The result was that, while the organizational arrangements of all administrations change, usually gradually, Nixon's were in a continual state of flux.
In the preinauguration period in 1968, the president-elect laid out plans for
a cabinet-centered government in domestic affairs and a White House-
centered government in foreign affairs. From January through September
1969, a period of policy formulation, the relations between cabinet and
White House staff remained in a volatile balance. Between October 1969
and June 1970, however, the administration's emphasis shifted to program
development and implementation, and internal power gravitated decidedly
toward the White House staff. In the next two years, control of government
became firmly centralized in the White House. The Domestic Council was
created, the Bureau of the Budget was converted into the Office of Management and Budget, functional and constituent offices proliferated in the
White House, and the president proposed fewer and larger domestic
departments. After his reelection in 1972, Nixon attempted to decentralize
power, primarily by transferring White House loyalists to the departments.
Finally, starting with the firing of H. R. Haldeman and John Ehrlichman
in April 1973, the administration disintegrated in response to the Watergate revelations, which culminated in the president's resignation on August
9, 1974.

Nixon began, as had other chief executives, with a plan to right the
wrongs of the previous administration's methods. When asked in May 1968
how he would operate if elected president, he replied:

> For one thing, I would disperse power, spread it among able people.
> Men operate best only if they are given the chance to operate at full
> capacity.
>
>   I would operate differently from President Johnson. Instead of tak-
> ing all power to myself, I'd select cabinet members who could do their
> jobs, and each of them would have the stature and the power to func-
> tion effectively. Publicity would not center at the White House alone.
> Every key official would have the opportunity to be a big man in his
> field. On the other hand, when a President takes all the real power to
> himself, those around him become puppets. They shrivel up and
> become less and less creative.

Actually, my belief in dispersal of power relates to the fundamental proposition of how to make a country move forward. Progress demands that you develop your most creative people to the fullest. And your most creative people can't develop in a monolithic, centralized power set-up.[3]

Indeed, Bob Haldeman, who was to be Nixon's chief of staff, told the first postelection meeting of his assistants, "Our job is not to do the work of government, but to get the work out to where it belongs—out to the Departments." One of those in attendance, speechwriter William Safire, later commented that this "was not a matter of being two-faced—Nixon and Haldeman honestly thought in the beginning that was the way it could and should be done."[4]

Nixon did, however, make a distinction in foreign policy operations, for which he wished greater presidential control. He looked back with enthusiasm on Eisenhower's extensive use of the National Security Council: "The process was, of course, not flawless, but it was the controlling element in our success in keeping the peace throughout our eight White House years." He considered subsequent foreign policy decisions, presumably those relating to Cuba and Vietnam, as flawed and the direct result of the demise of the NSC.

Since 1960, this Council has virtually disappeared as an operating function. In its place there have been catch-as-can talk-fests between the President, his staff assistants, and various others. I attribute most of our serious reverses abroad since 1960 to the inability or disinclination of President Eisenhower's successors to make effective use of this important Council. . . . I intend to restore the National Security Council to its pre-eminent role in national security planning.[5]

Still, if the impression given was that Nixon wished to be a latter-day Eisenhower, there was another clue in his campaign speeches to suggest otherwise: "The next President must take an activist view of his office."[6] But could an Eisenhower-style White House be adapted to the requirements of an activist president? Eisenhower's organization depended on staff-and-command routines that he had mastered in a lifetime of military service. Could they be fitted to the style of a politician whose managerial experience

with large organizations was limited? Moreover, despite the political usefulness of identifying himself with Eisenhower, Nixon is reported to have
told close associates that in his administration he wanted no Sherman
Adams, no James Hagerty, no John Foster Dulles.[7] Nixon, in short, was
more Johnsonian than he cared to admit, despite theories about the dispersal of power.

In the context, then, of an independent yet collegial domestic cabinet, a
retooled NSC that kept foreign policy control in the hands of the president,
and a White House staff of generalists, Nixon set out to choose his department heads and personal assistants. The results of his cabinet making were
announced on December 11, 1968: William P. Rogers, secretary of state;
David M. Kennedy at Treasury; Melvin R. Laird, Defense; John N.
Mitchell, attorney general; Winton M. Blount, postmaster general; Walter
J. Hickel, Interior; Clifford M. Hardin, Agriculture; Maurice H. Stans,
Commerce; George P. Shultz, Labor; Robert H. Finch, Health, Education,
and Welfare; George W. Romney, Housing and Urban Development; and
John A. Volpe, Transportation.

The president-elect presented the incoming cabinet to the American
people as men of "extra dimension." Others, such as Arthur Schlesinger Jr.,
criticized Nixon's appointees for their lack of national standing. "Historically, the Cabinet . . . has generally contained men with their own views
and their own constituencies," he wrote. "But who in President Nixon's
Cabinet will talk back to him?"[8] A more balanced assessment is to be found
somewhere between the two. The new cabinet displayed considerably more
diversity and political experience than had Eisenhower's. Nixon, too, had
his share of millionaires, but they were neither the patricians of the
Roosevelt and Truman administrations nor the corporation executives of
the Eisenhower cabinet. Rather, Nixon's appointees were generally self-
made business owners in the mold of Hickel, Volpe, and Blount. Even
Romney, a former president of American Motors, had started life poor and
had entered big business laterally by working for trade associations.

Nixon turned less to Congress for his department secretaries than
Truman had, but Truman was the exception, not Nixon. The trend was
clear: half the cabinet had come from Congress between 1828 and 1860;
40 percent from 1864 to 1896; 20 percent from 1900 to 1932; and only
15 percent since 1932.[9]

The Nixon cabinet showed the most similarities with Kennedy's initial
appointments. Each president chose three governors, appointed his cam-

paign manager to head the Justice Department, turned to one member of the House of Representatives, and gave Treasury to a banker, Post Office to a businessman, Interior to a westerner, and Agriculture to a midwesterner. Kennedy selected one person from the opposition party, which Nixon did not do until John Connally became secretary of the treasury in 1970, although Nixon did try to recruit Senator Henry Jackson as his first defense secretary. Both Kennedy and Nixon picked several cabinet officers who were personally unknown to them, but Shultz (whose surname Nixon did not know how to spell), like Robert McNamara before him, emerged as a cabinet strongman. Nixon also turned to two academics; there were none in the Kennedy cabinet.[10] In sum, Nixon selected a traditionally balanced cabinet. If it was a mite short on Washington experience, the reason was not difficult to locate. Republicans had had little opportunity for such experience in recent years, and many members of the Eisenhower administration, eight years previously, had been elderly even then. Yet three of Nixon's eleven cabinet officers had held high positions under Eisenhower.[11]

Some department under secretaries were selected by the cabinet officers and others suggested by the White House. Finch and Romney, for example, gave the number-two jobs to old colleagues from their states. But the White House balanced Hickel's Interior appointment, which had been subjected to heavy fire from environmentalists, with the appointment of Russell Train, a dedicated conservationist. Not surprisingly, the two were soon barely on speaking terms. As a rule—with a notable exception at Defense—the administration was better served when the secretary made the choice. An absurd attempt to expand the recruitment process by sending form letters to everyone listed in *Who's Who* (including Richard M. Nixon) resulted mostly in a lot of unanswered letters. Prospective assistant secretaries and other key aides were located in the usual manner, through participation in the campaign and other old-boy networks.

A number of people declined to serve in the cabinet, but Nixon's rejection rate was no higher than that of past administrations (other than Eisenhower's) and possibly even a bit lower than Franklin Roosevelt's and Lyndon Johnson's.[12] And only three members of the Nixon cabinet can be considered to have been close political allies: Mitchell, the 1968 campaign manager; Stans, the fund raiser; and Finch, the 1960 campaign manager. Rogers qualified as an old friend, not as a political activist. Finch and Rogers did not prove to be outstanding cabinet officers, but they did not contribute to and could not have prevented Watergate. Finch was the first department secretary that Nixon removed; Rogers was picked to be a compliant secretary of state so that the president could run foreign policy from the White House.[13] Mitchell and Stans were deeply involved in the events of Watergate, but this was a result of their campaign roles in 1972, not because they were cabinet officers. If Nixon was often better served by total strangers than by old friends in the cabinet—the experience of a number of other presidents as well—any generalization would have to be followed by a long string of exceptions.

In choosing his personal staff, Nixon was reported to have surrounded himself with "West Coast advertising executives and young merchandising types."[14] But this characterization, which has gained credence over time, ignores the degree to which White House functions and consequently the skills of their staffs have necessarily become differentiated. The Nixon White House operations were initially organized around eight discrete functions: a personal services staff, headed by Haldeman; two press relations staffs, under Ronald Ziegler and Herbert Klein; two domestic policy staffs, reporting to Arthur Burns and Daniel P. Moynihan; Henry Kissinger's national security staff; a congressional relations staff, directed by Bryce N. Harlow; a small political operations staff consisting of Harry Dent and John Sears; a personnel staff with Peter Flanigan in charge of high-level recruiting and Harry Flemming in charge of the larger number of more routine appointments; and a speechwriting staff with its own executive editor, James Keogh. Many of the traditional Executive Office staffs had become drawn into the White House operations by the beginning of the Nixon administration. And the Council of Economic Advisers and the Office of Science and Technology were on call, depending on the importance that the president chose to attach to such specialized advice.

The advertising-merchandising types were clustered, appropriately, on the president's personal services and public relations staffs. Haldeman had been vice president in charge of the Los Angeles office of J. Walter Thompson, and he had brought with him four young men who had been employed there, including Ron Ziegler. The other staffs were made up of people with backgrounds and skills appropriate to their specific functions. Harlow, who had been Eisenhower's congressional lobbyist, picked assistants with extensive experience on Capitol Hill. Three of the four chief members of the speechwriting team had been journalists. Kissinger largely borrowed from the Foreign Service and the Defense Department, and Burns and Moynihan tended to use people with academic backgrounds. As had been true in the past, the largest professional supplier of White House aides was the law. All of the president's political operatives were lawyers.

One noteworthy characteristic of Nixon's staff, other than the top echelon, was its youth—it was younger even than Kennedy's. While many of these aides, often in their late twenties or early thirties, served with distinction, a substantial number had the kind of weaknesses that allowed them to be sucked into the vortex of Watergate. Jeb Magruder wrote that Gordon Strachan, for instance, "was one of those people, like John Dean, who was capable and could be engaging, but who was obviously always studying all the angles and trying to manipulate events to his own advantage."[15] Yet not all these young men were mere seekers of the main chance. Herbert L. (Bart) Porter, another aide to Magruder, was to attribute his Watergate involvement to "fear of group pressure," desire to be considered "a team player," and unquestioning loyalty to the president.[16] The crimes of Watergate were not limited to the inexperienced, but beneath the surface of the Nixon administration was a stratum of staff, often young but not always so, that was particularly susceptible to the commands of others.

If Nixon's personnel were fairly conventional, his initial organization of the White House was more innovative, although some innovations were veiled from view at the time and the significance of others would not be perceived until later.

The Kennedy administration had attempted to coordinate the public relations activities of the various executive agencies, but there was a limit to how much attention press secretary Pierre Salinger could devote to these expanded duties.[17] Under Nixon the functions were divided. Ron Ziegler handled the traditional chores of press secretary. Herb Klein, director of communications for the executive branch, was vaguely empowered with coordinating the flow of information from the departments. Given Klein's reputation as a casual administrator, this arrangement may have been motivated by Nixon's desire to keep his old friend away from the daily routine of presidential press operations. By late 1969, however, the actual direction of the operation passed into the hands of Jeb Magruder. The office became obsessed with selling the president, and there followed a quantum jump in the scope and scale of White House public relations.

Speechwriting was again isolated from other assignments, as it had been under Eisenhower, although now the writers were more active participants in policy negotiations. The function was organized along the lines of a press newsroom; each writer had a beat, an executive editor made assignments, and researchers checked facts. Nixon's favorite writers were Raymond Price, Patrick J. Buchanan, and William Safire. Each held an ideologically distinct position, loosely corresponding to left, right, and center within the Republican party, and each had a special style. According to Safire, "When Nixon wanted to take a shot at somebody, he turned to Buchanan. . . . When Nixon wanted a vision of the Nation's future . . . he turned to Price . . . and when he wanted the complicated made simple, or a line to be quoted" he turned to Safire.[18] Nixon never merged their talents. Rather, he compartmentalized his staff to serve his separate needs. It was as if each chamber inside the president was to have its own reflection at the White House.

In addition to his speechwriting duties, Buchanan was responsible for presenting the president with a daily summary of the news, often fifty pages, which Nixon used as a supplemental source of information on what was going on within the federal government. In varying degrees, presidents have always looked to the press to tell them about their own administrations. Kenneth O'Donnell related how Kennedy phoned him early one morning about the closing of a government installation that he had noted in a Detroit newspaper article. "Call Bernie Boutin [administrator of the General Services Administration] right now and tell him that I want a written report . . . on my desk no later than nine o'clock this morning."[19] Nixon turned this process into a routine. His comments in the margins of the news summary, promptly transcribed, became a formal channel of command between president and staff.

A dark side of the desire for information was Nixon's use of private investigators. Jack Caulfield, an obscure member of the original Ehrlichman staff and a former New York City policeman, told the Ervin Committee that his job was to attempt to develop and supply political intelligence. He took special interest in the accident involving Senator Edward Kennedy and a young woman at Chappaquiddick, Massachusetts, that resulted in her death. He also arranged privately to place a wiretap on the phone of columnist Joseph Kraft because, as Ehrlichman told him, "the FBI is a sieve."[20] Clark Mollenhoff, a reporter, was also hired "to investigate any indications of wrongdoing or questionable ethical conduct" within the government.[21] Caulfield and Mollenhoff were on the White House staff because the president felt he needed information that he did not trust the usual mechanisms of the permanent government or his political party to supply.

Nixon's White House organization also had one very Rooseveltian touch—multiple advocacy in domestic policymaking. In this case, it was Daniel Patrick Moynihan versus Arthur Burns. Why the president chose Moynihan to be his assistant for urban affairs is a question that has not been satisfactorily answered.[22] Not only were they were strangers, but Moynihan was a Democrat, closely associated with the Kennedys, with a reputation as a colorful controversialist. Although the absence of a high-level Democrat in an administration that had not received a clear electoral mandate may have been a factor, the placement of Moynihan in an advocacy role at the president's elbow was overcompensation. As with Kissinger, Moynihan's colleague at Harvard, Nixon could also have been seeking a bridge to the intellectual community that had not been part of his electoral constituency. The appointments may thus have been an attempt to act presidential, for presidents, although chosen by only a part of the electorate, take office with the mandate to represent all the people, which often accounts for what may appear to be unlikely behavior—Eisenhower, the army officer, who warned of the "military-industrial complex"; Kennedy, the Catholic, who was accused of being the most anti-Catholic president since Millard Fillmore; and Johnson, the southerner, who became a champion of civil rights legislation. In the case of Kissinger, the risks were modest. Nixon had read Kissinger's books, agreed with him, and had considerable experience in foreign policy. But the appointment of Moynihan was to carry him down unfamiliar paths, often against his stated convictions.

On the other hand, Columbia University professor Arthur Burns was an elder among Republican economists and a chairman of the Council of Economic Advisers under Eisenhower. Nixon gave him responsibility for coordinating the development of domestic policies and programs.[23] The president also invented a new title, counselor, for Burns and bestowed upon him cabinet status.

With these two appointments the president gained contrasting academics, each with a small staff, to compete for his approval. It was a proven technique of presidential leadership, but it had never been Nixon's style, and he probably slipped into it inadvertently.[24] Burns had been promised the chairmanship of the Federal Reserve Board when it became available in 1970. In the meantime Nixon wanted his services, and there were not many positions in which to place a person of his background and prestige. That Burns and Moynihan were given vague and overlapping jurisdictions may have most reflected the president's limited attention to domestic policy.

In the competition between the two scholars, Burns should have been the winner. He had rank, the president's trust, and presumably a point of view that was ideologically sympathetic. That it did not always work out this way is a commentary on the importance of chemistry in doing business with a president. Burns was ponderous, and while his long monologues had fascinated Eisenhower, they bored Nixon. The glittering style and wit of Moynihan, however, engaged the president and became a weapon of considerable utility. Moreover, Moynihan's proposals were dramatic; they appealed to the presidential instinct to "do something."

Moynihan also had a vehicle, the Council for Urban Affairs, that provided him with regular access to the Oval Office. This cabinet-level council was chaired by the president, with Moynihan as its executive secretary. As long as Moynihan could keep the weekly meetings interesting and important, Nixon would keep them on his schedule. If the president kept coming, the cabinet members would keep coming, and policy would be debated through a mechanism that was run by Moynihan. Burns had no comparable process for initiating policy. He was in charge of seeing that preinaugural task force recommendations worked their way through the departments, and later would create a series of outside task forces, but these quick reports could not compete with the recommendations of the Urban Affairs Council's subcommittees, which harnessed the desires of the domestic cabinet officers. When the secretary of commerce wanted to create a minority enterprise program or the secretary of agriculture wanted to increase the food stamp program, the recommendation came to the president through the council.[25] Burns was thus placed in the position of having to react to the proposals of others, but he performed the task with thoroughness, often to the betterment of the proposals under discussion.

On August 8, 1969, Nixon announced his support for Burns's revenue-sharing plan (a proposal that had come from a task force) and Moynihan's family assistance plan, a form of guaranteed income. Burns and Moynihan shed the veneer of neutral competence and became forceful advocates for their beliefs. But within a month the president was turning away from the system that had produced the two most important domestic proposals of his administration. On October 17 the White House announced that Burns was to be the next chairman of the Federal Reserve Board, in effect "promoting" him prematurely. On November 4, Moynihan was promoted to counselor, a member of the cabinet without specific duties. At the same time, John Ehrlichman, who had entered the White House as counsel to the president, handling routine legal matters, was named chief domestic assistant. By late fall the Burns and Moynihan staffs had been disbanded. Some went to work for Ehrlichman, others left the White House.

Why had Nixon chosen to dismantle the loose, somewhat Rooseveltian system that had produced proposals he believed would "bring reason, order, and purpose into a tangle of overlapping programs, and show that Government can be made to work"?[26]

Certainly one reason was that the Urban Affairs Council was a flawed instrument. For a mechanism that did not even have jurisdiction over all domestic policy, it consumed a tremendous amount of the cabinet's time—justifiable, perhaps, in the beginning when all policy was under review but difficult to sustain as the demands of department management built up. Another vehicle was needed at a lower echelon to turn proposals into draft legislation, executive orders, and presidential messages. As the administration moved from forging policy to implementing it, the president shed his scholars in favor of a manager. Another reason Nixon scrapped the system was that it made him uncomfortable. For a president to choose a system of staff conflict, he must be prepared to assume a major role in making assignments, mediating disputes, and unruffling feathers. This Nixon was unwilling to do.

Furthermore, to rely on the Urban Affairs Council was to rely on the cabinet, and Nixon had come to realize, as do all presidents, that his cabinet was a mixed bag, full of pleasant surprises and serious disappointments.[27] Quiet, calm George Shultz was the biggest surprise. Being secretary of labor was not overly taxing, and as in the case of Arthur Goldberg under Kennedy, the secretary was available for additional assignments. Nixon soon engaged him in such matters as school desegregation policy and welfare reform. Agriculture Secretary Hardin and Treasury Secretary Kennedy, however, did not seem to have the extra dimension necessary to be forceful political executives. HEW Secretary Finch, who had surrounded himself with assistants considered too liberal by the White House, increasingly appeared ideologically out of phase with the president. And Nixon's former governors were often long-winded and apt to promote their department's interests beyond what the president felt was reasonable. A system that relied so extensively on face-to-face dealings with these people was highly inefficient.

There was also before Nixon the example of foreign policy development, which was free of the internal turmoil that characterized domestic policy-making. Secretary of State Rogers did not make excessive demands. The staff of the National Security Council reported to Kissinger, and Kissinger alone reported to the president. Could not a similar orderly arrangement be devised for the domestic side of government?

In each year of the Nixon presidency the White House looked different from the year before. To some extent this is true of every administration. A White House staff is constantly changing, reflecting the changing abilities and interests of those who leave and those who join, the rise of favorites and the falls from grace, the new priorities of the president and new pressures on him. But added to this, the Nixon White House engaged in an endless search "to improve the processes by which our Nation is governed." It had become clear, the president said in the middle of his first year, "that one of the principal requirements is for new mechanisms."[28] After creating the Council for Urban Affairs as his first executive order, Nixon went on to establish the Office of Intergovernmental Relations, the Council on Environmental Quality, the National Goals Research Staff, and the Council for Rural Affairs. Later he would create the Office of Telecommunications Policy, the Council on International Economic Policy, and the Special Action Office for Drug Abuse Prevention. Each new office added to the girth of the presidency and multiplied the number of people purporting to speak in the president's name. The White House was becoming increasingly compartmentalized, with each office or council operating in isolation. As more and more specialists were added, there was less and less room for generalists.

While the activities around the fringes of the White House often appeared frenetic, at the core there was a growing stillness. The president wanted to be alone. In 1963 in his book on presidential decisionmaking, Theodore Sorensen wrote, "It is commonly said that our Presidents need more time set aside to do nothing but think" (a view with which he took exception).[29] Now the word went out that the president was reserving Wednesdays for thinking time. In part this need resulted from Nixon's overarching interest in foreign policy; great chunks of time were needed to plan disengagement from Vietnam, resumption of relations with the People's Republic of China, and détente with the Soviet Union. It also resulted from the way Nixon liked to receive information. Eisenhower found committee meetings congenial; Kennedy preferred small, informal sessions with a few advisers; Johnson would accept any format as long as the information was presented orally. Nixon told an interviewer, "My disposition is to see that the President's time is not frittered away. I've found a way to do it. I'm a reader, not a buller. Most of the boys at the Law School had long bull sessions about cases. I studied my cases alone."[30] But the reasons for the president's solitary behavior went deeper. Clues are spread throughout his *Six Crises*, the most self-revealing book written by an active American politician. Together amounting to a study in crisis management, each of the six cases suggests to the author a lesson of personal behavior. On his confrontation with Alger Hiss: "The ability to be cool, confident, and decisive in a crisis is not an inherited characteristic but is the direct result of how well the individual has prepared himself for the battle." Other lessons speak to "the necessary soul-searching of deciding," to "the tension which builds up in a crisis," and to "concentrating completely on how to meet the danger."[31] Solitude seems to have been necessary, not only because of the importance Nixon placed on preparation and planning, but also as a method of keeping within the limits of his endurance and of controlling or overcoming what became known as the president's "darker side."[32]

This characteristic, more than any other, dictated and defined the position of H. R. Haldeman. Initially Haldeman was not a powerful figure—at least, he had no major voice in policy. He was the staff manager, a neutral, almost pedestrian, assignment. He oiled the machinery of the presidential office, arranging space, transportation, dining room privileges, and the like. He made sure that deadlines were met and that papers reaching the president were adequate for their purposes.

As the president spent less time in meetings with his staff and cabinet officers, more of the business of the presidency was conducted in writing, and the function of the gatekeeper became more important. The role also grew in direct proportion to the growth of the White House staff. Most of the original staff had been transplanted from the campaign organization, and their long-standing relations with Nixon could serve to put his wishes in some useful context. As the size of a White House staff increases, the standard complaint is that it exceeds the span of a president's control, and aides go into business for themselves, a concern that is not unfounded. Yet in the Nixon White House another type of problem arose. New people moved in who did not know the president intuitively and were likely to accept presidential directives too literally.[33] Such memos, when they are not supplemented by an opportunity to probe the president's intent, can take on the stark, absolute quality of a command. Communication was still a two-way process in the White House at the end of 1969, but through Haldeman, and in writing, the process screened out subtleties. Moreover, Haldeman lacked the intuition and instincts of Washington power that might have compensated for the absence of the staff's direct dealings with the president. In some ways, such as his deep suspicion of the press, "a darker side to Haldeman [was] reflective of Nixon's darker side."[34] Thus Haldeman often failed to protect his chief from those impulses that the system of solitary confinement was meant to moderate. The White House became an echo chamber that magnified the voice of the president but sacrificed true pitch.

One new person managed to move past the gatekeeper into the inner circle. Charles W. Colson was hired in late 1969 to serve as liaison with nongovernmental lobbying groups. Since 1970 was an election year, Colson, by turning his limited mandate into a theory of a new Nixonian majority, was able to capture the president's attention. If an election coalition could be built around lower middle-class ethnics and other aggrieved minorities, then Colson's special interests office was a logical place to start. The operation was to reach sizable dimensions by the 1972 campaign. As one of Colson's assistants testified before the Ervin Committee,

> he had responsibility for all special interest groups such as veterans, the labor, youth, Jewish vote, the ethnic, Catholic, women, elderly, Spanish speaking, black, and I think there were several other groups. All of us had the mandate to develop programs that would best benefit our respective constituencies and within that umbrella was included appointments to high level positions . . . generating grants and contracts, and . . . trying to publicize all of these accomplishments and achievements under the Nixon administration to our respective constituency.[35]

This was an extension of Johnson's resident concept, whereby each White House assistant, in addition to his major responsibilities, served as liaison with some outside group, usually one with which he shared membership. The Nixon variation, as orchestrated by Colson, was a staff of junior-level people with full-time assignments as White House advocates for definable groups. A common worry of presidents has been that their domestic agency appointees would become representatives for special interests, and Nixon had tried to protect himself by isolating himself from his most nattering cabinet members. Yet at the same time he nullified the protection by allowing Colson to move such representatives into the White House. Assistants who were expected to be loyal to the president were also being forced to divide their loyalties and in effect pitted one against the other. They were employees of the president whose status would be determined by how successfully they could win victories from the president for their outside constituents.

Yet while group representation was having the effect of moving White House aides away from the president, a counterpull was also developing, a sort of macho theory of staffing, which in a less virulent strain can be found in all administrations. Those who could display their toughness—measured by the most unquestioning opposition to forces and people that were thought to be against their president—were most likely to prosper. Magruder identified the losers as those who were considered soft on the media, soft on Congress, or soft on "liberals in general." He put Klein, Harlow, and Finch in this category. The winners were Haldeman, Mitchell, and Colson.[36]

But Harlow and Burns (another loser) were not liberals. Rather, what distinguished losers from winners was that the losers tended to be persons of substantive interests. The winners were largely interested in the techniques of politics. "Moynihan and Burns were believers," John Osborne wrote in 1971, "they fought with each other and for their beliefs, and the likes of them are no longer to be found at the Nixon White House."[37]

The president and his White House loyalists increasingly saw themselves as pursued by three demons: the press, Congress, and the federal bureaucracy. A study of Washington reporters during the Nixon administration did conclude that most of the press corps probably voted Democratic (although it does not necessarily follow that their stories were slanted).[38] Both houses of Congress were controlled by the Democrats. And interviews with supergrade civil servants in the domestic agencies documented "a career bureaucracy with very little Republican representation . . . a social service bureaucracy dominated by administrators ideologically hostile to many of the directions pursued by the Nixon administration" (although it does not necessarily follow that they sabotaged the president).[39] George Christian, Johnson's last press secretary, wrote, "President Nixon inherited a governmental apparatus that was predominantly Democratic, and there was very little he could do about it unless he desired to devote his entire time to the task." (Johnson, according to Christian, recommended that Nixon employ a strong loyalty test to those in policymaking roles.)[40] One might conclude, as do Joel Aberbach and Bert Rockman: "Even paranoids may have real enemies."[41]

To deal with Congress, Nixon settled on a three-pronged approach. Rather than try for conciliation and compromise, he would take on the legislators frontally, as he did in attacking the Senate for being biased against southerners after it rejected the Supreme Court nominations of Clement Haynsworth and G. Harrold Carswell. He also increasingly attempted to accomplish his goals through administrative actions instead of asking for legislation. And he pushed beyond the limits of past interpretations in using those means that supported the concept of a strong presidency, such as impoundment, executive privilege, and the war powers of the commander in chief.

Nixon's response to the press was also multifaceted. To minimize the importance of what he considered a hostile Washington news corps, he held only twenty-eight presidential news conferences in the capital in four years. Another defensive tactic was to keep White House reporters occupied with briefings that suited the interests of the administration. The genius of Eisenhower's press secretary, James Hagerty, had been not only to recognize that the flow of news could be adjusted in a measurable way, a major breakthrough in the history of news management, but also to realize that, all things being equal, White House reporters take the stories they are given. This technique was expanded by Ron Ziegler. In March 1971, for example, there were seven briefings at the White House that had no direct bearing on the activities of the president, ranging from the plans for the recreational use of Camp Pendleton to a visit by the astronauts to college campuses. But the major evasive tactic in this war with the press was the president's greatly increased use of television. As James Keogh explained, "Richard Nixon believed . . . that the best way to communicate with the people was to appear on live television and speak directly to them. This was, in effect, going over the heads of the newsmen so that what was said would not be strained through their political bias."[42] Whereas Kennedy had made four prime time TV appearances during his first nineteen months in office, Nixon made fourteen.[43]

The counteroffensive was a public relations campaign of unprecedented scale. Magruder, a "winner" and a "merchandising type," was given actual, though not formal, command of the Office of Communications. Herb Klein was relegated to making speeches, a sort of perpetual traveling salesman for the administration. Magruder's greatly expanded operation used a computer programmed with 150,000 names that enabled staff to send presidential statements to people in categories as specific as "middle-aged black dentists" if that was considered desirable. It also was used to "stimulate letters to the editor and to members of Congress in support of the President."[44] A White House aide ran a speaker's bureau. A White House aide lined up TV appearances for administration spokesmen. A White House aide wrote speeches for members of Congress. A White House aide named E. Howard Hunt, directed by Colson, prepared phony State Department cables implicating President Kennedy in the assassination of South Vietnam's Premier Diem, and these were leaked to journalists.

As for Nixon's third demon, the bureaucracy, his New Federalism program was intended to weaken the power of the permanent government in Washington. Revenue sharing, for example, was meant to transfer federal tax dollars to the states and localities with few strings attached. This was in keeping with traditional Republican doctrine, and the president would have proposed it even if the civil service had been dominated by Nixon enthusiasts. That this was not the case undoubtedly made his proposals even more personally satisfying.

Nixon's other serious effort to keep from becoming the hostage of government careerists was to attempt to create a "counter-bureaucracy."[45] The president turned to the Advisory Council on Executive Organization, under the chairmanship of industrialist Roy L. Ash.[46] The proposals of the Ash Council, incorporated in Nixon's Reorganization Plan 2 of March 12, 1970, called for the creation of a Domestic Council and the conversion of the Budget Bureau into the Office of Management and Budget. "The Domestic Council will be primarily concerned with what we do; the Office of Management and Budget will be primarily concerned with *how* we do it and *how well* we do it."[47]

The first director of the Office of Management and Budget was George Shultz, who stepped up from his $60,000-a-year job as secretary of labor to a more important assignment at $42,500: the federal salary scale had as yet failed to adjust to the flow of power in government. Nixon was reported to have spent about forty hours working on the 1971 budget and to have been bored by the exercise. The appointment of Shultz would not only relieve him of this chore, but would also reduce the independence of the departments. Traditionally, cabinet officers had the right to appeal to the president when negotiating their budgets; now this right was to be denied them.

Shultz and Ehrlichman became the final arbiters. Shultz was given an office in the west wing of the White House, emblematic of his relationship with the president, and OMB, with more political appointees, would gain additional power over the departments.[48]

Nixon described the new council as "a domestic counterpart to the National Security Council." The analogy was strangely apt. Both councils had been approved as cabinet-level advisory groups to the president. But in fact under Kissinger the NSC had become primarily a White House staff operation, expanding to 132 staff members (fifty professionals) by the administration's fifth year. And the Domestic Council, under its executive secretary, John Ehrlichman, was to serve a comparable staff purpose; Nixon seems never to have meant it as a collegial body.

By 1972, the Domestic Council had about the same number of professionals on its staff as the Johnson administration had employed to cover similar duties, and they seemed equally qualified: twelve of the twenty-one staff members had law degrees, seven had Ph.D.s, and the other two had degrees in business administration.[49] Each of the six assistant directors was responsible for one or more specific concerns—crime and transportation, for example, or energy, environment, and agriculture. There was something akin to an annual process. Issues were generally identified in late spring and studies were completed early in the fall so as to be integrated into the budget and the legislative program.[50] An ad hoc working group, created to develop each program, might consist of a member of the Domestic Council staff; an official of OMB, the Council of Economic Advisers, or the Science Adviser's office; and an assistant secretary from each of the departments concerned. As Richard Nathan pointed out, "In important ways they were becoming more like Johnson's White House under Joseph Califano, a model that President Nixon at the outset had explicitly rejected."[51]

There was, however, an important distinction: Johnson measured his success largely by legislative enactments, while Nixon decidedly did not. The Johnson style was to reach the greatest consensus possible with those whose approval was necessary. The Nixon style, reflected in the composition of the working group, was exclusionary; no outsiders were welcome, not even members of the permanent government. Chester Finn, a member of the White House staff working on education programs, recalled that the group kept civil servants "in an adjoining room during the meetings, summoning them only when their expertise was required. Every time we invited one in, I could sense a certain coolness and reserve descend upon the room.

After the presentation, the staffer would be thanked and invited to leave, whereupon the Group members loosened up and talked frankly once again." Finn concluded, "This is not an administration that relies on outside advice for much of anything."[52] Thus Nixon's proposals had few supporters when support was needed. The one exception was the general revenue-sharing package, which had been negotiated with mayors and governors before its introduction in Congress and was the major legislative success of the administration.

The Domestic Council staff increasingly became involved in the most routine departmental operations. One relatively minor matter, making veterans aware of benefit programs, took three or four months of the time of one White House aide. As he recalled, "The Veterans' Administration administered most of the benefit programs; the Defense Department had the best list of discharged servicemen; the Postal Service had to be involved because of the increased work load. . . . I acted as a go-between with these agencies."[53] More and more department decisions required White House clearance. Presidential assistants worked longer and harder with less to show for their efforts. Cabinet officers became increasingly disgruntled. Interior Secretary Hickel's break with the president, for instance, probably had less to do with policy differences than with being locked out from personal contact with Nixon and forced to take orders from junior White House aides. (Hickel had only two private meetings with Nixon in fifteen months.) By the time he was elected to a second term Nixon recognized that trying to create a counterbureaucracy at the White House had failed.

Nor had he succeeded in regrouping the executive departments along functional lines. The president's 1971 State of the Union message, following suggestions made by the Ash Council, proposed merging the eight domestic departments into four new superagencies: the Departments of Natural Resources, Human Resources, Economic Affairs, and Community Development. It was a plan similar to the one offered to Johnson in 1967 by the President's Task Force on Government Organization. But Johnson knew by instinct what Nixon had to learn the hard way—Congress would have nothing to do with such a drastic reorganization, even after Nixon agreed to keep the Agriculture Department intact. His only victory was to remove the Post Office Department from the cabinet, a proposal made by Johnson in his last State of the Union message.[54]

After defeating George McGovern, Nixon announced that he planned to overhaul the government. His statement of November 27, 1972, perhaps the most remarkable ever made by a president who had just been reelected, proclaimed that he had lost confidence in his appointees and in the organization he had constructed to serve him. The White House staff, he said, had "grown like Topsy. . . . It is now time to reverse that growth." A cabinet member eventually "becomes an advocate of the status quo; rather than running the bureaucracy, the bureaucracy runs him." He would attempt to reverse the "historical pattern," which was for "an administration to run out of steam after the first 4 years, and then to coast, and usually coast downhill." Nixon did not blame himself. On the contrary, he saw no connection between the administration's operations and the pattern of solitude that had left him physically removed from his appointees and increasingly removed from the seat of government. Speaking from his retreat at Camp David, he said that each president "must work in the way that . . . best fits his own patterns." For him this meant "getting away from the White House. . . . I find that up here on top of a mountain it is easier for me to get on top of the job."[55] The solution would not be to change his patterns but to make massive changes in personnel and structure.

Between November 28 and December 22, Nixon announced fifty-seven resignations and eighty-seven other personnel decisions. He nominated six new cabinet officers and appointed five White House assistants to under secretary, assistant secretary, or agency head. The Executive Office of the President was to be streamlined by eliminating the Space Council, shifting the advisory functions of the Office of Science and Technology to the National Science Foundation, and transferring the duties of the Office of Emergency Preparedness to other agencies. Nixon also sought to abolish the Office of Economic Opportunity. To compensate for the failure of Congress to approve his design for superagencies, he named four of his cabinet members as counselors to the president—Treasury Secretary Shultz, Agriculture Secretary Earl Butz, HEW Secretary Caspar Weinberger, and HUD Secretary James Lynn—with overall functional responsibilities, respectively, for economic affairs, natural resources, human resources, and community development. This meant, for example, that in some matters the secretary of the interior would be reporting to the secretary of agriculture.

Part of the top-level reorganization was accomplished by internal shifts. The chairman of the Atomic Energy Commission became the director of the Central Intelligence Agency; the CIA director became the ambassador to Iran; the deputy secretary of defense became the deputy secretary of state; the under secretary of commerce became the secretary of HUD; the director of OMB became the secretary of HEW; the deputy director of OMB became the under secretary of HEW; the secretary of HEW became the secretary of defense, and so forth. This elaborate game of musical chairs reflected the limited number of people who had gained the president's trust. But these circulating executives were also among the most competent of Nixon's first term. Changing assignments is a sensible technique for prolonging the vitality of political appointees. Yet the personnel problem in the Nixon administration was ultimately of a different nature. Consider the experience of Elliot Richardson, possibly the most skilled political executive in the president's inner circle. He served successively as under secretary of state, secretary of HEW, secretary of defense, and attorney general. In being moved from HEW to Defense at the beginning of the second term, Richardson was leaving behind an unfinished agenda in a department that would now have its third secretary in less than three years. From 1933 to 1965 the median length of service for cabinet officials was forty months; during Nixon's presidency it dropped to eighteen.

Nor was there always a powerful rationale for bringing some of the new people into government. Efficient managers at Commerce and Labor were dismissed and the Transportation and Commerce portfolios were given to relatively obscure businessmen. The new secretary of labor, Peter Brennan, was the head of the building trades union in New York and a political ally of the president. Nixon apparently had not learned the lesson of Martin Durkin, the ill-fated union leader whom Eisenhower had appointed in the hope of not having to deal directly with the AFL-CIO. George Meany made it clear that he would not be fobbed off on some unionist at the Labor Department and turned Brennan's life into "if not a hell, at least an existence in limbo."[56]

The planned changes in the Nixon cabinet were completed in September 1973, when Henry Kissinger became secretary of state without having to relinquish his White House duties. This was one way to reconcile the growing feud between Kissinger and Rogers. As the president told William Safire, "I'm sorry about how Henry and Bill go at each other. It's really deep-seated. Henry thinks Bill isn't very deep, and Bill thinks Henry is power-crazy. . . . And in a sense, they're both right."[57] The foreign policy of the first term was based on the Nixon-Kissinger assumption that the most pressing world issues could be best resolved by direct negotiations among the superpowers, each represented by a strong leader. The participants were limited, the means were secret. Kissinger, as the president's agent, was the prime operator in the preliminary stages; a series of summit meetings followed.

But the system was not without detractors. Congress felt increasingly left out, especially since, as a White House aide, Kissinger could not be forced to testify before congressional committees. (Senator William Fulbright even introduced a bill that would have required Kissinger's appearance before his Foreign Relations Committee.) The State Department also felt left out. Senator Stuart Symington complained that Kissinger's ascendancy created an "obvious decline in the prestige and position of the Secretary of State and his department," proving, perhaps, that even the State Department has friends.[58]

The two-man system of conducting foreign policy also encountered serious problems. It limited the number of issues that could be handled at any one time. During the first term this had meant that such questions as U.S. relations with less developed countries were unattended.[59] Then too, the needs of the administration had changed. Kissinger had once written that "the spirit of policy and that of bureaucracy are diametrically opposed. . . . Good administration thrives on routine, the definition of relationships which can survive mediocrity."[60] Foreign policy during Nixon's first term had "required, to a considerable extent, secret diplomacy . . . conducted on a rather restricted basis." But in the second term, Kissinger implied, the need was for "good administration" that would consolidate gains and build "a structure that we can pass on to succeeding Administrations."[61]

Whether Kissinger's dual responsibilities could lead to conflicts of interest in the internal negotiations of the NSC was not addressed by the president. Eventually, Kissinger's two hats would be attacked by Senator Lloyd Bentsen and others as "dangerously [centralizing] power in the hands of one man."[62] Yet in the short term, as the administration crumbled, the elimination of rivalry between the secretary of state and the assistant to the president for national security affairs was a fortunate break for the United States.

Nixon's final strategy for taking control of government by shifting proven loyalists to the departments had no chance to succeed or fail. The last year of his presidency was a fight to survive, not to innovate, and the White House was organized around the defense of the president. By the summer of 1974 a team of fifteen lawyers, under James St. Clair, was trying to stave off impeachment. Another group, with Dean Burch and Ken

Clawson as its key members, was engaged in a political and public relations counteroffensive. Nixon himself spent longer periods away from Washington. While he was able to concentrate on foreign policy, domestic planning, to the degree that presidential approval was necessary, seemed to come to a standstill. Donald Santarelli, director of the Law Enforcement Assistance Administration, was quoted as saying, "There is no White House."[63] Yet most of government went on without presidential attention and continued to function properly.

The president brought into the White House a series of advisers of independent stature, wise in the ways of politics and Washington—John Connally, Melvin Laird, Bryce Harlow. But he never told them of the extent of his complicity in the Watergate cover-up, and so their advice was irrelevant and unheeded. Soon he stopped seeing them altogether. After Haldeman and Ehrlichman left, Nixon had even fewer direct contacts with even fewer people. At the end he limited those with whom he regularly met to Alexander Haig and Ron Ziegler.

Some were to blame Nixon's downfall on the people around him. "They entered into government, all of them," Theodore White said, "with no greater knowledge of how power works than the intrigues of the political antechambers and the folklore of advance men—and were quickly off into a dark land."[64] But while the tragedy of Nixon was intimately connected with actions taken by his subordinates, they were not all pols and hucksters. Columnist Joseph Kraft noted that "as the Nixon administration presents its 1974 face to the world, it turns out to be a government by—of all things—professors [who] command among them more influence than intellectuals ever had in Washington."[65] Kraft cited Shultz, Kissinger, James Schlesinger, and John Dunlop, and over the life of the administration there had been such others as Burns, Moynihan, Paul McCracken, Herbert Stein, Lee DuBridge, Murray Weidenbaum, and Arnold Weber. The president's helpers cannot simply be dismissed as a collection of intellectual ciphers; they represented a substantial reservoir of talent at hand. But Nixon was inclined to draw on it for specialized and technical advice and then, as had his White House working groups, invite his advisers to leave the room. The decisions that ended his career were taken alone.

Nixon's relations with Congress were also as he wanted them to be, despite a liaison staff—Harlow, Clark MacGregor, William Timmons— deeply versed in the sensitivities of Capitol Hill. Even of Haldeman it was said, "If he didn't exist, Nixon would have had to invent him."[66] Nixon's staff was, then, ultimately irrelevant to the root cause of Watergate. "He peopled his office himself," Safire wrote, "and was the captive of nobody; he made his fate the extension of his character."[67] Comparing White House operations under Haldeman and Haig, John Osborne wrote in May 1974:

> Haig and his predecessor, Bob Haldeman, are very different individuals. Haldeman was secretive, inaccessible, vengeful, a worker in the dark. Haig is open in manner, moderately accessible, much more visible than Haldeman was. Yet the White House with Haig isn't very different from the White House with Haldeman. The reason is obvious. It wasn't Haldeman's White House and it isn't Haig's White House. It was and is Richard Nixon's White House and that is the trouble.[68]

Nixon later recalled, "With all the problems I was having with Watergate, I could not become embroiled in a massive partisan slugging match over the selection of the new Vice President." He had wanted John Connally to succeed Spiro Agnew when the disgraced vice president was forced to resign in 1973. Republican party leaders were evenly split between Nelson Rockefeller and Ronald Reagan. "Ford was fourth," wrote Nixon. "Ford, however, was first choice among members of Congress, and they were the ones who would have to approve the man I nominated."[69] Thus was Gerald R. Ford put in the position from which he was automatically elevated to president of the United States on August 9, 1974.

For twenty-five years Ford represented Grand Rapids, Michigan, in the House of Representatives; since 1965 he had been Republican leader of that body. According to *Congressional Quarterly,* "To his colleagues in Congress, Ford built a reputation for being solid, dependable and loyal—a man more comfortable carrying out the programs of others than in initiating things on his own." And Democratic Senator William Proxmire concurred: "A man of integrity and character. Of course," he added, "I think he has been consistently wrong on almost every issue. . . ."[70] Fortunately, rather than intellectual brilliance or special expertise, the qualities of integrity and character were exactly what the nation now most needed. The new president, at ease with people and not notably obsessed with power, would have sought an open administration, short on "the trappings of an 'imperial' Presidency," even if he had not followed Richard Nixon.[71]

The situation Ford found himself in differed fundamentally from that of the two other modern vice presidents who unexpectedly attained the nation's highest office. The first task before Harry Truman and Lyndon Johnson had been to reassure a shocked nation by reaffirming the principles and policies of their predecessors. Ford had to try to rebuild public faith in the presidency itself and at the same time avoid any policy lurches that might further call into question the government's stability. This tension between change and continuity dominated the early days of his administration.

As early as May 1974 a small group of White House officials had begun to meet in anticipation of a possible change in the Oval Office. Headed by the vice president's longtime friend and adviser, Philip Buchen, this rudimentary transition group met without Ford's knowing of its existence. The day Ford assumed the presidency, the group had ready for him a list of immediate priorities and decisions to be made. Assuming that the old White House staff would tender their resignations, it made recommendations for key White House posts. Although the Haldeman stigma made the group chary of recommending a titled chief of staff, it did suggest a staff coordinator, Donald Rumsfeld, a former Illinois congressman then serving as U.S. ambassador to NATO. The group also advised Ford to retain Alexander Haig through the transition period.[72]

Ford immediately appointed a formal transition team, headed by Rumsfeld, to arrange the details of how the new president would assert mastery over the White House. Rumsfeld set out to organize an administration compatible with the new president's style that also would symbolize the difference between Gerald Ford and Richard Nixon. Because many believed that the Nixon White House, and especially the power given to Haldeman as chief of staff, contributed to Watergate, decentralization of executive authority became an organizational and thematic imperative.

Specifically, Rumsfeld's group recommended strengthening the cabinet and giving cabinet officers greater access to the president. Their authority would be restored by eliminating presidential micromanaging of cabinet department operations, which had been done through OMB and the Domestic Council. Another priority was to build in many channels of communication to the president so as to avoid isolating him. Both Rumsfeld and Haig, however, urged Ford to designate someone to coordinate White House paper flow and presidential scheduling. But Ford, grown comfortable with the way he had interacted with a small congressional staff, wanted to be his own chief of staff. "The President had to go through his period where he got that out of his system," observed Rumsfeld.[73] Ford enthusiastically envisioned himself the hub of a structure he called "the spokes of the wheel" and left it to Rumsfeld to work out the details of the organization.

By the end of August, Rumsfeld had devised a system with nine spokes going into the president: staff coordinator (Haig and later Rumsfeld) in charge of the offices of cabinet secretary, staff secretary, and presidential personnel; legislative and public liaison (John O. Marsh Jr., a former Virginia congressman); editorial matters such as speeches and other presidential statements (Robert T. Hartmann, a former newspaper reporter who had been Vice President Ford's chief of staff); legal counsel (Buchen); press secretary (Ronald H. Nessen);[74] national security adviser (Kissinger, who continued to serve as secretary of state); domestic affairs (Ken Cole, a Nixon holdover, subsequently succeeded by James M. Cannon); economic affairs (L. William Seidman, from Grand Rapids and a major accounting firm); and budget (Roy Ash, subsequently succeeded by James Lynn). When Rumsfeld replaced Haig at the end of September, he asked for the authority of a chief of staff, though not the title, and Ford finally agreed, admitting that "without a strong decision-maker who could help me set my priorities, I'd be hounded to death by gnats and fleas."[75]

The sudden transition produced organizational problems. John Casserly, a White House speechwriter, observed at the time that "one of the major reasons why the Ford White House is so disorganized is that it did not join and weld itself together in the heat of a political campaign out of genuine respect and admiration for the candidate."[76] But worse, according to Robert Hartmann's bitter book, was the "internecine warfare" between "proven Ford loyalists" and "Haig's espionage net."[77] Hartmann urged the president to fire all Nixon appointees with any authority at all and led the charge by dismissing the entire Nixon speechwriting staff. But Ford balked at a Stalinlike purge, as he called it. While he told Haig and Rumsfeld to see to it that unwanted Nixon holdovers left by January 1, every effort had to be made to help them relocate and find employment: "Nobody was going to be thrown off the airplane without a parachute."[78]

Although the genesis of the infighting at the White House was the mix of two different staffs, it lingered into 1975 because "Ford simply hated to lay down the law." Unlike Roosevelt, he "was not deliberately pitting people against each other"; it was just that he "seemed unable to control his staff."[79] As the House minority leader, Ford's skills as a consensus builder and compromiser were practically a job description. Running the White House required a more commanding approach.

Ford's stated goal of reducing the size of the White House staff complicated the aim of surrounding himself with his own people. Simply replacing Nixon's people would keep the White House as bloated as before. Many posts therefore were allowed to die with the outgoing staffer. As of October, for example, about seventy Nixon people had departed while only fifty appointees had come abroad. By January the White House staff had been cut from 540 to 485, where it stayed for the duration of the administration.

Ford chose New York Governor Nelson Rockefeller as vice president. Perhaps as a lure to attract a man of such stature, perhaps as a way to take advantage of his talents, perhaps recalling the limited use that Nixon had made of him as vice president, Ford promised to put Rockefeller in charge of domestic policymaking. It was a mistake. What happened is recounted by Richard Cheney, Rumsfeld's deputy and then his successor:

> [A]t his regular Wednesday afternoon meetings, the vice-president would come in with a new policy proposal for the president, new health insurance scheme or new economic policy initiative of some kind. . . . At the end of the day, you'd go down for the final close-out session, and the president would hand it to you and say, "What the hell do we do with this?" Your responsibility at that point was to say, "Well, we'll staff it out," and then take it and send it out through the system. The answer would always come back—it never failed—it always came back exactly the same way, "This new policy is totally inconsistent with the basic policy of the Ford administration."[80]

In other words, by putting the vice president in charge of a staff operation, the Domestic Council, the president had chosen to ask for advice that was awkward to reject from a man that he could not fire and that he certainly did not want to dishonor.

In the interest of maintaining continuity, Ford retained the Nixon cabinet until January 1975, when he made the following changes: Edward Levi, president of the University of Chicago, replaced William Saxbe as attorney general; William Coleman, a prominent Philadelphia attorney, took over Claude Brinegar's spot at Transportation; Harvard professor John Dunlop moved into Peter Brennan's place at Labor; HUD Secretary James Lynn succeeded Roy Ash at OMB; and assistant attorney general Carla Hills became the new HUD secretary. Ford did not fire anyone; he was pleased, however, to put his own mark on the cabinet. Of his five appointees, two came from academia, one from private practice, and two from within the government; all had law degrees. While upgrading the intellectual caliber of the body, Ford also added a woman and a black appointee.

The president initially met with the cabinet once a week. But the usual problems of large meetings were exacerbated by Ford's easygoing style, which often allowed the gatherings to degenerate into unresolved talk sessions, and the meetings were gradually reduced to one a month. At the same time, however, the White House was designing a subgroup of the cabinet that Ford would ultimately call "the most important institutional innovation of my administration." In contrast to the full cabinet, the Economic Policy Board (EPB), as it was named, was to meet more than 500 times. The group was chaired by Treasury Secretary William Simon, with William Seidman of the White House as its executive director. According to Roger Porter, who served on the staff, Simon was "Mr. Outside" (advocate and principal spokesman) and Seidman was "Mr. Inside" (honest broker and process manager). Besides Treasury, the main participants represented OMB, the Council of Economic Advisers, the special trade representative, and the Departments of State, Labor, and Commerce. Most of the work was conducted by an executive committee that met three or four times a week for an hour or so.

> While the EPB's primary function was organizing the flow of information and advice to the President for his decisions on economic policy issues, the Executive Committee also produced and cleared presidential speeches and messages, exchanged information among the administration's leading economic officials, coordinated administration presentations to congressional committees, resolved disputes between member departments and agencies, coordinated the activities of several statutory councils and committees, and served as the place where the major White House policy-making entities responsible for advising the President met and coordinated their activities.[81]

Although Rumsfeld became the president's de facto chief of staff, he never felt that Ford granted him the authority he really needed to make things run properly. Still, he was able to develop a certain degree of regularity in decisionmaking. "He's another Bob Haldeman," grumbled one staffer, "only he smiles."[82] Rumsfeld did not hesitate to expedite things by playing the role of the genial president's alter ego. "With the spokes coming in," remarked Rumsfeld later, "the President is in the center and the chief of staff is the grease. All the grease does is get overheated and have to be replaced."[83]

Labor Secretary John Dunlop's resignation in the spring of 1975 reinforced the impression that the Ford White House was not a smoothly functioning operation. In this case it was what Cheney called an "oh-by-the-way decision." That is, a cabinet member goes to see the president on matter X and as he heads out the door he turns and says, "Oh, by the way . . ." and raises matter Y. Dunlop's oh-by-the-way had managed to get Ford's verbal support for pending legislation permitting common situs picketing. The result was an avalanche of opposition from the business community. By the time the legislation passed Congress, senior White House advisers and cabinet members opposed it almost unanimously. Ford decided to veto the bill, thereby angering labor and embarrassing Dunlop, who resigned in protest.

If domestic policy formulation was often disorganized, foreign policy remained firmly under Henry Kissinger's control. Ford felt more confident dealing with domestic policy and therefore preferred hearing options from a wide range of advisers before making a decision. Less sure of his foreign policy knowledge, he generally deferred to Kissinger's judgment: "I respected his expertise in foreign policy and he respected my judgment in domestic politics."[84] Emblematic of Kissinger's influence was the hour-long meeting he held with the president each morning. Although presidential advisers feared that Ford would be eclipsed by his illustrious secretary-of-state-cum-national-security-adviser, the mid-May seizure of the American merchant ship *Mayaguez* by Cambodia gave the president a first opportunity to demonstrate foreign policy prowess.

Still, after a year in office, the national perception of the Ford administration was of "a genial indecisiveness, spreading from the President outward through his subordinates."[85] Frustrated, Ford decided to combat this problem with a drastic and sudden high-level shake-up. On Sunday, November 2, he fired Defense Secretary James Schlesinger and CIA Director William Colby. The next day he announced that Kissinger would step down as national security adviser while remaining as secretary of state. Although the press quickly criticized the firings as the Sunday morning massacre, and the criticism was severe, Ford's simple and appropriate explanation was that "I wanted my own team."[86] Schlesinger, although highly competent, rubbed the president the wrong way, an incompatibility that would have distorted national security advising if it had been allowed to continue. Kissinger's divestiture was a proper restoration of the NSC as an independent advisory body and a symbolic declaration of who was in charge. As the new NSC head, Ford selected deputy national security adviser Brent Scowcroft, an Air Force general with a doctorate in international relations. He brought George Bush back from China to run the CIA, gave the Defense post to Rumsfeld, and, in January 1976, named Elliot Richardson secretary of commerce. So in the last year of the Ford administration there were only three Nixon holdovers in the cabinet—Kissinger, Simon, and Agriculture Secretary Butz. At the White House, Rumsfeld's position devolved to the thirty-four-year-old Cheney, whose low-key demeanor reduced the level of tension around the president. Indeed, Cheney was so unassuming that eventually he was able to drop the pretense of being staff coordinator and take up the title chief of staff.

The 895-day presidency of Gerald R. Ford can be assessed as the final two and one-quarter years of an eight-year administration—reflecting the two elections of Richard Nixon—with all of the hazards of winding down that are associated with the seventh and eighth years of a second term. Or Ford's administration can be thought of as the initial years of a presidency without benefit of the afterglow that comes from an election victory. Either way, there are debilitating consequences.

In *The President's Agenda*, Paul Light described two patterns of presidential resources. One is a "cycle of decreasing influence," meaning that the longer a president is in office, the more of his capital, time, and energy he uses up. A second "cycle of increasing effectiveness," however, offers hope: presidents learn and, therefore, may become more effective.[87] But Gerald Ford got decreasing influence without the increasing effectiveness. Moreover, never having sought the presidency, he lacked the communication skills that are sometimes honed during that process.

Management expert Frederic Malek blamed Ford for a host of "managerial failures."[88] But given the disadvantages that he had to work under, failures of management made little difference, and he actually deserves considerable credit for the quality of his top appointments. Critics have been especially hard on Ford's spokes-in-the-wheel idea. Yet few have noted that it was not a guiding principle for long. Within two months of taking office he had Rumsfeld imposing a system of accountability in the White House that was not very different from that of presidents who have been judged a success. Equally criticized was Ford's turning over the Domestic Council mechanism to Rockefeller. Yet budget belt-tightening would have scuttled any new initiatives regardless of the system that might have produced them.

Ford came remarkably close to winning the 1976 election, an indication, perhaps, that the American people thought government had come a hopeful distance from where Nixon had left it. If so, it should not be interpreted as a vote of confidence in Ford's policies, nor in his management, but in what Richard Cheney thought of as "the calming, therapeutic nature" of the man.[89]

CHAPTER 9

Jimmy Carter
1977–1981
Ronald W. Reagan
1981–1989

 Jimmy Carter, former governor of Georgia, and Ronald Reagan, former governor of California, moved into the White House bereft of Washington experience. As outsiders they had pitched their campaigns on anti-Washington rhetoric, and their elections reflected a dialectic at work among American voters, who often choose new presidents to make up for the shortcomings of incumbent or past presidents. Anti-Nixon sentiment helped elect Carter, who pledged not to lie to the voters; disillusionment with Carter's perceived incompetence helped elect Reagan, who promised leadership.

The same dialectic is reflected in the way presidents organize their administrations. Gerald Ford and Jimmy Carter reacted against the secrecy and imperial quality of Richard Nixon's White House and sought to broaden the decisionmaking process. Ronald Reagan reacted to the inconsistent and chaotic Carter administration with a focused, ideological policy apparatus. By examining, side by side, the ways Carter and Reagan organized their presidencies, one can better grasp the reactive nature of presidential organization while also identifying often surprising constants.

Transforming his outsider status into a political virtue, Jimmy Carter took advantage of Americans' lost faith in the ability of the central govern-

---

This chapter was written by Stephen Hess with Andrew Cowan.

ment to be responsive, effective, and trustworthy. At the 1976 Democratic convention he blasted Washington insiders as a major cause of the lost faith: "Too many have had to suffer at the hands of a political and economic elite who have shaped decisions and never had to account for mistakes or suffer from injustice."[1] He pledged to shake things up in Washington by bringing new faces, especially women and minorities, into government, by reorganizing the bureaucracy, and by instituting "cabinet government." With adroit use of symbolic actions—he walked the route of his inaugural parade instead of riding in a limousine—Carter sought to project the image of a nonimperial presidency. But although he wished to bring a new attitude to government and indicated the urgency of achieving energy conservation and the primacy of human rights in international relations, the new president did not have a coherent policy agenda. Rather, he brought to the White House a commitment to process. Carter believed that a good process—open and comprehensive—would produce wide-ranging policy options, the best of which would prevail on the strength of their merits.[2]

Ronald Reagan did not need a process to identify what he thought was good policy. More than any other modern president, he came to office with a clear ideological agenda, including lower taxes, a massive military buildup, fewer federal regulations, and a reduced government role in domestic concerns. The agenda enabled his administration to set priorities and focus its energies. Domestic adviser Martin Anderson remembered, "Some of the people who worked for me . . . wanted to develop new policy, to be creative. Subsequently, they were upset when I insisted we focus our available time and energy on policies that Reagan already had decided on. They never seemed to understand or appreciate how easy it would be to fragment our policy efforts, and to end up trying to do everything at once, as President Carter had done, accomplishing nothing."[3] The guidance for President Reagan's appointees was the policy statements of candidate Reagan (budget director David Stockman called them The Scrolls), and Reagan had been running for the office since 1968. All that could guide the Carter appointees was their president's commitment to developing the "best policy."

The management styles of Carter and Reagan have become for most observers the Scylla and Charybdis of presidential organization. Future presidents must successfully navigate between Carter's obsessive attention to detail and Reagan's cheerful obliviousness to it. Carter's Naval Academy training in nuclear engineering had imbued him with an appreciation for the importance of minutiae: "[M]y ability to govern well would depend upon my mastery of the extremely important issues I faced," he wrote in his memoirs.[4] Griffin Bell, his attorney general, called Carter "about as good a President as an engineer could be."[5] He could absorb and understand vast amounts of detail and impressed department heads with his intimate knowledge of the workings of their fiefdoms. "Carter read hundreds of pages of material on welfare programs and did almost everything but draft the legislation," recalled Joseph Califano, his first HEW secretary, who added that the president was "the highest paid assistant secretary for planning that ever put a reform proposal together."[6]

Carter wanted to be his own chief of staff, and he organized the White House to identify and create options and then leave final decisions to him. Relatively few decisions in the first half of the administration were made outside the Oval Office. "Whenever I tried to relieve him of excessive detail," national security adviser Zbigniew Brzezinski remembered, "Carter would show real uneasiness, and I even felt some suspicion that I was usurping authority."[7] Power centers existed in the White House—in the Office of Management and Budget, the Domestic Policy staff, the National Security Council, and the Council of Economic Advisers—but no hierarchy. No one supervised how all the pieces fitted together philosophically or operationally until halfway through the president's term.

Like Nixon, Carter preferred to reach decisions in private from options presented to him in writing. He did this to conserve time, not to sequester himself from critics behind a protective gatekeeper. Time studies of his first year showed that he averaged an astounding seventy hours of work each week, not including paperwork done at home or at Camp David.[8] Predictably, perhaps, his first solution to the overwhelming onslaught of memoranda was not to modify the White House organization but to take speedreading lessons. His effort to exert personal control over his administration would come to represent all cramped management styles, as when an associate of Michael Dukakis said in 1988, "Michael won't waste time deciding who gets to use the White House tennis court."[9] Submerged in details, Carter "focused his energies on decision making rather than public leadership."[10] He seemed unable to articulate a larger vision to inspire the country—or at times even his own subordinates—nor did he appear to see that as his role.

Ronald Reagan kept his administration directed by strongly voicing general goals and letting his subordinates work out the details. Bert Rockman described the Reagan administration as "an activist presidency without a highly active and involved president."[11] Reagan's supporters praised his ability to delegate authority; his detractors denigrated his detachment. Both were right. "He worked us hard so he could do his job and still be relaxed. That is the mark of a skillful executive. He knew how to delegate and when to monitor," wrote Terrel Bell, his first education secretary.[12] Reagan described his managerial system in this way: "you surround yourself with the best people you can find, delegate authority, and don't interfere as long as the overall policy that you've decided upon is being carried out."[13] The praise that surrounded Reagan's style for the first six years of his administration culminated in a *Fortune* magazine article headlined "What Managers Can Learn from Manager Reagan." Hosannas, however, turned to ridicule soon after the Iran-Contra scandal revealed a national security apparatus in disarray and exposed extreme delegation as Reagan's Achilles' heel. Relying on underlings to interpret presidential intentions ultimately created what Donald Regan, the deposed chief of staff, called a "guesswork Presidency."[14]

Displaying little comprehension of or interest in the details of his administration's policies, Reagan "was content to exercise the symbolic powers of his office."[15] When Edwin Meese, the president's counselor, decided not to wake him after Libya fired on two U.S. fighter planes in August 1981, the action suggested to the public that this was a president whose expectations of his White House staff differed markedly from those of his predecessors. Reagan rarely spoke at policy meetings, preferring to stay aloof as the experts battled it out; but "when he has made a decision, he lives with it," observed Regan. "He doesn't fret over it. And most of all, he doesn't change his mind. Therefore he doesn't confuse Congress or the public as to what he stands for."[16]

Judging from the testimony of former aides, Reagan's style grew out of a way of thinking that was basic to his character. "Reagan's body of knowledge is primarily impressionistic: he registers anecdotes rather than concepts," explained David Stockman. "I soon learned that it made less sense to tell him that you were eligible for a 35-cents-a-meal lunch subsidy if your income was above 190 percent of the poverty line than to tell him, 'The kids of cabinet officers qualify.'"[17] Because of his lack of knowledge, Reagan had to rely more than most presidents on the opinions of his aides. He provided general direction; specific policy came exclusively from the bottom up. He "made decisions like an ancient king or a Turkish pasha," observed Martin Anderson, "passively letting his subjects serve him, selecting only those morsels of public policy that were especially tasty."[18] He thus required aides whose opinions he trusted, since he usually lacked the grasp of information to evaluate policy himself. "The degree of trust involved in this method of leadership must be unprecedented in modern American history," remarked Regan. "Kennedy might call up a minor bureaucrat to check on a detail; Johnson might twist a senator's arm; Nixon might discuss the tiniest details of China policy with his staff; Carter might micromanage a commando raid in the Iranian desert from his desk in the Oval Office. But Reagan chose his aides and then followed their advice almost without question."[19] Thus when his views were well known—largely because of his prepresidential statements—it was a relatively simple matter for staff to work out the details. When his views were not clear, his officials had to fall back on guesswork. As more and more issues resisted resolution by reference to prepresidential pronouncements and fewer and fewer aides had the advantage of intimate knowledge of what the president thought, a system that had at first worked very well began to fall apart.

All presidents people the White House with longtime friends and assistants from their campaigns. But Carter excluded others to an unusual degree. Virtually all the members of his inner circle were Georgians. Of these, Hamilton Jordan, his former campaign manager, was top aide but shunned the often tedious and detail-oriented job of running the staff. He focused instead on political strategy. The other key adviser was press secretary Jody Powell. Jack Watson, an Atlanta attorney, held the titles of assistant for intergovernmental affairs and cabinet secretary, the latter a traditionally minor position that became more significant because of the increased responsibility Carter gave the departments in developing policy. Other Georgians included OMB director Bert Lance, chief congressional lobbyist Frank Moore, and chief counsel Robert Lipshutz, who had been campaign treasurer. Stuart Eizenstat, a Georgian with Washington experience and the campaign's issues director, headed the Domestic Policy staff. The only non-Georgians initially in top jobs were Columbia University professor Brzezinski (national security adviser), Charles Schultze (CEA chairman) from the Brookings Institution, and Margaret Costanza, formerly vice mayor of Rochester, who became public liaison director. "It was something of a puzzle why so many capable individuals didn't coalesce more effectively as a working body," noted Hedley Donovan, the journalist who later served as an adviser to Carter. "If the White House staff was not really an effective arm of the Carter Presidency, it was in part, paradoxically, because most of them individually were *too* devoted to the President, without enough perspective on the country or even on Washington itself."[20]

Carter's chief advisers, euphoric over their electoral victory, came to Washington disdaining the folkways of the capital. The rhetoric of the campaign had been infused with a personal antipathy toward Washington bigwigs, who had scoffed at Carter when he declared his candidacy and had ignored his campaign until its success forced them to live with it. Carter's top advisers made it abundantly clear to the Democratic establishment that their participation was not needed. They also rejected the experiences of previous administrations. Believing that Nixon's White House organization contributed significantly to the Watergate debacle, Carter distrusted on principle a strong chief of staff. Instead he endorsed a structure ensuring more or less equal access to him by eight senior advisers, a scheme that strongly resembled the spokes-of-the-wheel concept that Ford had had to abandon for a strong chief of staff. But Carter had defeated Ford and, as one top Carter aide proudly noted, "The only thing I know about [Ford chief of staff] Dick Cheney is that he has a nice wife."[21] This willed naiveté meant, according to James Fallows, Carter's chief speechwriter, that "a year was wasted as we blindly groped for answers and did for ourselves what a staff coordinator could have done."[22]

Lacking any top advisers with broad experience, "Carter tended to look to whoever had the formal responsibility for a topic for advice in that area."[23] The usual result was that decisions were made case by case, with little consideration given to grander questions of how policies relate to one another. While this did not differ markedly from the experiences of other presidents, many of Carter's policies seemed inordinately at cross purposes. Complicated energy tax proposals belied attempts at tax simplification, new social programs compromised the vision of a balanced budget, the creation of new federal departments scuttled the promise to reduce the size of the bureaucracy. The Domestic Policy staff proposed a liberal task and OMB pursued a conservative one.[24] Califano's vigorous antismoking campaign was in full swing before the White House realized the enormous political problems it was causing for Carter in tobacco-producing states. "Carter had not given us an *idea* to follow," Fallows observed. "The central idea of the Carter Administration is Jimmy Carter himself, his own mixture of traits, since the only thing that finally gives coherence to the items of his creed is that he happens to believe them all."[25] Not surprisingly, John Kessel's study of the Carter White House staff indicated a low level of agreement among its members about what direction policy should take.[26]

The Carter administration gradually learned from its mistakes. The president learned to manage his time more effectively, and finally in the summer of 1979 formally appointed Jordan as the primus inter pares of his staff. White House units, such as congressional liaison, steadily improved through on-the-job training and the addition of some Washington veterans. The administration began to reach out to the establishment it had earlier ignored as the president hired experienced people—Anne Wexler (public liaison), Robert Strauss (special representative for trade negotiations), and Lloyd Cutler (chief counsel). By its final year Carter's operation ran almost glitch-free. But it was too late to overcome public perceptions of White House amateurism and incompetence. Moreover, if there was such a thing as Reagan luck, there was also Carter unluck, notably Iran's taking American embassy personnel hostage in Tehran.

Although the Reagan administration had its share of staff squabbles, policy conflicts were tame compared with Carter's. Reagan's aides avoided some of Carter's worst problems. The White House organization chart was sharply hierarchical, and the staff had a clear ideology and agenda. Despite its anti-Washington stance, the administration sought to supplement its ranks with experienced Washington hands, and the president used his charm to make peace with the capital's movers and shakers. During the transition, for example, the Reagans dined with such establishmentarians as Katharine Graham, chairman of the Washington Post Company, and Lane Kirkland, head of the AFL-CIO.

For his chief of staff Reagan chose James Baker, a Texan who had served in the Ford administration and had managed George Bush's presidential bid. The wealthy and urbane Baker, according to Michael Deaver, would have been "an asset to any political leader because he doesn't need the job and he is secure enough to say no."[27] Reagan's other two top aides were Californians: Edwin Meese oversaw the administration's ideology, and Deaver was in charge of the president's schedule, travel, and public image.

The selection of other important aides reflected a judicious mix of trusted Californians and savvy insiders. Meese's staff was initially made up of proven ideologues, including chief domestic adviser Anderson, who had served in Nixon's White House and later as a senior fellow at Stanford's Hoover Institution, and national security adviser Richard Allen, who had briefly been Henry Kissinger's deputy at the NSC. Eight senior aides answered to Baker: E. Pendleton James, personnel, a California head-hunter; Max Friedersdorf, congressional liaison, a veteran of both the Nixon and Ford liaison teams; David Gergen, communications, who had held that post under Ford; Fred Fielding, chief counsel, who had been deputy counsel for Nixon; Lyn Nofziger, politics, Reagan's California press secretary; Rich Williamson, intergovernmental affairs, a former congressional assistant; James Brady, press, Reagan's campaign press secretary; and Elizabeth Dole, public liaison, a former member of the Federal Trade Commission. All possessed at least some Washington experience.

The difference between the backgrounds of the Reagan and Carter staffs was stark. At OMB, Carter had a Georgia banker and Reagan had a Michigan congressman; as chief congressional lobbyist, Carter picked the head of his Georgia legislative liaison team and Reagan chose a veteran of Capitol Hill. The posts of chief counsel, cabinet secretary, and press secretary were filled with Georgians under Carter; Reagan chose relative strangers who had experience. And, partly because California is a larger and more diverse state, partly because Reagan had been a two-term governor, even the aides who followed Reagan east tended to have broader governmental experience than their Georgia counterparts.

The organization chart in the Reagan White House was unique, a hybrid of a pyramid and spokes of the wheel. The president's top three advisers— Baker, Meese, and Deaver—enjoyed unlimited access to the Oval Office. Known alternately as the Troika, the Triumvirate, and the Three-Headed Monster, they and the arrangement created intense internal competition, especially during the first year when responsibilities were still being defined. The three jealously guarded their prerogatives: "During the Baker-Meese-Deaver days no one was allowed in the Oval Office unless one of them was present," remembered White House spokesman Larry Speakes.[28] None of the three had qualms about leaking information to the press to advance their interests.[29] In effect, they balanced each other's influence—the American tenet of separation of powers, perhaps, on a smaller scale. Dispersing authority in this way, however, made taking action on issues cumbersome. "You generally have to build consensus for things to go forward," one aide commented. "You have to check here and here and here. . . . We tend to be very, very good when we have one major problem out there that we all have to work on together. . . . We have much more difficulty coping with three or four simultaneous problems."[30] When the Troika agreed on a course of action, it executed effectively—witness the dramatic legislative success of Reagan's first-year economic plan.

Decisionmaking came to be focused in the Legislative Strategy Group (LSG), described by Speakes as "the engine that ran the White House." Created by Baker's influential deputy Richard Darman, who also supervised the quality of options papers, the LSG met each morning and limited its number to those who could squeeze around the small conference table in the chief of staff's office. Besides Baker and Darman, frequent attendees included Stockman, Anderson, and Friedersdorf; others were invited depending on the subjects discussed. Although its original mandate was limited to devising ways to implement policies developed by Meese's policy planning group, the LSG inevitably expanded its role. "Meese had the policy apparatus," noted Speakes, "but it was slow and creaky. Baker's legislative strategy group had to react immediately to legislative developments. His group quickly became a policy group as well as a legislative group. . . ."[31]

After the first term the Troika was replaced by a system that looked better on paper and fared worse in reality. The new, more streamlined setup was installed by Donald Regan, the new chief of staff.[32] The White House quickly assumed a different character under the imperious former Wall Street executive. Whereas Baker had acted as a facilitator and a broker, Regan "apparently saw himself as the chief operating officer in an administration where the President played a hands-off role."[33] Regan's high profile, which, for example, eclipsed the vice president's when President Reagan underwent surgery for cancer, earned him the unwanted nickname of the Prime Minister. He restructured the White House so that all lines to the president except one ran through him (NSC chief Robert McFarlane still maintained direct access). Decisionmaking structures that had ensured a broader hearing were axed in the interests of efficiency and centralization. Regan brought a hard-charging, combative approach to White House policy, particularly in choosing a confrontational right-wing newspaper columnist, Patrick Buchanan, as communications director.

By the administrator's sixth year, the president was receiving advice from a smaller, shallower, and politically less savvy pool at the White House. Congressional lobbyist Friedersdorf and political director Edward Rollins both left, frustrated by their decreased influence. Given Regan's poor political instincts, this was a draining of advisory resources that the president could ill afford. "Hanging tough" often became the preferred response to criticism, such as the furor that arose when Reagan was scheduled to visit a cemetery in Bitburg, West Germany, in which, it was revealed, SS troops were buried. "That situation could have been cleared up in a few days instead of being strung out for weeks," remarked a former aide to Baker.[34] When the Iran-Contra debacle finally forced Regan's resignation, a fitting epitaph came from a former presidential aide: "He's represented himself for two years as an all-knowing and all-powerful chief of staff who boasted that nothing happened without his sign-off. The flip side of that is you have to be all-responsible, too."[35]

Regan's replacement was former Senate Republican leader Howard Baker, who did not impose any major structural changes when he took over in February 1987, although the White House operated more in the style of the first term. Tom Griscom, Baker's Senate press secretary, became the new communications director, and Kenneth Duberstein, another Capitol Hill veteran, was appointed deputy chief of staff. The low-profile Baker, skilled at accommodating Congress, pursued no agenda of his own; rather, he returned the chief of staff's role to that of mediator, while opening access to the president and broadening the decisionmaking process.[36] Yet, regardless of the chief of staff's style, things did not run as smoothly in the second term. Organizational problems included poor preparation for the summit meeting in Iceland and Supreme Court nominations for Robert Bork and Douglas Ginsberg that could not clear the Senate.

A clear agenda, the responsiveness of the Legislative Strategy Group, and the expertise of Friedersdorf's operatives gave Ronald Reagan an early reputation for legislative prowess. During his first year he enjoyed a legislative success rate of more than 82 percent—the highest since Lyndon Johnson launched the Great Society in 1965—even though Democrats controlled the House of Representatives. The importance of good congressional relations was symbolized by moving Friedersdorf's office into the west wing of the White House, where the president also had his office. Reagan's success, of course, required extraordinary cooperation from legislators, who were being asked to slash or eliminate programs they had created and defended over the years. The White House communications unit helped convince Congress that public opinion was behind the administration's initiatives. The White House Office of Public Liaison also helped sway members of Congress by producing timely phone calls from business and other interests in their communities.[37]

Just as Reagan's reputation for legislative skill survived even after his success rate turned dismal later in his first term, Carter's bumbling first-year legislative strategy and tactics caused a lasting impression of incompetence that lingered even after his congressional relations began to run smoothly. Carter displayed little initial aptitude for congressional relations: "He did not know how congressmen talked, worked, and thought, how to pressure them without being a bully or flatter them without seeming a fool," observed Fallows.[38] Besides the initial insensitivity to congressional folkways, the president proposed more legislation than the Congress—especially the House Ways and Means Committee—could handle at one time. Welfare reform, for example, was introduced while Congress was already swamped with complicated energy and tax reform proposals. The failure to prioritize, as well as poorly conceived scheduling, led to a legislative logjam as cabinet departments raced each other to be first to submit their congressional bills, and White House lobbyists seemed like rookie cops trying to direct rush hour traffic at National Airport. Carter managed a legislative success rate of 75 percent, but that was only respectable considering the Democratic majorities in the House and Senate. Eventually some of Carter's problems in legislative relations were eased by the backup work of Anne Wexler, who took over the Public Liaison Office in 1979.

Carter wanted to lead by standing above the tangle of normal politics. He wanted to advocate policies solely on merit. He saw himself as "doing what's right, not what's political," in the words of Charles O. Jones, who depicted him as a rationalist convinced that thinking people will always follow the best policy and as a trustee because he thought that the public interest could best be served by separating policy politics from electoral politics.[39] These attitudes are most clearly seen in Carter's quixotic crusade against new dams and other water projects, bastions of pork-barrel politics protected by members of Congress who had clear ideas about what was in their constituents' best interests.

The two presidents relied extensively on television to garner support for their initiatives. "What do a peanut farmer and a movie actor have in common?" asked Samuel Kernell. "The answer is their lack of interest in active negotiation with fellow politicians and their confidence in speaking directly to the voters."[40] This confidence gave the White House Office of Communications (the Office of Media Liaison under Carter) a prominent role in legislative battles. Carter pursued appeals to the electorate because of his disdain for legislative politics and his belief in his own ability to manipulate the media. According to Lester Bernstein, "He owed more to the engines of publicity for his emergence from obscurity to a Presidential nomination than any politician since Wendell Wilkie in 1940."[41] In his administration the Media Liaison Office played a pivotal role in building public support for ratifying the Panama Canal treaties, initiating the energy program, and eliminating water projects. Carter's principal media adviser, Gerald Rafshoon, who had created the media campaigns for his gubernatorial and presidential races, symbolized to many an emphasis on image over substance. But rafshooning, as White House public relations packaging came to be called, failed to reverse the president's downward slide in the polls. Although Rafshoon wanted to emphasize fewer policy themes more strongly, Carter remained reluctant to commit himself significantly to one program at the expense of another.[42]

Reagan's Communications Office orchestrated publicity even more thoroughly than did Carter's, but the former actor's skill made much of it seem natural. "Standing in virtual awe of his acknowledged communications skills, both press and public often tended to forget what he was communicating."[43] Reagan's cheerful and reassuring demeanor helped sell policies that polling data suggested did not have wide popular approval.

Deaver and Gergen tried to keep the president away from environments that they could not control. If he were bereft of a script or the elaborate preparations that preceded news conferences or debates, Reagan often revealed a tenuous grasp of facts. Primarily to avoid embarrassing gaffes, he scheduled fewer press conferences than any other modern president. (Carter, for example, held fifty-nine press conferences compared with twenty-six during Reagan's first term.) Frustrated at Reagan's inaccessibility, reporters were reduced to shouting questions at him as he walked through the Rose Garden to his helicopter. "And that suits the administration just fine," wrote Bill Plante of CBS. "The president can snap back one of his one-liners if he chooses, or make an easy getaway if he doesn't."[44] It was a unique way of managing the news. The hallmark of the administration's media policy, according to ABC's Sam Donaldson, was a Larry Speakes slogan: "You don't tell us how to stage the news, and we won't tell you how to cover it."[45]

Carter and Reagan followed contrasting strategies in selecting personnel. Carter's notion of a nonideological process that would create the best of all possible policies required, above all, the best of all possible people—experienced, intelligent, open-minded. His instructions, therefore, were for the transition staff to identify the most qualified people available, which resulted in a confused and redundant talent search that generated 125,000 résumés, not including 16,000 suggestions from Congress. Because he thought experience and considerations of affirmative action more important than he did political philosophy, the administration he cobbled together showed a wide range of opinion that ultimately caused turmoil.

Reagan was not interested in diversity and had two good reasons for seeking a cadre of distilled conservatives. The success of his hands-off management style would depend on trusted subordinates in tune with his policies. And his presidency was to be geared toward policy implementation instead of policy development, since the policies were to be those that he had spent two decades promoting. Diverse opinions would only get in the way. Personnel director James scrutinized résumés to find loyal and ideologically pure applicants—expertise was a secondary consideration. In fact, after testing administration officials, John Kessel recorded an extremely high level of agreement on policy, far more than he had noted in his study of Carter's government.[46] Enforcing ideological conformity did not end with hiring. "Lower-level appointees were thoroughly socialized about agency programs and operations before assuming their positions; and they were socialized by Reagan aides and the conservative task forces, not by the career agency personnel whose corrupting influences were to be minimized."[47]

Overall agreement did not, however, translate into a strife-free Reagan White House. Especially during the first term, a constant battle simmered between what the news media dubbed the movement conservatives, led by Meese, and the pragmatists, led by Baker. Disputes were generally over tactics, not goals. For the movement conservatives, "compromising rather than waging a fight to the end was a failure to keep the faith and a sign of weakness and wishy-washy convictions."[48] Thus the president's core constituencies always had a built-in demonology to blame when the administration was forced to settle for less than a whole loaf. The Baker-Deaver-Darman faction was accused of not letting Reagan be Reagan. But although he appeared to sympathize with the hard-liners, the president said, "I've never understood people who want me to hang in there for a hundred percent or nothing. Why not take seventy percent or eighty percent and then come back another day for the other twenty or thirty percent?"[49]

If Reagan campaigned on the need to reduce the role of the federal government, Carter campaigned on the need to reduce its size. To set an example, he decided to cut the White House staff and reorganize the Executive

Office of the President. He centralized administrative functions and reduced the number of EOP units from twenty-one to twelve, yet budget and staff were virtually unscathed.[50] Although White House employees numbered 351 (100 fewer than under Ford), Carter had simply shifted operational staff onto the EOP payroll.[51] The White House also made extensive use of detailees from other departments, a stratagem presidents have long used to hide the real growth of their operations. Reagan's White House staff was somewhat larger than Carter's.[52]

For two presidents who arrived in Washington speaking the language of insurgency, vowing to challenge the power of the Washington establishment, Carter and Reagan ended up appointing supremely conventional cabinets. During Carter's transition, Hamilton Jordan was widely quoted as saying that he would quit if Cyrus Vance became secretary of state and Zbigniew Brzezinski national security adviser. Jordan never carried out his promise, although the Carter cabinet, including Secretary of State Vance and NSC adviser Brzezinski, fell far short of the president's pledge to bring new faces into government. With the exception of Attorney General Griffin Bell, a former judge and Carter confidante, those filling the top slots would likely have been included in any Democrat's administration. And although Bell had outstanding credentials, his nomination provoked criticism because of his weak record in support of civil rights and because of post-Watergate sensitivity to appointing a crony to head the law enforcement agency. Besides Vance, who had been Lyndon Johnson's deputy secretary of defense, other establishment figures were Harold Brown, president of Caltech and former air force secretary, at Defense; Michael Blumenthal, president of Bendix Corporation, at Treasury; and Joseph Califano, Lyndon Johnson's top domestic adviser, at HEW. Carter redeemed his campaign pledges to women's groups and minorities by appointing Patricia Harris, the black former ambassador to Luxembourg, for HUD, and Juanita Kreps, Duke University's vice president for academic affairs, at Commerce. A third academic, University of Texas economist F. Ray Marshall, became labor secretary. Carter kept tradition by selecting a westerner, former Idaho Governor Cecil Andrus, at Interior. Vice President Walter Mondale suggested a second politician, Minnesota congressman Bob Bergland, who became secretary of agriculture. Carter selected the familiar face of James Schlesinger as his secretary of energy, pending creation of that department, and elevated Brzezinski to cabinet rank. Three cabinet members came from academia, two from government, and four from law. Geographically, the cabinet tilted slightly to the South, but most of the heavyweights were best known for their accomplishments in Washington.

Reagan's cabinet was also well within the ideological parameters of his party. Movement conservatives whose enthusiasm had helped put him in the White House found little to cheer about in a cabinet whose reading preferences were more likely to be *Business Week* than *National Review*. Two inner-cabinet appointees had long-standing ties to the president: Defense Secretary Caspar Weinberger, HEW secretary and OMB director under Nixon, had been in his California government; and Attorney General William French Smith was his personal lawyer. The new treasury secretary, Donald Regan, lacked government experience and was not personally known to the president but had an impressive record on Wall Street. Alexander Haig returned to Washington as secretary of state. Despite his phenomenal résumé, the former NATO commander's name created controversy because of lingering doubts over his role in the Nixon White House during Watergate.

Outer-cabinet appointments rewarded past loyalty. Labor Secretary Raymond Donovan, a New Jersey contractor, and Transportation Secretary Drew Lewis, a Pennsylvania businessman, had been active during the campaign. Retiring U.S. senator Richard Schweiker, Reagan's preemptive running mate in 1976, became HHS secretary. New York attorney Samuel Pierce took over HUD. The only black member of the cabinet, he also would be the only secretary to serve the full two terms. Connecticut businessman Malcolm Baldridge was appointed commerce secretary. Former South Carolina governor James Edwards became secretary of energy. Despite a lack of Washington experience, Illinois agriculture director John Block was named secretary of agriculture. Reagan threw a sop to the Republican right wing and a right hook to environmentalists by selecting James Watt as interior secretary; conservation groups decried handing the henhouse keys to the fox, but they could not block the nomination. Terrel Bell, a Utah educator, was chosen to run the fledgling Department of Education, which Reaganites had sworn to abolish. The position of UN representative, a post that presidents elevate to the cabinet at their discretion, went to Jeanne Kirkpatrick, a Democrat and Georgetown University professor whose foreign policy views had caught Reagan's attention. She was the only woman in the cabinet as well as the only academic.

Reagan also gave cabinet rank to OMB director David Stockman and to CIA director William Casey, his campaign manager. Stockman's elevation, while accurately reflecting the institutional clout of OMB, was calculated to impress Congress and department heads with the importance accorded budget slashing. Including the head of the CIA in the cabinet, which made little sense in institutional terms, was a consolation prize to Casey, who had set his hopes on being secretary of state. Assessing the character of the appointments, Laurence Barrett observed that Reagan "did not attempt to stretch his cabinet across all the mainstream political factions, but he avoided the trap of narrow ideological confinement."[53]

Both Carter and Reagan pledged to institute cabinet government, although by this they meant somewhat different things. Carter envisioned a plenary cabinet devising broad policy objectives, another reaction against Nixon's administration, which had attempted to bypass cabinet departments by creating a White House counterbureaucracy. To emphasize the importance he accorded his cabinet, he released their names before formally announcing any of his appointments to the White House staff and gave them authority to choose their own subordinates. The latter decision, intended to ensure compatibility between department deputies and their superiors, gave away a good deal of presidential prerogative, especially in being able to distribute political patronage. Even though the White House retained veto power over prospective appointees, applying the veto generated acrimony. The president subsequently felt that some of his cabinet officers did not use their appointment powers in his best interests, a view seconded by Griffin Bell, who wrote that Carter unwittingly "staffed the government with McGovern people, with Kennedy people—people with no feelings of loyalty toward him and, more important, with a different view of government."[54] Although the White House encouraged cabinet officers to give special consideration to qualified women and minorities, subcabinet appointments fell short of the administration's goals. "Privately the White House had relinquished the authority to ensure that the selections were good," Bruce Adams and Kathryn Kavanagh-Baran observed. "But publicly, they had to take the blame for bad appointments."[55]

Carter's grand experiment in cabinet government began with two-hour weekly meetings, an arrangement that continued for the first year. Collegiality required a group of friends and equals, and "Jimmy" attempted to foster this camaraderie by emphasizing informality.[56] The result, according to Bell, was that "the discussions were too disjointed, given the range of Cabinet positions, to produce any coherent themes. It was adult Show-and-Tell. . . ."[57] Despite the president's injunctions, from the start the cabinet was an advisory body, not a generator of policy. Cabinet government under Carter found its expression in the increased independence of the agencies rather than in consensual decisionmaking among them and the White House. Administration policy rarely transcended the sum of the departments' positions.

In the second year, although Carter tenaciously continued the pretense of governing by cabinet, he made efforts to rein in the departments. Cabinet meetings were cut to twice a month. All proposals from cabinet members were routed to the president through either Stuart Eizenstat (domestic affairs) or Zbigniew Brzezinski (international affairs). Hamilton Jordan also started meeting weekly with cabinet representatives to monitor the departments and consolidate second- and third-tier hiring. But some cabinet officials resented Jordan's slipshod work habits, especially his failure to return their calls, and his ill-tempered remarks to journalists. Before long, the White House staff doubted the cabinet's loyalty and the cabinet questioned the competence of the White House staff.

HEW Secretary Califano, in particular, clashed with the White House over appointments and pursued his own policies with vigor; he was thus branded disloyal. But much of the disloyalty of department heads stemmed from the president's inability to demand loyalty and to articulate priorities. "Often he alternated between giving his Cabinet members little policy guidance and becoming overly involved in the details of their jobs."[58] The need for greater White House assertiveness became more pressing as secretaries repeatedly disagreed with administration policy or with each other. Treasury Secretary Blumenthal, for instance, publicly contradicted policy statements made by other senior economic advisers, and HUD Secretary Harris was publicly critical of administration monetary policy. The administration seemed unable to speak with one voice. Carter said he felt "like the referee between the Cabinet and the White House staff."[59]

In the summer of 1979, as lines grew at gas stations and inflation soared, Carter's pollster, Pat Caddell, measured a national lack of confidence in the president, a sentiment echoed by editorial cartoonists, who drew him progressively smaller as his ability to deal with problems seemed to diminish. These chronic economic ills merged with conflicts within the administration to prompt Carter to reexamine his methods. He responded by retiring to Camp David to seek solutions from a variety of national noteworthies and government officials. The reassessment resulted in the long-overdue installation of Hamilton Jordan as official chief of staff, with all the attendant authority, and the replacement of five cabinet officers. Loyalty rather than competence had become the main criterion for evaluating department heads. Califano had failed to support the creation of a department of education, Adams had retained his deputy despite explicit White House disapproval, Blumenthal refused to mute disagreements with other economic advisers. Califano, Adams, and Blumenthal were fired; Bell and Schlesinger resigned.[60] The cabinet was told to fill out evaluation sheets on subcabinet officers, which Jordan later used to target about fifty for replacement. The fact that the departing secretaries were generally considered among the most effective made it seem as if Carter were blaming the cabinet for his own shortcomings. As Democratic congressman Charles Wilson of Texas remarked, "They're cutting down the biggest trees and keeping the monkeys."[61] Most observers agreed that the president badly botched the firings by demanding pro forma resignations from his entire cabinet, which invited comparison with Nixon's identical action in 1972.

Ronald Reagan's version of cabinet government enjoyed greater success. He spoke of treating his cabinet like the board of directors of a corporation. Virtually all the members felt at home with this definition since virtually all were successful businessmen, many of them epitomizing Reagan's ideal of the self-made man. Though from geographically diverse backgrounds, they shared a fundamental business ethos that coincided with the president's vision of a shrunken federal government (except at the Pentagon). Reagan made it clear that secretaries were to represent his views to the departments, not vice versa. "Cabinet appointees met frequently with the President-elect to establish a bond that Reagan hoped would prevent them from 'going native' later on," wrote Terry Moe.[62] Reagan and Meese stressed the importance of teamwork in early cabinet meetings. The pledge of cabinet government, largely kept in Reagan's first term, together with frequent access to the president, helped counteract the natural centrifugal tendencies of cabinet officers. "The difference in this presidency," Meese remarked in 1982, "is that Reagan has used his system so that the Cabinet members all feel closer to him than they do to their departments. And he gives them a lot of opportunities to remember that."[63]

Meese established an innovative cabinet system that effectively involved secretaries in policymaking while maintaining White House control. The main feature was five cabinet councils, later six, each composed of four to six department heads who met to review policy and develop options. The president chaired a fifth of the council meetings in the first year; the others were chaired by the official with primary responsibility for the issues. During the first term there were more than 500 meetings, over half of them relating to economic affairs.[64] The councils also functioned at the subcabinet level through a staff secretariat composed of a representative of each relevant department. These meetings were chaired by an executive secretary, a high-ranking White House official. Martin Anderson called the executive secretaries "a superb control and monitoring instrument."[65] Collectively, the councils were especially good at bringing into the White House a variety of important second-echelon issues that might otherwise have escaped presidential attention. During Reagan's second term, chief of staff Donald Regan, in the interests of centralization, replaced the six cabinet councils with two—an economic policy unit, chaired by Baker, and another for domestic policy, chaired by Meese—but these units played a more limited role.

Reagan had a secret weapon for keeping department secretaries in line: the Office of Management and Budget. David Stockman, the director, wielded his 610 traditionally nonpartisan staffers like a chainsaw, slashing away at domestic discretionary spending as if it were so much underbrush. "Government by OMB" best describes the atmosphere of Reagan's first year, as Stockman forced cabinet secretaries to streamline operations and cut back services. As Donald Regan recalled,

> Stockman and his people, working in phalanx, overwhelmed the rest of the members with statistics, rapid-fire argument, and a brassy confidence in their own expertise. . . . He believed that the federal budget should run the economy and thereby shape social policy. This was a philosophical position designed to be executed by bureaucratic means. His plan of action was correspondingly simple: by controlling the flow of money into the Cabinet departments, the Director of the Office of Management and Budget would starve certain programs (for instance, welfare) and feed others that were more productive in economic terms.[66]

Stockman's assault can be seen as a successful reincarnation of Richard Nixon's stalled attempt to control the bureaucracy from the White House, although Nixon was more interested in controlling policy than in controlling money. To circumvent the tendencies of cabinet officers to complain to the president, Stockman established a budget working group to review disputed cuts with the aggrieved department heads. Martin Anderson, a group member, described it as a "hanging jury."[67] It rarely rescinded cuts, and secretaries rarely brought matters to the president. Stockman imposed "top-down" budgeting, ending the era when budgets resulted from the collective proposals of the various departments and agencies.

Stockman left behind him a transformed OMB when he departed in 1985. During his tenure the office had made the most of its new power to review existing and proposed federal regulations, pruning about 20 percent of some 10,000 rules that existed in 1981. Stockman also involved OMB in lobbying Congress for the passage of the budget, a first for an agency whose role traditionally ended with the submission of the budget in January or February. The politicization of the office did not begin with Reagan's administration, of course. Nixon's directors, George Shultz and Roy Ash, had been active in departmental policy decisions, activity well beyond the Budget Bureau's function of doing its job with "neutral competence." Nixon even moved the director's office into the White House west wing, symbolizing the status of its occupant as a presidential assistant.[68]

OMB also had a high profile in the Carter years, partly because of Bert Lance's closeness to the president, partly because of the president's deep interest in budget details and his desire to reorganize the executive branch, an OMB project. Carter and Reagan both increased the number of political appointees in OMB, and as it became more and more embroiled in partisan politics its credibility as the source of objective numbers plummeted.[69]

Vice President Walter Mondale had a more prominent role in Carter's administration than did Vice President George Bush under Reagan. As a former senator, Mondale helped compensate for Carter's lack of Washington know-how, serving as a "vital political barometer for the President."[70] Although he had no administrative or policy duties in the manner of Rockefeller, Mondale was consulted on all major decisions. This role of senior adviser had its detractors, however. Griffin Bell thought that Mondale's influence on the more conservative Carter helped to "produce the unclear, all-things-to-all-people voice that the public heard so often from the administration."[71] The same criticism was not leveled at Bush. Even though he had differed with Reagan when they ran for the 1980 presidential nomination, as Reagan's vice president he won high marks for unobtrusiveness. His duties—with several exceptions, such as heading a crisis management team—were of the representational and ceremonial sorts that traditionally devolve on a vice president.

As in domestic affairs, Carter insisted on controlling the conduct of his foreign policy. The unprecedented power wielded by Henry Kissinger in the previous two administrations disturbed him. To be a strong foreign policy president, Carter believed, required a strong national security adviser who could counter the institutional weight of the State Department. His approach seemed reminiscent of Nixon's efforts to deal the permanent bureaucracy out of decisionmaking and was certainly at odds with his own profession of cabinet government. But because Cyrus Vance protected State Department prerogatives more aggressively than had William Rogers under Nixon, the formulation of Carter's foreign policy appeared turbulent in a way that Nixon's did not. Brzezinski quickly developed the habit of making public statements at odds with those of the State Department, especially in setting the tone of U.S.-Soviet relations. Although Hedley Donovan, among others, saw foreign policy being conducted by two secretaries of state,[72] Carter thought the competition healthy. The conflict, as he intended, left the president as the only player in a position to resolve disputes between his chief advisers.[73]

Yet Carter did not appreciate the importance of keeping these disputes internal. In Vance's opinion, Brzezinski's conduct "became a political liability, leaving the Congress and foreign governments with the impression that the administration did not know its own mind."[74] The outspoken U.S. representative to the UN, Andrew Young, increased the confusion with statements at odds with both Brzezinski and Vance. Despite frequently sending mixed signals to other governments, the foreign policy tempests wreaked most damage on domestic shores, further eroding the administration's battered image of competence. Still, Vance remained Carter's main foreign policy adviser until 1979, when events in Afghanistan and Iran prompted the president to take Brzezinski's harder line. Foreign policy mirrored domestic policy in the sense that Jimmy Carter himself was the common denominator. His total immersion paid off in negotiating the Camp David accords between Egypt and Israel. But his refusal to distance himself from the day-to-day trials of the Iranian hostage crisis drained his energy and fatally associated him in the public eye with ineffectiveness.

If Carter created difficulties by having a strong NSC chief sparring with the secretary of state, Reagan caused problems by diminishing the importance of the NSC too much. He initially vowed to restore the secretary of state as primary formulator of foreign policy, and Alexander Haig, sensitive to the realities of bureaucratic skullduggery, quickly drafted a document laying out the proposed relationship between NSC and State. (The paper vanished into the briefcase of Ed Meese, to whom NSC adviser Richard

Allen reported.) Haig soon concluded that, presidential rhetoric aside, he was not getting the access to Reagan he needed to function effectively. "I had to proceed on the assumption that our principles and our instincts were roughly the same," he complained, not realizing that this phenomenon characterized most aspects of policymaking in the Reagan administration.[75]

Two factors frustrated Haig's quest to be the sole vicar of foreign policy. First, the White House Troika distrusted his ambitions, especially following his heavy-handed behavior when the president was shot in March 1981 and he announced on TV that he was in charge. Second, although the NSC's Richard Allen was not a Zbigniew Brzezinski, Caspar Weinberger was a contender for power, and the outspoken defense secretary clashed with Haig on such issues as arms control and policy toward Poland.

The secretary of state's authority was further diminished in 1982 when William Clark took over at the NSC. By virtue of a long-standing relationship, Clark enjoyed direct access to the president, displacing Meese's influence in foreign policy formulation. Haig later accused Clark of "conducting a second foreign policy" in Lebanon, "using separate channels of communication . . . [and] bypassing the State Department altogether."[76] Frustrated by the confusion produced by Clark's activities, particularly during the Argentine invasion of the Falklands and the war in Lebanon, Haig resigned in June 1982. His successor fared better. Although George Shultz also had his share of run-ins with Weinberger, the high turnover of national security advisers in the Reagan White House ensured that his authority would not be threatened on a second front.

An irony of Reagan's administration was that the NSC, which he had wanted to downgrade, ultimately became the center of the scandal over secret arms sales to Iran and the funneling of profits to the Nicaraguan Contras. Reagan was to have six NSC advisers during his two terms and the first four—Allen, Clark, Robert McFarlane, and John Poindexter—were not of the quality of previous occupants of the office, who had tended to be distinguished academics. It seemed to Larry Speakes as if "the President and his top aides . . . had such low regard for the position of NSC director that they paid little attention to those who held the post."[77] If so, the president's indifference cost him dearly. For the cause of the Iran-Contra scandal did not lie in NSC's institutional shortcomings but in the men who worked there. Poindexter and Oliver North disregarded the traditional guidelines that defined proper NSC conduct, particularly that of keeping the NSC out of covert operations.

But a deeper cause of the scandal was improper management. Reagan's underlings routinely interpreted presidential intentions according to their own best guess. A Donald Regan in the Treasury could faithfully serve Reagan, even while being "free to interpret his words and implement his intentions in my field of policy and action according to my best judgment."[78] So could a David Stockman, though he later wrote that Reagan "conveyed the impression that since we all knew what needed to be done, we should simply get on with the job. Since I *did* know what to do, I took his quiet message of confidence to be a mandate."[79] John Poindexter and Oliver North, of course, exemplified this attitude in their undercover initiatives and nearly destroyed Reagan's presidency as a result. If hands-off management is to work, it requires that key subordinates be picked with loving care. At the beginning of the administration, they were. But McFarlane and Poindexter, who had been deputies, were elevated because they were there rather than because they were deemed the best persons for the job.

After the Iran-Contra debacle, Frank Carlucci, a veteran public administrator, was brought in to clean up the mess. When he left the NSC to replace Weinberger at Defense, his position defaulted to his deputy, Lieutenant General Colin Powell. This time Reagan got lucky. "In his lame duck days," wrote Fred Barnes, "Reagan . . . stumbled onto the kind of national security adviser he always needed but never had, a tough guy without an independent streak."[80]

The process of governing may have concerned Jimmy Carter more than any president before him. Almost scientifically, giving great weight to theory, he structured what he thought would be a supremely rational administration, an open process producing good results. But process should only be a tool for getting from here to there, not a substitute for substance, not an end in itself. Carter trusted process to create policy and was adverse to ideology, which in his view would contaminate rational selection of policy. All modern presidents, whether liberal or conservative—no matter what their other faults— have had some programmatic view of government in which the specific parts could usually fit. This was not the case with Carter's domestic program, although defense and foreign policy seemed more consistent.

Ronald Reagan, in contrast, entered office as the most ideological president in history. Knowing exactly what he wanted to accomplish, he geared his administration toward achieving those goals. The clarity of the Reagan domestic agenda is what maintained so much unanimity among key administration players; he never had a loyalty problem with his cabinet. The vagueness of Carter's goals fostered confusion and dissent, even among his appointees. Political executives and high-level civil servants prefer to be loyal to a president. But if they do not know what to be loyal to, they may go into business for themselves. Certainly, Reagan benefited from Carter's mistakes. After Carter's experience, certain needs were obvious: a skilled chief of staff, basic agreement among advisers and cabinet, and hiring people who know their way through the Washington thicket.

Looking back over the two presidencies, Jeremiah O'Leary, a journalist who served briefly in the Reagan White House, wrote, "Jimmy Carter was too immersed in the trivia of paperwork to be effective and Ronald Reagan is noted for nothing so much as his ability to rise above the nitty-gritty of running a great nation."[81] Their managerial techniques have come to represent the polar extremes of how to run a White House. As such, neither is an appropriate model for future presidents. Surely there is an appropriate balance somewhere in between. It is a question I shall return to in the last chapter.

CHAPTER 10

George H. W. Bush
1989–1993
William J. Clinton
1993–2001

 George H. W. Bush and William Jefferson Clinton provide sharp contrasts in experience, presidential persona, and approach to organizing the White House. Bush, the last president of the World War II generation, volunteered for the Navy in 1941, when he was eighteen years old, and ultimately flew fifty-eight combat missions in the Pacific. Clinton, born in 1946, was the first president of the post–World War II baby boom. While every president since Harry Truman had served in some way in the military, Clinton opposed the Vietnam War, the major war of his generation, and avoided military service in it. George Bush was sixty-four years old when he was elected; Bill Clinton, at forty-three, was the third-youngest president, after Theodore Roosevelt and John Kennedy.

Bush was a scion of the eastern establishment and heir to a political heritage: his father, Prescott Bush, had been a United States senator from Connecticut. Clinton was born William Jefferson Blythe and grew up in small-town Arkansas. His father died before he was born, and he was adopted by his stepfather, Roger Clinton.

Bush came to the presidency with exceptional federal government experience: he had been a member of Congress for two terms, ambassador to the

This chapter was written by James P. Pfiffner.

United Nations, chief of mission in Beijing, director of the CIA, and vice president for eight years. Clinton's government experience was limited to Arkansas, where he was governor for twelve of the fourteen years between 1978 and 1992. While Bush had wide experience in international affairs and knew many foreign leaders on a first-name basis, he was impatient with domestic policy; Clinton, on the other hand, was fascinated with the nuances of domestic policy and was an excellent policy analyst, but he was impatient with foreign policy. Bush had trouble with syntax when speaking in public; Clinton had a silver tongue and could speak at length about a broad range of topics (and often did). Bush was a reserved Yankee who once mistakenly read his cue card literally: "Message: I care." Clinton was known for his empathetic words when speaking to the less fortunate. His message: "I feel your pain."

Although widely respected by voters, Bush was denied a second term. Clinton was reelected soundly, even while most citizens deplored his personal conduct. Bush and Clinton: studies in contrast with respect to party, experience, and persona.

Still, Republican Bush and Democrat Clinton faced similar political situations, which were characteristic of national politics at the end of the twentieth century: a closely divided electorate, a polarized and contentious Congress, and budget constraints. Each entered office with limited political capital. Bush ran in 1988 on a platform of policy continuity with the Reagan administration and comfortably defeated Democrat Michael Dukakis, but Bush had not laid out a policy agenda and did not pursue an active agenda upon coming into office. Clinton ran in 1992 on a platform of "change," which helped him win. Yet more than half of the voters opposed him, choosing either Bush (37 percent) or independent candidate Ross Perot (19 percent).

Each president faced a Congress that had become severely polarized over the past two decades of the twentieth century, a state of affairs that would have created difficulties for any president, regardless of political skill.[1] Bush's promise of a "kinder and gentler" approach to governing won some goodwill, but it could not overcome the problem of partisan polarization. With Democrats controlling both houses, Clinton initially had the advantage of a unified government. But as a self-styled "New Democrat," he did not have the support of all of his congressional partisans for his policy priorities. And after the 1994 elections he faced six years of a Congress controlled by hostile Republican majorities.

Each president had to confront mounting budget deficits that severely limited his policy options. Each acted responsibly against significant opposition within his own party to reduce the deficits (Bush in 1990, Clinton in 1993), and each suffered politically for doing so. Yet their combined deficit reduction actions made possible the unprecedented economic expansion of the late 1990s and the first balanced budgets in decades.

In choosing their cabinets Bush and Clinton appointed competent secretaries, yet neither president reversed the post-Eisenhower trend of shifting power from the cabinet to White House staff. The expanding role of government and the need for policy integration and central control led to the growth of the White House at the expense of the cabinet. John Kennedy wanted a "little State Department" in the White House under the direction of McGeorge Bundy; Lyndon Johnson developed his Great Society initiatives in the White House; Richard Nixon wanted Henry Kissinger to be his deputy for foreign policy and John Ehrlichman to control domestic policy. Thus were created White House counter-bureaucracies that ensured that the president would not be dependent on the departments and agencies for expert advice or policy development. Cabinet secretaries still played an important role as manager of their department and often as advisers to the president, but policy development has moved to the White House, where staffers broker disagreements among cabinet members and control their access to the president.[2]

President Bush came to office as the first sitting vice president to be elected in his own right since Martin Van Buren in 1836 and as the first president elected to succeed a predecessor of his own party since Herbert Hoover in 1928. His eight years as Reagan's vice president gave him a familiarity with White House operations and organization that few other newly elected presidents have had. President Reagan had campaigned vigorously for him, in contrast to President Eisenhower, who provided only lukewarm support for Vice President Nixon in 1960, and Lyndon Johnson, who maintained tight control of Hubert Humphrey in 1968. Yet succeeding President Reagan was a mixed blessing. Bush had run on a platform of policy continuity, but a president has to put his own stamp on the office or risk being perceived as merely a weak carbon copy of his predecessor. So for Bush the challenge was to strike the right balance between continuity and change.

The Bush transition was a "friendly takeover" in that loyal, fully cooperative Republicans were in office when the vice president assumed the presidency, yet some Reagan appointees wanted to stay and resented being replaced by Bush associates. Bush took sixty-five days to designate the full cabinet, one of seasoned executives who together had more than a hundred years of experience in previous administrations and with whom the president had close personal or professional relationships.[3] Reagan had helped Bush by making three cabinet appointments in his last two years in office that were clearly acceptable to Bush and that Bush retained: Attorney General Richard Thornburgh, Secretary of the Treasury Nicholas Brady, and Secretary of Education Lauro Cavasos. Bush appointed three other Reagan administration cabinet-level executives: Baker went from Treasury to be secretary of state; Elizabeth Dole, who had been secretary of transportation, became secretary of labor; Clayton Yeutter moved from U.S. trade representative to secretary of agriculture. Three cabinet appointees had been Republican members of the House of Representatives: Jack Kemp, the new secretary of housing and urban development, was a supply-sider from the conservative wing of the party; Edward Derwinski became secretary of veterans affairs; and Manuel Lujan was appointed secretary of the interior. Robert Mosbacher, a Texas friend and campaign fundraiser, became secretary of commerce. Retired admiral James Watkins took over the Department of Energy. Samuel Skinner, campaign chairman in Illinois, became transportation secretary. Dr. Louis Sullivan, a hematologist at Morehouse Medical School, was appointed secretary of health and human services, the only African American in the cabinet.

The Senate's rejection of John Tower, Bush's nominee for secretary of defense, was a serious setback. Tower had been a Texas political ally of the president's since Bush ran for the Senate in Texas in 1964. As a U.S. senator from 1961 to 1985, Tower had been a strong supporter of defense spending, and he had been a member of the Armed Services Committee for twenty years, the last four as chairman. But after he left the Senate he earned big bucks in defense consulting, prompting charges of potential conflict of interest, and he also was accused of being a heavy drinker and a womanizer. When grumbling began to be heard from Armed Services Committee chairman Sam Nunn, Bush ignored it and decided to stick with Tower. The ensuing battle became Bush's first fight with the Democratic Congress and ended in defeat, with the Senate rejecting Tower 47 to 53. Bush then nominated Dick Cheney, and with wide respect on both sides of the aisle, the Wyoming congressman was confirmed 92 to 0 eight days after the Tower defeat.

Bush's relations with his cabinet were in marked contrast to those of Reagan, who let his White House staff deal with the cabinet much of the time. Although Bush, unlike his four immediate predecessors (Reagan, Carter, Ford, and Nixon), did not promise cabinet government, he may have come closest to achieving a working relationship with his cabinet, both because he knew them personally and liked to keep in touch and because he was familiar with the policies he expected them to implement. As president-elect, Bush had said he wanted cabinet members to "think big" and "challenge the system." "I want them to be frank; I want them to fight hard for their position. And then when I make the call, I'd like to have the feeling that they'd be able to support the president."[4] Early in his administration, members of the cabinet enjoyed a certain amount of leeway and some took initiatives without first clearing them with the White House.[5] But the influence of individual cabinet secretaries did not extend to the cabinet as a collective body. Cabinet meetings were "used more for a briefing session" than for policy deliberation, according to David Bates, secretary to the cabinet.[6]

Initially, Bush continued the second-term Reagan administration's operation of the Domestic Policy Council and the Economic Policy Council. These were useful forums in which White House staffers and cabinet members could consult directly on policy development, but they did not dominate the policy process, especially in regard to the most important administration priorities.[7] The domestic and economic councils never have reached the level of institutional coherence of the National Security Council, which has been around since 1947. Bush's national security team was particularly effective, with little of the institutional and personal rivalries that marked the administrations of Nixon, Carter, and Reagan. In part, this was the result of personal relationships that had previously developed among Secretary of State Baker, Secretary of Defense Cheney, and President Bush. In part, it was the personality and expertise of national security adviser Brent Scowcroft, who had played the same role with the same understated competence that had characterized his performance in the Ford administration. Scowcroft and Bush developed a close personal bond that aided the whole policy process. The smooth-running process and close personal relationship were to pay off during the successful conduct of the Gulf War in 1990 and 1991.

Even though Bill Clinton's 1992 victory over Bush was decisive, he came to office with relatively little political capital. His share of the vote was only

43 percent. The two other twentieth-century presidents who won comparable shares of the vote also had to contend with third-party candidates: in 1912, Woodrow Wilson won 42 percent of the vote; in 1968, Richard Nixon won 43 percent. Each of these minority presidents won reelection, and each had a disastrous second term: Wilson lost Senate ratification of the Versailles Treaty and had a stroke; Nixon resigned; and Clinton was impeached.

Clinton's transition was not auspicious. He stayed in Little Rock to emphasize his outsider status, but with part of the operation in Washington and part in Arkansas, much time was lost.[8] Some preelection transition planning had been done by people who had been involved in previous transitions, yet much of the effort was wasted when a power struggle erupted between Mickey Kantor and George Stephanopoulos over who was to run the transition. Clinton ultimately chose Warren Christopher and Vernon Jordan to preside over the transition, but he refused to delegate full authority. The division of effort between Washington and Little Rock was cumbersome, and the jockeying for positions in the new administration diverted efforts from planning its organization.[9]

The initial cabinet selections were made by a small group of advisers who met with Clinton in the governor's mansion: Christopher, Hillary Clinton, Al Gore, and Bruce Lindsey. As the lists for each position were narrowed, candidates were invited to Little Rock for discussions with the president-elect. Personal chemistry was an important factor. A large portion of transition time was taken up with cabinet selection, yet a significant amount of juggling continued as the self-imposed deadline of Christmas approached. On December 24, four final names were announced: Michael Espy at Agriculture, Federico Peña at Transportation, Bruce Babbitt at Interior, and Zoë Baird at Justice. With those choices, Clinton felt that he had achieved his goal of appointing "a cabinet that looks like America." There were four African Americans (Espy, Hazel O'Leary at Energy, Jesse Brown at Veterans Affairs, and Ron Brown at Commerce); three women (Donna Shalala at HHS, O'Leary, and Baird); and two Hispanics (Henry Cisneros at HUD and Peña). Two appointees were congressional committee chairmen: Lloyd Bentsen of the Senate Finance Committee, Treasury, and Les Aspin of the House Armed Services Committee, Defense; two were state governors: Arizona's Babbitt and South Carolina's Richard Riley at Education; and two were mayors: Cisneros from San Antonio and Peña from Denver.

Despite the usual vetting, the Baird nomination blew up when it was publicized that she and her husband had employed immigrants who did not have work permits to care for their children and had not paid Social Security taxes for them.[10] A nomination battle over a wealthy lawyer and a prospective attorney general breaking the law and not paying taxes was too much political weight, and Baird withdrew on January 21. Determined to break precedent by nominating a woman for attorney general, Clinton stumbled a second time when he settled on federal judge Kimba Wood, who also had employed an undocumented alien to care for her child, before it was illegal. She had paid Social Security taxes and had broken no law, but the president decided the situation was too similar to Baird's.[11] Finally, Janet Reno, Florida state attorney for Dade County, was nominated and easily confirmed. She turned out to be a problem for Clinton later when they clashed over the appointment of special prosecutors; by that time, however, it was too politically sensitive for Clinton to fire her.

In spite of the time and careful effort that Clinton put into selecting his cabinet, the reality of the modern presidency is that power has flowed from the cabinet to White House staff since the Eisenhower administration. Thus Clinton blundered in putting off the selection of White House staffers until late in the transition. His final choices were not announced until the week before inauguration.[12] Despite all of the time he spent on cabinet selection, Clinton did not revert to "cabinet government." The major policy initiatives of the administration were developed in the White House (e.g., health care reform, national service, trade policy, and deficit reduction). Nor did Clinton use his cabinet as a deliberative body, as Eisenhower had. In his first year as president, the cabinet met only seven times.

In line with his inclusive style of leadership, Clinton accorded cabinet-level rank to eleven top officials in addition to the fourteen department secretaries.[13] This near doubling of the "cabinet" was indicative of its decline as an advisory or deliberative body. Although policymaking was centered in the White House in his first term, later in his second term Clinton and his top White House staff were so preoccupied with scandal and impeachment proceedings that cabinet members ran their departments with minimal White House involvement.

Presidents Bush and Clinton took contrasting approaches to organizing the White House, particularly at the beginning of their terms. Bush's White House was run in a buttoned-down, orderly fashion, as most modern Republican administrations have been. Clinton began his administration, as had all modern Democrats, intending to act as his own chief of staff, even though Thomas McLarty was given the formal title. While Bush ended his administration having to fire his domineering chief of staff, Clinton was well into his first term before he realized that it was necessary to delegate to his chief of staff the authority necessary to run the White House.

Bush's intent to involve his cabinet in policymaking fit with his ideas about the appropriate role of White House staffers: to facilitate and support cabinet officers, not direct them. In contrast to those in the Reagan administration, Bush White House aides—with the infamous "Sununu exception"—did not try to dominate the cabinet. According to one senior Bush White House official, "The staff is precisely what Bush wants: nice people who will not handle him or try to, people who are technically competent and without much ideology, people who will not usurp power that belongs to the President and cabinet."[14] Most of the Bush staff (twenty-four of twenty-nine members) had previous White House experience, and Bush knew most of them personally.[15]

The role models for White House assistants were Brent Scowcroft on the national security side and Roger Porter on the domestic side. Porter, a Harvard professor, had run the Economic Policy Board when Ford was president and had been an assistant to President Reagan. Under Bush his title was assistant to the president for domestic and economic policy. Despite his title and stature, he did not attempt to dominate the White House staff or cabinet. He provided experience, expertise, and policy analysis without engaging in public disputes or trying to strong-arm members of the cabinet or pursue his own agenda. Porter's attitude was that "nobody elected me to make policy. I'm here to provide my best advice."[16] Because Bush knew his cabinet appointees well and, unlike Reagan, made it a habit to keep in touch with them with phone calls, personal notes, and informal meetings, his White House staff tended not to interpose themselves between president and cabinet or have major fights with cabinet departments.

The Bush administration did not begin with a large domestic agenda, and after the United States invaded Panama to depose General Manuel Noriega, the main focus shifted to foreign policy. With Saddam Hussein's invasion of Kuwait and threat to Saudi Arabia in August 1990, the administration was on a war footing until the summer of 1991. Decisionmaking during the war was not always perfectly coordinated, but it was effective and the principals worked as well together as any national security team since World War II.[17] Bush and his staff must also be given credit for their handling of the demise of the Soviet Union and the reunification of Germany.

The Bush White House staff exhibited few major ego problems or conflicts with the cabinet, with the major exception of chief of staff John Sununu, who, often in tandem with OMB director Richard Darman, tried to dominate the policy agenda.[18] Sununu, who typically spent 35 to 45 percent of his day with the president, performed many of the traditional roles of the chief of staff well.[19] He made the trains run on time. He was the enforcer with respect to White House staffers, the cabinet, and Congress. He fired people. One of his useful functions was as a visible keeper of the conservative flame. Bush had been viewed with suspicion by social conservatives since he ran against Reagan in the 1980 Republican primaries. Sununu assured them that their interests were represented at the highest levels. Bush must have thought it useful to let Sununu stake out a very conservative policy position while he himself took a more moderate stance.

One danger of a domineering chief of staff is that a president may become isolated from his cabinet and other advisers. This danger was minimal with Bush because he was not hesitant to call up cabinet secretaries on particular issues. Yet that did not keep Sununu from trying to control access to the Oval Office and shut out policy perspectives with which he disagreed. The problem became public when *Time* and *Newsweek* ran reports that senior aides were so upset at being cut off by Sununu that the president was forced to open a post office box at his summer home in Kennebunkport, Maine, so that they could contact him without having Sununu censor their communications.[20] That Bush felt compelled to set up this back channel was an admission of organizational failure: Sununu was not acting as a "neutral broker." In the fall of 1991, for instance, Michael Boskin, chairman of the Council of Economic Advisers, wanted to see the president and had to threaten to resign before Sununu would let him talk with Bush.[21] Sununu's style grated on Congress too. During the 1990 budget summit with the congressional leadership, his behavior was so boorish that Senator Robert Byrd was prompted to tell him: "Your conduct is arrogant. It is rude. It is intolerable."[22] Sununu's eventual downfall began in spring of 1991, when information was leaked to the *Washington Post* about more than seventy trips that Sununu took around the country on military aircraft.

Although he designated almost all of them as official business, the purpose of some seemed to be to provide skiing vacations for the Sununu family. In addition, ski-industry organizations paid for his meals, lodging, and lift tickets, and air fare for his wife.[23] When the disclosures caused a public scandal, the president ordered him to clear all future flights with the White House counsel's office.

Furthermore, in an eerie parallel to a previous chief of staff and governor of New Hampshire, Sherman Adams, Sununu made several calls to the Environmental Protection Agency and the U.S. Forest Service to ask about the status of applications to double the size of the Loon Mountain ski resort owned by a friend. While he did not demand a favorable outcome for his friend's applications, his actions were described by an official as "a lot of bullying and bluster" that "made it clear what outcome the White House wanted in this case."[24] (Ironically, Sherman Adams, whose acceptance of favors from a New England businessman forced his resignation from the Eisenhower administration, was one of the founders of the Loon Mountain resort.) The last straw came in November 1991 after Bush gave a speech in New York in which he remarked that interest rates on credit cards might be higher than necessary. The stock market fell 120 points. Distancing a president from ill-considered remarks is a common task of the White House staff, and it can be done in a number of ways. But when Sununu was asked how the remarks got into the speech, he answered that the president "ad-libbed" them. His attempt to blame the president was rebutted by press secretary Marlin Fitzwater, who told reporters that the lines were in the printed text, not ad-libbed. Other Bush aides said that Sununu himself was the author of the offending lines.[25] Shortly after the incident, Sununu was asked to leave the administration.

The striking thing about Sununu's term as chief of staff is how long he was allowed to stay. It speaks of Bush's gratitude for Sununu's support in the New Hampshire primary and of the president's loyalty to his subordinates. It also demonstrates that Sununu was performing highly valued functions for the president. For despite the "Sununu problem," Bush was getting what he wanted from his White House staff—low-key, high-quality analysis.

Clinton's White House was marked by youth, inexperience, and diversity. He naturally turned to his campaign, as most presidents do, for his personal staff. Of 450 initial White House assistants, sixty-three were twenty-three years old or younger and many others were under thirty.[26] Yet at the top levels of the Executive Office, the age of Clinton appointees, about forty-five, did not differ significantly from the average age of Reagan, Bush, or George W. Bush appointees.[27]

The top staffers at the Clinton White House were not particularly experienced in the ways of Washington. Exceptions included George Stephanopoulos, Howard Paster, and NSC director Anthony Lake. While it is true that in 1993 the Democrats had a shallow bench of former White House professionals—Republicans having occupied the White House for twenty of the previous twenty-four years—there were Carter aides who might have been tapped. But in addition to the natural bias in favor of one's own campaigners, there was an unfortunate bias against those associated with the Carter White House. After four months in office, Clinton admitted his need for expert Washington hands and recruited David Gergen, who had served presidents Nixon, Ford, and Reagan. Gergen was seen as a turncoat by Republicans and as too conservative by liberals in the White House. Yet he lent a ballast of experience and maturity (some said "adult supervision") that helped stabilize the Clinton White House.[28]

White House organization always reflects the personality of the president, and the disorder of the early days of the Clinton White House reflected the wallowing of a notorious policy wonk in the details of domestic policy. Clinton resisted "premature closure," or what others would call "making up his mind." Willing to listen to continued debate and unwilling to cut it off, Clinton, according to one staffer, could "have a 10-minute meeting in two hours."[29]

Ordinarily, a president's chief of staff imposes order on the policy development process, insists that all issues are "staffed out" before they reach the president, and runs meetings in an orderly and disciplined manner. But Clinton's first chief of staff was not able to play the traditional role. Thomas ("Mack") McLarty, the president's boyhood friend, was the antithesis of John Sununu. With no agenda of his own, a gracious manner, and no psychological need to dominate the White House, he was known as "Mack the Nice."

Clinton was the first Democratic president to come to office admitting that he needed a chief of staff—it took Carter until 1979 to abandon his "spokes-of-the-wheel" approach—but Clinton admitted it only intellectually; viscerally, he was not willing to delegate sufficient authority to McLarty to do the job. McLarty did not have a major say in the selection of White House personnel nor did he control office space in the West

Wing. In addition, much of his time was spent as an emissary to Capitol Hill and the business community. Being a special troubleshooter meant that he could give only part of his time to actually running the White House, a job that takes a time commitment of 110 percent. Some said McLarty did not have the right personality to be chief of staff, but the real reason that he was unable to control the White House was that Clinton would not delegate enough authority to him to do the job. Also, the president was not the only power center in the White House. As McLarty told Gergen when he came on board in 1993, "In this White House, as you will find, we usually have three people in that top box: the President, the Vice President, and the First Lady. All three of them sign off on big decisions. You'll just have to get used to it."[30] The Clinton White House was unique in the way that power was shared from the beginning.

Most vice presidential candidates have been chosen for electoral reasons—what they can add to the ticket—and, as a result, vice presidents seldom have been part of the president's inner circle. Carter was the first president to give his vice president an office in the West Wing and a place among his top advisers. Vice presidents Bush and Quayle did not play similar roles. But Clinton chose Gore for personal compatibility and like-mindedness rather than ticket balance, and he gave Gore unprecedented influence, especially in national security affairs, science and environmental policy, and management initiatives. Later, in George W. Bush's administration, Dick Cheney's broad influence and participation in policymaking exceeded even Gore's.

Similarly, Hillary Rodham Clinton was to play an unprecedented role. Eschewing the traditional first-lady jobs—social director, behind-the-scenes adviser, and doer of good deeds—Hillary Clinton took on a full range of policy, political, and personnel chores, as she had in the campaign. She had her own office in the West Wing; her chief of staff's title was "assistant to the president." The positive and negative sides of the first lady's status were illustrated by her leadership of the health care reform task force in 1993. She was able to speak authoritatively for the president and prevailed on most issues. On the other hand, other staffers were hesitant to disagree with her, and when health care reform died, she carried a large share of the blame.

The bottom line is that during the first year President Clinton was not willing to delegate enough power to anyone else to manage the policy process and that the administration consequently suffered from poor organization. McLarty's challenge was described by Secretary of Labor Robert Reich: "Nothing gets done in this wildly disorganized White House unless B [Bill Clinton] orders it done (and even then there's no guarantee)." Reich was sympathetic to McLarty's plight: "Poor Mack has been unable to impose discipline on a chronically undisciplined president and a chaotic White House staff."[31] With no disciplined policy process, members of the cabinet and White House staff become tempted to build their own back channels of communication. Reich felt that his memos were not getting to the president and went to the First Lady for help. "Send them to *me*," she said. "I'll make sure they get to him. Use blank sheets of paper without any letterhead or other identifying characteristics. Just the date and your initials."[32]

Clinton came to understand that the lack of discipline was hurting him, and in summer 1994 he replaced McLarty with Leon Panetta, his OMB director, who had had a long career in Congress. Panetta tightened White House operations by insisting that he himself clear all staff work for the president, that all decision memoranda be routed through him, and that any presentations to the president be rehearsed. He reduced the size of senior staff meetings from thirty to ten attendees. Access to the Oval Office was reduced from ten staffers who had walk-in privileges to one or two; others had to clear access through Panetta. He took control of staff hiring and payroll decisions, set tighter agendas for staff meetings, and insisted on closure for the matters considered.

One of McLarty's problems in controlling the White House had been that Clinton had allowed Oval Office access to several former campaigners who lobbied him on his budget and domestic priorities without monitoring from McLarty or other White House aides. A similar situation developed on Panetta's watch when, after the 1994 takeover of Congress by Republicans, Dick Morris—under the code name "Charley"—secretly began advising Clinton. Policy proposals and speech drafts would appear with no known provenance. Finally, in March 1995, Panetta discovered the source of this external advice and Morris was brought into the White House to advise the president openly. The point is not to deny the president advice, but to permit those who are sensitive to the budget and implementation implications of policy proposals to monitor and leaven the advice. Presidents need balanced perspectives before making important decisions.

One exception to the general organizational laxity of Clinton's first year was the National Economic Council. The president concluded that the country's economic health was essential to national security, especially after the Cold War, and created the NEC by Executive Order 12835 on January 25, 1993. The council, which had a staff of about twenty professionals, stood out as a successful advisory structure because of the stature of its initial director, Robert Rubin, and the role he established for the council as neutral broker in the economic policymaking community (Treasury, OMB, CEA, Labor, and the Fed). If others were not convinced that their advice was getting fairly presented to the president, they would have created back channels that would have disrupted the policy process. Rubin said that his policy on advising the White House was that he was willing to offer his own judgment to the president but only "as long as you are excruciatingly careful to make sure your own views do not taint the fairness of the process."[33] One notable NEC success was Clinton's early decision to pursue deficit reduction rather than a middle-class tax cut in his first budget. The $500 billion deficit reduction package reassured financial markets and contributed to the historic economic expansion of the 1990s. The analog to the effectiveness of the national security policymaking process in the Bush administration was Clinton's economic policy team and the NEC.

In 1996 Panetta announced that he would leave at the end of the first term. He was succeeded by Erskine Bowles, an investment banker from North Carolina who had been director of the Small Business Administration in 1993 and 1994 and was brought in as Panetta's deputy in 1994. By then Clinton was convinced that someone short of the president had to be in charge, and Bowles gave the White House a more organized and buttoned-down tone. Bowles recruited two deputies, designated his own chief of staff, and hired an executive assistant, a national security assistant, and a press secretary. This was a more elaborate superstructure for the chief of staff office than had existed in any earlier White House. The general consensus was that Bowles finally imposed order in the Clinton White House. When he resigned in 1998, his deputy John Podesta became chief of staff and stayed until the end of the term.

The last years of the Clinton administration were dominated by the legal battles brought on by the accumulation of scandals beginning with Whitewater and culminating in impeachment. The role of the counsel's office took on added importance as its stable of forty lawyers struggled to distinguish

Clinton's personal interests from the institutional interests of the presidency. Clinton's legal troubles were reflected in counsel office turnover. Clinton had six counsels and seven deputies; George Bush had one counsel and one deputy.[34]

In its early months the Clinton White House was marked by a lack of organizational structure and discipline, but the president soon learned the costs of his freewheeling approach to policymaking. He replaced McLarty with Panetta, and by the end of his first term the White House was running relatively smoothly. Organizational discipline was reinforced in the second term by Bowles and Podesta, but the whole White House was overwhelmed when impeachment defense overrode all other priorities in 1998.

Communicating with the American people is crucial in every presidency, and the image of a president depends in important ways on how the administration is portrayed in the media. The relationship is symbiotic: reporters rely on the White House for the news that is their raison d'etre and the White House depends on reporters to project its message to the country. The media tend to be sympathetic to a new administration, but that sympathy is tempered by an innate skepticism and fear of being manipulated. Reporters respect professionalism on the part of the White House staffers; on the other hand, they do not want the president's staff to be too skillful at handling the press.

President Bush began his administration with the conscious intention to distinguish himself from his predecessor. That was a delicate task. He had run on a platform of continuity, yet he had to establish his own persona. One of the ways he did so was to present himself as an authentic, unscripted president who eschewed the elaborate orchestration of media events and photo-ops of the Reagan presidency. Bush made a key move when he persuaded Marlin Fitzwater, who had been Reagan's press secretary, to stay on in the same role; Fitzwater was a true professional who was able to serve two very different presidents effectively. Ronald Reagan had been "the great communicator" and Michael Deaver had been a master orchestrator of symbolic events and photo-opportunities that highlighted the policy agenda of the Reagan administration. But George Bush resisted being "managed" or "handled."[35] Fitzwater recalled Bush's aversion to artifice:

> It represented a kind of phoniness to him, or fakery, that repelled him. There was the basic old-New England, Yankee honesty of spirit about George Bush that made him distrustful of anything that was staged.

He used to say to me, "don't tell me what to do Marlin, I'm not a piece of meat . . ." So he just resisted any efforts to stage manage him or to do the basic public relations things that we wanted him to do.[36]

President Bush contrasted himself with his predecessor by actively scheduling press conferences in which he could personally interact with reporters and demonstrate his mastery of the policies of his administration. Bush held more news conferences in his first eighty days in office than Reagan had during his last two years in office. Reagan's news conferences were usually highly structured and lasted thirty minutes; Bush's usually were more freewheeling and often went beyond the allotted time.[37]

Thus Bush began his presidency with relatively favorable coverage by reporters who respected the professionalism of his press secretary and who admired Bush personally for his ability to answer their questions directly. On the other hand, several months into the administration, criticism began to surface in the press: the administration lacked strategic direction. Bush had emphasized a number of priorities—the environment, education—but had no overarching theme or direction. The administration was dealing with the savings and loan bailout, the Latin American debt crisis, and the war on drugs, but no sense of momentum developed. The contrast with Reagan was vivid, and the press corps did not help. The media tend to focus on the initial 100 days of a new administration and remember the major accomplishments of newly elected presidents like FDR, LBJ, or Reagan. Such inflated expectations work to the detriment of presidents who do not have large agendas for change or who have modest policy aspirations. Bush's treatment was ambivalent: he got credit for his modest persona and his impressive competence in foreign affairs; he was criticized for a lack of "the vision thing" and the seeming lack of an activist economic agenda at the end of his administration.

In contrast to Bush, the press gave Clinton virtually no honeymoon, yet his longer-term focus on (or obsession with) communications was effective in winning reelection and sustaining his approval ratings, even through impeachment. After running a transition from Little Rock during which very little effort was made to provide fodder for the reporters stationed there, the new administration made several other mistakes in its press relations. Reporters were denied the access to the upper press offices in the White House to which they had grown accustomed. They felt that they were being pushed away by staffers who did not respect them. The president added insult to injury when he publicly "dissed" White House reporters by telling a Washington press dinner: "You know why I can stiff you on press conferences? Because Larry King liberated me by giving me to the American people directly."[38] It also became evident that George Stephanopoulos was not the best spokesman for the president and that his successor, Dee Dee Myers, was not close enough to the president to command the respect of the press corps.

Of course, a miffed press corps had plenty of fodder for negative stories on the new administration. Clinton had promised a large and active agenda to be pursued collaboratively with the Democratic Congress, and expectations for performance were high. But minor blunders (Zoë Baird, gays in the military) took center stage in the early days of the new administration when the major Clinton agenda items (health care reform, welfare reform) were not ready to go. A *Time* cover on June 7, 1993, featured "The Incredible Shrinking President," towering over a tiny picture of Clinton.

Yet just as Clinton learned from early problems with White House organization, his press office became much more effective over time. Pannetta was able to bring the widely respected Mike McCurry from the state department to be press secretary. Clinton provided a sharp contrast with Bush in his willingness to use all of the techniques of "the permanent campaign" in his efforts to sell his governance to the American people. He continued to actively seek advice from the advisers he had used in his campaign, and the Democratic National Committee spent millions of dollars conducting polls to advise on the appeal of different policies. When he became chief of staff, Pannetta was able to limit the access of the campaign consultants, but after the 1994 elections Dick Morris heavily influenced Clinton's reactions to the Republican takeover of Congress. In 1995 pollster Mark Penn and Morris conducted Wednesday night meetings in the White House solarium to map out communications strategy. The weekly meetings (without Morris) continued even after Clinton was reelected. It seemed that Clinton had everything polled, from the phrases in his public addresses to where he should vacation to whether he should tell the truth about Monica Lewinsky.[39]

In its early years the Clinton administration also brought in the "war room" tactic from the 1992 presidential campaign when it wanted to focus on a specific policy initiative, such as health care reform or an economic package. Leaders of different parts of the policy campaign came together in one room to coordinate media tactics (TV and radio ads, talking points for administration surrogates, supporters on the Hill, and so forth) so that reactions could be made quickly, preferably within one news cycle. The advantage of the war room tactic is that it allows an administration to counterattack immediately, as is crucial in a campaign. But it also slights deliberation, compromise, and depth of policy knowledge, and it undercuts the regular lines of White House authority and communication.[40] The trappings of the permanent campaign—war room, integration of campaign apparatus into the White House, instant counterattack, aggressive polling—are likely to be permanent fixtures of the presidency.

A president has many more important things to do than "manage" the White House. Still, the White House must be managed, and the president's agenda will suffer if it is not done well. This became abundantly clear in the first months of the Clinton presidency and was addressed only after Panetta became chief of staff and fully solved only in the second term under Bowles and Podesta. The Bush White House was better managed except for the distorting impact of John Sununu. While Sununu imposed the necessary discipline on the policy process, Bush paid a steep price for Sununu's personal excesses and policy biases. The bottom line is that presidents should not be managers, but they must ensure that the White House is well managed.

The institutional constraints of the modern presidency are relatively constant, while each president's personality and abilities are unique. Thus the White House staff and its organization must be molded to the strengths and weaknesses of each president. Clinton's staff needed to impose more discipline on the policy process early in his administration. Bush's staff served him well, but he was forced by Sununu's policy biases to be his own neutral broker much of the time. Ultimately, the good judgment of the president is the only assurance that the staff will serve the president and compensate for his weaknesses. The good judgment of the president also is necessary to strike the right balance between attending to the substance of governing and maintaining the symbols of popular support.

CHAPTER 11

George W. Bush

2001–

 The contested presidential election of 2000 was a virtual test-tube experiment to determine what might be gained or lost by cutting the traditional ten- to eleven-week transition period in half. Although George W. Bush quickly attempted to assume the mantle of president-elect, he soon realized that that was a public relations blunder. As long as the race's outcome was still in doubt, the media regarded his transition planning as arrogant. In other words, until the U.S. Supreme Court announced its decision on December 12 and Al Gore made his concession speech, Bush could not officially assemble his administration.

Bush's only transition-related announcements between election day, November 7, and his victory speech on December 13 were those appointing Andrew Card his chief of staff and putting the vice president–elect, Dick Cheney, in charge of the transition, with Clay Johnson as the transition's executive director. Card had had considerable Washington experience, including a stint as secretary of transportation; Johnson had been the governor's chief of staff in Austin. Cheney was assuming a role that no incoming president had ever turned over to his running mate, dramatically

Based on Stephen Hess, "First Impressions," in G. Calvin Mackenzie, ed., *Innocent until Nominated* (Brookings, 2001), and Kathryn Dunn Tenpas and Stephen Hess, "The Bush White House: First Appraisals" (Brookings Working Paper, 2002).

foreshadowing the influence that he would have in the administration. On matters of personnel, Bush, Cheney, Card, and Johnson were the transition's inner circle.

On December 16, Bush announced his first cabinet appointment, the long-expected selection of Colin Powell to be secretary of state. The next day Condoleezza Rice, his chief foreign policy aide, was named national security adviser, although she was not given cabinet rank. To complete the national security cluster, Bush appeared to be leaning toward giving the defense portfolio to Dan Coats, a former senator from Indiana. The question was whether Coats would be strong enough to represent the institutional needs of the Pentagon, given the wattage of Powell at State and the closeness of Rice at the White House. Bush concluded that the answer was no and turned instead to Cheney's old mentor, Donald Rumsfeld, who had been secretary of defense under President Ford. When reporters asked Bush about this equation, he replied, "General Powell's a strong figure, and Dick Cheney's no shrinking violet *[laughter from the reporters]* . . . but neither is Don Rumsfeld, nor Condi Rice. I view the four as being able to complement each other."[1]

The White House staff was chosen promptly and with no surprises—no James Baker, no John Sununu. Clay Johnson said that Bush "did not want someone to be chief of staff who was over-territorial or was a control freak."[2] Andy Card had been a Bush family loyalist since 1980. Personnel director Johnson had been the president-elect's friend since they were students at Phillips Academy, Andover. White House counsel Alberto Gonzales, a Texas Supreme Court judge, had served for three years as counsel to Bush when he was governor. Of the triad that ran the campaign, Karen Hughes would oversee the offices of communications, press secretary, and speechwriting; Karl Rove's responsibilities would include political affairs, intergovernmental affairs, and public liaison; and Joe Allbaugh was to head the Federal Emergency Management Agency. Ari Fleischer, an experienced Capitol Hill hand, had proved his worth during the campaign and was elevated to the role of presidential press secretary. Perhaps the staff's most interesting characteristic, according to Dana Milbank, was that there were "more women with more power than in any previous administration." Of Bush's top twenty aides, eight were women.[3]

The closeness of the election made it politically appropriate for Bush to seek at least one Democrat for his cabinet. John Breaux, whom he would have liked for energy secretary, chose to remain in the Senate. In a

December 28 press conference, Bush was asked whether he was having trouble getting a Democrat to join the administration:

> Bush: That's an interesting question. *[Laughter]* I'm not having trouble getting Democrats to return my phone calls.
> Reporter: That's a different question, sir.
> Bush: Yes, it was, but the same answer.[4]

The president-elect finally found his Democrat on January 2, in President Clinton's cabinet: Secretary of Commerce Norman Mineta would serve as the next secretary of transportation.

The matter of which federal jobs, in addition to the leadership of the fourteen executive departments, deserve cabinet status has become increasingly negotiable in recent years. Clinton created eight honorific cabinet offices. Bush limited himself to four: budget director and White House chief of staff (two positions that clearly rate inclusion), director of the Environmental Protection Agency, and U.S. trade representative. Making the EPA director a member of his cabinet was necessary to lure a sitting governor to Washington. The trade representative's status was the subject of lively discussion within the transition. "The position needs to remain a Cabinet-level position," Bush concluded, "because of the importance of trade in the global economy. It should reconfirm our nation's commitment to free trade."[5]

When Bush finished his cabinet selections, on the first working day of the new year, it was clear that his three staunchest conservatives—John Ashcroft (Justice), Gale Norton (Interior), and Linda Chavez (Labor)—would not be looked upon with favor by many in the Democratic Party, which now held half the seats in the Senate. Although confirmation hearings are conducted by different committees, composed of individuals with different interests and egos, there seems to be something holistic about the way the Senate considers an administration's initial slate of appointments. Perhaps the energy expended in fighting one nominee cannot be recycled. Perhaps there is a point past which opposition is perceived as obstructionism and becomes politically counterproductive. Bush understood this when he answered a reporter's question about the Ashcroft nomination: "Well, I expected at least one member of my Cabinet to get a pretty tough hearing. You know, it could've been John, it could've been somebody else."[6]

The syndicated columnist Linda Chavez, a foe of affirmative action and bilingual education, also could expect a pretty tough hearing, presided over by Senator Edward Kennedy. Nevertheless, in the history of confirmations, ideological opposition is generally not sufficient to defeat a person who serves at the will of the president; it takes a skeleton in the closet. Chavez's skeleton was that she had taken a battered woman into her home, an illegal immigrant from Guatemala, who in the course of two years had done occasional chores for the family and had been given at least $1,500 in spending money. Did the work make her an employee? Although the facts were vastly different, was this Zoë Baird redux? Admitting to "bad judgment" in not telling the Bush vetters or the FBI, Chavez withdrew her name from consideration.[7] Senate Democrats were delighted. Yet it came at little cost to Bush. The situation was unlike the senior Bush's unsuccessful fight to confirm John Tower as his secretary of defense—the Labor portfolio is not significant in a Republican cabinet, and Chavez was not a member of Bush's inner circle. Two days later Bush announced a replacement and was given credit for acting expeditiously.

Senators would find no skeleton in the closet of straight-arrow John Ashcroft, their recently defeated colleague from Missouri, whose views on abortion, gun control, and the death penalty were deeply controversial, as were his actions in blocking the nomination of a black state judge to the federal bench. What two weeks of anguished debate in the Judiciary Committee did produce, however, was a set of Ashcroft commitments to policies he had opposed as senator, including a statement that *Roe* v. *Wade* was "the settled law of the land" and "as attorney general I don't think it could be my agenda" to overturn it.[8] The nomination was approved 10 to 8, with all Republicans plus Democrat Russell Feingold voting for Ashcroft. The full Senate favored him 58 to 42. No Republican deserted, and Bush won a big victory. So too did the Democrats, who showed that they had the votes to sustain a filibuster if Bush ever proposed a Supreme Court nominee who they felt was beyond their tolerance level. Senator Charles Schumer pointedly reminded the president that "what has happened with the Ashcroft nomination in terms of divisiveness would look small compared to the divisiveness that would occur if someone of Senator Ashcroft's beliefs were nominated to the United States Supreme Court."[9]

The undoing of Chavez and the intense attack on Ashcroft seemed to shield the Norton nomination. Environmentalists waged an expensive campaign, said to cost nearly $1 million, that portrayed her in the pro-business image of her mentor, James Watt. But she was easily approved by the Senate Energy and Resources Committee, 18 to 2, partly because of her silken performance as a witness and partly because of skilled lobbying by her Denver law firm and a bipartisan group of states' attorneys general.[10] The Senate vote was 75 to 24 in her favor.

The Bush cabinet ultimately included two African Americans, a Japanese American, a Cuban American, a Chinese American (who was the replacement for a Hispanic American), and an Arab American. There were four women in the cabinet, and the national security adviser was a black woman. The press made favorable comparisons with Clinton's tortured 1992 efforts to create a cabinet that "looks like America."

In announcing his nominees, Bush kept remarking on their "wonderful stories." Mel Martinez, his choice for Housing and Urban Development, left Cuba at the age of fifteen, speaking no English, and lived with foster families until he was reunited with his parents. Colin Powell was the son of immigrants from Jamaica. Elaine Chao, labor secretary–designate, came from China when she was eight years old. Norman Mineta was forced into an internment camp during World War II. The hallmark of Clinton's cabinet was representativeness: it was imperative to have a woman attorney general, just as it was necessary to have more than one Hispanic American. Strangely, given the similar end result, that was not the primary thrust of Bush's labors. In mid-December, Bush was asked: "Mr. President-elect, in the last two days you have appointed two women, two African Americans, a Hispanic American. Aside from the fact that these are incredibly competent, qualified people, is there another message that you are sending to America with these first choices?" He replied, "You bet: that people that work hard and make the right decisions in life can achieve anything they want in America."[11]

Rather than striving for representativeness, Bush seemed to be honoring true grit. While Clinton's outstanding record of opening high-level government positions to minorities could not be matched by a conservative administration, Bush freed his minority appointments from tokenism. He had received only 9 percent of the black vote, yet Powell and Rice would be his premier advisers on foreign relations and Rod Paige was made secretary of education, Bush's number-one domestic priority.

When Bush finished selecting his cabinet, a reporter asked, "What does your Cabinet say, do you think, about your management style, about how you intend to make decisions as president?" The president-elect replied, "First, it says I'm not afraid to surround myself with strong and competent people. . . . I hope the American people realize that a good executive is one that understands how to recruit people and how to delegate, how to align authority and responsibility, how to hold people accountable for results, and how to build a team of people."[12]

Bush had picked some highly competent people in a very short time. Ann Veneman, the first woman to be secretary of agriculture, was more than a "first"—she had been deputy secretary in the first Bush presidency as well as head of California's agriculture department. Secretary of Transportation Mineta was intimately involved in his subject from his days as chairman of the Public Works and Transportation Committee in the U.S. House of Representatives. Anthony Principi had the best résumé of any secretary in the brief history of Veterans Affairs as a cabinet department. Christine Todd Whitman, a two-term governor of New Jersey, brought more political clout to the EPA than any past administrator. Don Rumsfeld at Defense and Paul O'Neill at Treasury, as did Vice President Cheney, combined vast government experience with experience as chief executives of Fortune 500 corporations.

Perhaps Ed Meese, the director of Reagan's successful 1980 transition, was right: the 2000 transition was proving that the corollary to "work expands to fill the available time" is "work can be compressed to fill the available time." Yet is there not a downside to cutting a presidential transition period in half? Linda Chavez thought her downfall was partly the result of the Bush staff's not having the time to follow the "normal procedure" of conducting a lengthy background check.[13] Previous transitions that went full term, however, notably those of George H. W. Bush and Bill Clinton, had made more serious vetting mistakes. The real problem was that there had not been enough time to carry the selection process deeper into the administration's second ranks. So the inauguration came and went without deputy secretaries, under secretaries, and assistant secretaries in place. By March 1, 2002, Brookings's Presidential Appointee Initiative released data showing that the administration had become "the slowest in modern history to fill its top appointee positions . . . just three-quarters of the administration's 510 Senate-confirmed officers were on the job."[14]

Although Bush's White House staff possessed qualities similar to those of his predecessors, he imposed his own ideas about running an executive office by making structural changes reflecting his priorities, goals, and general approach to governing. He began his term by adding two new White House units: the Office of Strategic Initiatives and the Office of Faith-Based and Community Initiatives. He bolstered the Office of the Vice

President, and his cabinet was given both standard and nontraditional functions.[15] The events of September 11, 2001, imposed additional structural and procedural changes that affected cabinet and White House staff. Each innovation represented a break with the Clinton presidency, although in some cases there were roots in prior administrations.

The Office of Strategic Initiatives (OSI), led by Bush confidant Karl Rove, was established to allow staff to think ahead and devise long-term political strategy. "It is an effort to solve the problem that consistently dogs White House staffs: the pressure to respond to unexpected events and to react to daily news cycles, which causes presidential advisers to lose sight of the big picture,"[16] wrote Dana Milbank. The equivalent during the Reagan administration could have been the Office of Planning and Evaluation, led by Richard Beal, a colleague of pollster Richard Wirthlin. It is hardly unusual for presidents to create offices designed to ensure their political longevity. For instance, Reagan's Office of Political Affairs, initially led by Lyn Nofziger, was charged with maintaining and expanding his electoral coalition, but it was not given a long-term strategic mandate.

The unique feature of the OSI was that it was run by the president's political adviser. Although George H. W. Bush relied on the strategic advice of Lee Atwater, he did not provide Atwater with a White House perch. Atwater resided at the Republican National Committee until health problems forced him to resign. After his death, the absence of political insight and strategy became a serious weakness in the administration and reelection campaign. President Clinton used outside consultants James Carville, Paul Begala, Mandy Grunwald, and pollster Stanley Greenberg until the disastrous 1994 midterm elections. Subsequently, Dick Morris provided strategic input while running a consulting firm in which he offered advice to politicians of all stripes. The Bush administration clearly took a different approach by thoroughly integrating Rove into the White House chain of command. Would this be a sensible organizational solution to a persistent presidential problem? According to one aide in the post-terrorism crisis period, "You can't predict events more than 72 hours out at most. . . . We pretty much have a game plan for next week, but that could change."[17]

The White House Office of Faith-Based and Community Initiatives (OFBCI) was meant to demonstrate Bush's commitment to "compassionate conservatism" by reaching out to faith-based and community organizations in an effort to help the needy. The initial legislative initiative endorsed by the administration primarily sought to ease government restrictions on religious organizations so that faith-based groups could more easily provide government-subsidized services such as day care and alcohol rehabilitation programs. Numerous presidents have created offices for the sake of pursuing a single policy objective (Clinton for the Y2K problem, for example). But the establishment of such an office by means of an executive order was unusual and perhaps unwise since it can be eliminated only by issuing another executive order.[18] Special White House offices create unreasonable expectations for constituencies that previously lacked a White House contact; moreover, those expectations create problems for an overburdened White House staff.

The stature of vice presidents had risen markedly since Jimmy Carter selected Walter Mondale in 1976, and Al Gore was clearly the most engaged vice president of the twentieth century. But Cheney's vast Washington experience, as well as his formidable role in the transition, catapulted the vice presidency to new heights. According to James A. Barnes, "Hardly anyone would minimize the enormous role Cheney plays in running George W. Bush's administration."[19] The vice president's activities included devising energy policy, congressional lobbying, and diplomacy. After 9/11, while intermittently staying in an "undisclosed location" for security reasons, the vice president continued his integral role, even creating the initial plan to set up the Office of Homeland Security. At the same time, his aides worked closely with the president's staff. His chief of staff attended most of the A-level meetings at the White House, and two aides—Mary Matalin and Lewis Libby—were given the added title of "assistant to the president."

President Bush's reputation as one who likes to delegate authority, along with the impressive résumés of some cabinet members, led observers to expect the cabinet to play an enhanced role in the administration. According to one early forecast, "With their golden resumes, long years of public service, strong personalities and close ties to Mr. Bush, Vice President-elect Cheney, and the Republican establishment-in-waiting, the men and women of the emerging cabinet can be expected to exert just as much influence over the administration as the staff in the White House exerts, if not more."[20] The supposition was that these department heads would need little direction from the White House, particularly on day-to-day matters. But students of American politics remembered Jimmy Carter's failed attempt to form a "cabinet government" and how his White House staff rejected that approach in favor of centralizing control, maintaining the authority to rein in cabinet members when necessary.

Just days before the September 11 attack, *Time* magazine declared Colin Powell the "odd man out," but the events of that fateful day enhanced and strengthened his status as well as that of a number of other cabinet secretaries, notably Attorney General Ashcroft and Defense Secretary Rumsfeld. Indeed, any department with important homeland security concerns instantly moved up a notch on the power ladder in Washington. Scholars have noted the presence of an "inner" and "outer" cabinet arrangement in which the original departments (State, War, Treasury, and Justice) dominate the president's time and attention, and the events of September 11 created an expanded inner cabinet. At the same time, however, the White House staff promptly moved in when it perceived weaknesses in the cabinet.[21] So by the end of his first year, Bush had created his own variation on the inner/outer cabinet model, while adjusting White House control on a case-by-case basis.

After 9/11, Bush's organizational challenge was how to respond to the urgent need for homeland security. He had to choose between two basic approaches: the department model, a single operating agency with overall responsibility for preventing, protecting against, and responding to terrorist attacks; or the National Security Council model, a White House office responsible for coordinating the activities of various operating agencies and getting them to work as a team.[22]

Bush opted for the NSC model and chose a good friend, Governor Tom Ridge of Pennsylvania, to be his homeland security adviser. But because Ridge had no authority over the operating units, observers calculated that his chances of success would depend importantly on his perceived clout with the president and his personal leadership skills. At the same time, many in Congress were pushing a bill to create a new cabinet department whose secretary would be confirmed by the Senate and who would be expected to testify before congressional committees.[23]

The most important test of whether the NSC model under Ridge's leadership would work came in December 2001, when he proposed to the president a new agency merging those parts of government with responsibilities for protecting U.S. borders, such as the Coast Guard and the Customs Service. What happened next, according to the *Washington Post*, was that the proposal was leaked to the press and "the bureaucracies erupted . . . scuttling the border proposal." The lesson learned by Bush's team was that "ideas introduced piecemeal will be killed piecemeal."[24]

This began a top-secret White House operation that eventually produced a surprising mega-proposal. Reversing course, the president on June

6, 2002, asked Congress to join him in creating a Department of Homeland Security, which would have 169,154 employees and a budget of $37.5 billion. The major components of the new department—the third-largest unit of the federal government—would be the Coast Guard, Transportation Security Agency, Immigration and Naturalization Service, Customs Service, Secret Service, and the Federal Emergency Management Agency. Bush would continue to have a cabinet-level Homeland Security Council and a homeland security adviser in the White House, both created by executive order.[25]

Another element of Bush's response to 9/11 was to create a White House office designed to challenge Americans to commit themselves to 4,000 hours of public service during their lives. The new program, USA Freedom Corps, would have a council similar to the Homeland Security Council and a presidential assistant, John Bridgeland, charged with coordinating the activities of other government agencies in the volunteer business, such as the Peace Corps, AmeriCorps, and Senior Corps.

Aside from these more ambitious innovations, the events of September 11 altered "business as usual" in the White House. Whether in the offices of communications, public liaison, and political affairs or the OFBCI, aides assumed additional responsibilities pertaining to the attack and recovery.[26] Deputy chief of staff Josh Bolten was put in charge of the Domestic Consequences Principals Committee, assessing the impact of the attacks on domestic policy. Presidential confidant Karen Hughes created a White House–based public relations operation aimed at winning international support, particularly in the Islamic world, for the antiterrorist campaign.[27] The ability to respond quickly in a crisis once again illustrates an advantage of the White House staff.

Mistakes are endemic to the start of any administration. A lethal combination of early arrogance and euphoria often derail the best intentions. Bush's first stumble was over the nomination of Chavez to be labor secretary. Some blamed the debacle on a lax vetting process. But she withdrew quickly and a less controversial successor was named and confirmed without incident. Having recovered from that mishap, Bush received a blast of criticism over the delayed stock divestitures of senior staff and cabinet members, especially those of Treasury Secretary O'Neill. The heat was turned up even more when Karl Rove met with lobbyists for Intel, a company in which he owned stock, thereby opening the door to political opponents' demands for a prompt investigation. These missteps resulted in bad publicity that may have distracted the White House operation, but they did not prove disabling.

In contrast, the newly established White House OFBCI attracted controversy from day one, when Republicans and Democrats alike began to question the constitutionality of government financial assistance to religious institutions to provide certain social services. The mission of this office not only created opposition within both parties, but it also created some enemies within the religious community—the very group that supposedly had the most to gain. Compounding their tribulations was a summertime leak from an employee of the Salvation Army who revealed that the White House was seeking to protect the organization from cities' domestic partnership benefit requirements. The uproar created even more suspicion. However, the events of 9/11 relegated the issue to the sidelines, and OFBCI pursued the less controversial component of its agenda—tax incentives for charitable giving.

Those missteps pale in comparison with the shock waves following Senator Jim Jeffords's defection from the Republican party, which caused the party's loss of majority status in the Senate, jeopardized the president's legislative agenda, and, for the first time, cast serious doubt on the performance of the White House staff. Why didn't they know about Jeffords's apparent dissatisfaction? If they did know, why didn't they do something?

Successful presidents have to respond to personnel weaknesses and cracks that appear in their administrative structures. Time will tell whether staff innovations designed to meet the challenges of "America's New War" against terrorism can achieve the necessary level of integration and cooperation. Nevertheless, the Bush team initially established an advisory system that reflected a unique balance of White House staff and cabinet input, a system nicely fitted to the country's crisis atmosphere after 9/11.

In the end, it is impossible for any administration to be mistake free. Stumbling is inevitable. Still, Bush benefited from his predecessors' mistakes. His transition and first year were a cakewalk compared with the unrelenting criticism faced by Clinton or the Senate confirmation defeat of a key cabinet nominee suffered by his father. If Bush's administrative innovations fail to live up to expectations—or worse, if they create new problems—they must be quickly discarded. Presidents are rightly cautious when it comes to adding or subtracting White House offices and responsibilities. Unfortunately, they are often less adept at correcting their own mistakes.

PART *Two*

Redefining the
Presidential Task

CHAPTER 12

The White House/
Cabinet Nexus

The organization of the White House depends largely on the style of the president, which obviously changes from one administration to another. But basic guidelines can be established concerning the size and configuration of the White House—which functions belong there and which do not—as well as the types of people who should be selected as presidential assistants and what a president should have a right to expect from various kinds of advisory systems.

Ever since 1937, when the Brownlow Committee concluded that "the President needs help," there has been an unremitting effort to help him by increasing the size of his staff. If he followed sound management principles, the reasoning went, a president, like any other executive, would be measurably assisted through the sensible delegation of his workload to an enlarged body of intelligent and loyal assistants.

That something went wrong is hardly in dispute. The risks of imposing a large staff between the president and the departments have proved greater than in other types of large organizations. Presidents as political executives must bear special responsibility for the actions of those who work for them, for the "dirty tricks" or the secret arms sales. More important from a management standpoint, however, is the serious potential for distortion. When the wishes of a president are passed along an extended chain of command, the message loses definition until, as in the children's game of "Telephone," the last relay (presumably to the person who must carry out the command) may bear little resemblance to the original message. Simple messages have the best chance of surviving intact. But presidential messages are rarely simple, and in the modern White House fewer and fewer aides hear directly from the president what he really wants done.

The problem of a White House staff grown beyond the personal attention of a chief executive was well illustrated by the testimony of John Dean before the Senate's Watergate Committee. Although Dean held the exalted title of counsel to the president, he revealed that he had had no direct contact with Nixon for nearly two years after his appointment. Yet during that period he dealt with others in and out of government in the name of the president.

Control by staff is premised on a naiveté about power in Washington: that a president has a greater chance of taking charge if there are enough assistants to act on his behalf. But a president's reach cannot extend indefinitely through White House surrogates. Enlarging the staff beyond a certain point ensures that more problems are drawn to the White House for resolution, limits the number of problems that might be resolved below the White House level, cuts the time that a president can give to any one problem, forces him to spend more time on the care and feeding of his staff, and increases the potential for aides to misspeak in his name. "As with the ships of the Spanish Armada, size is a crippling handicap, not a source of strength," commented Ben Heineman and Curtis Hessler, two Carter administration officials.[1]

Expanding the White House also builds pressure for further expansion. Each group that is rewarded with representation on the staff—youth, the aged, labor, women—sets a precedent for the next group to apply for similar recognition. A president agrees to additional group representation because there are no political benefits to be derived from denying such requests. Presidential assistants, in keeping with the bureaucratic imperative, measure their importance by the size of their staffs. Each new staff member finds ways to keep busy.

Such special-interest representatives at the White House create further problems in that they often come from the ranks of those interests and can be expected eventually to return to them. "Having chosen men because of their affiliations with particular constituencies," wrote Roger Hilsman, "a president can hardly be surprised if they speak for that constituency in the internal policy debate."[2] Yet a president expects an aide to be his representative *to* a client and is surprised to find that his aide has become the representative *for* a client. Outside interests discover that they can circumvent the departments and take their demands directly to their representative at the White House, thus affecting morale in the departments. The problems with having an Office of Public Liaison in the White House are outlined by Robert A. Bonitati, who served in the office under Reagan: "It raises the visibility of many issues that do not deserve such attention; it brings issues into the White House that should be settled elsewhere in the government; it enhances the importance of the 'interest groups' being represented; and it raises some troublesome questions about interest groups' advocates participating in policy-making decisions impacting their constituencies."[3]

While the original theory was that each new special assistant relieves the president of some responsibilities and shields him from some outside demands, in practice each assistant bargains for a portion of the president's time, thus luring the president into accepting additional responsibilities and adding to the demands made on him. As the White House takes on the characteristics of a bureaucracy, the president's time is increasingly allotted to whoever comes out on top in the internal bureaucratic politicking and trade-offs between staff members. This pecking order does not necessarily reflect the relative importance of issues.

We cannot simply abolish the representation of special interests, however. Although government designed around group representation has been seriously questioned by Theodore Lowi and others,[4] the government, and particularly the president, must be continually made aware of the hopes and frustrations of different segments of society. The least powerful, especially, should have a right to expect that a president, the only elected official with the whole nation as his constituency, understands their concerns. The clash of interests is healthy if all interests are adequately represented. Still, there are many ways to be heard other than through a permanent representative at the White House.

Presidents, then, can increase their effectiveness by shortening the chain of command, thus eliminating some of the causes of delay and distortion. They can attempt to limit the number of White House aides to those who can be kept reasonably apprised of their intentions and try to keep their personal staffs from trying to implement policy.

Although there is still a hazy distinction between White House personnel and those in the Executive Office of the President, the presidential complex can better be imagined as two concentric circles, the outer staff and the inner staff, with the chief executive at the center. On the perimeter is the outer staff, whose assignments require little personal attention by the president or who deal with matters in which his political stakes are modest. Sometimes they have been placed in the presidential orbit by an act of Congress, as in the cases of the Council on Environmental Quality and the Office of the U.S. Trade Representative. Other outer staff units may reflect accommodations that have little to do with the proper functioning of the presidential office, such as solving a sticky personnel problem (Kennedy's wanting to get Chester Bowles out of the State Department) or conferring status on an important constituent group (Nixon's creating a special assistant for the aged). As a rule of thumb, these presidential assistants, who rarely see the president, should not be on the White House staff. Almost all outer staff offices could easily be relocated elsewhere in the government.

Inner staff assistants are those who perform personal services for the president, those who are engaged in matters requiring close presidential involvement, such as national security and economics, and those whose opinions are often sought or who are given a wide variety of assignments, especially in matters on which they are not expert. Occasionally inner staff people—Robert Kennedy in his brother's administration—are not even located in the White House. Then, too, titles can be deceptive: as special counsel, Theodore Sorensen was inner staff; John Dean, with the same title, was not, until he was given responsibility for the Watergate cover-up.

The problem with the inner staff is not in the function that it performs, but rather in that the wrong people have too often been allowed to get too close to the president. Inner staff people have usually known the president for a long time. Unlike cabinet officers, they often are friends a president has gathered on the way to the presidency. If the president is a former member of the Senate or House, he will bring with him the small staff that he accumulated in the legislature.

Often the staff will have been through a presidential election together. Aside from being a matter of obligation, choosing presidential assistants from the campaign organization has a certain superficial logic. Some personal services performed on the campaign trail, such as scheduling and press relations, are also necessary in the White House. But in picking inner staff assistants, the easy choice often is the wrong one. Once in the White House, campaign aides become drawn into governance, and often the skills required for campaigning and governing are quite different. The freewheeling attitudes useful in a campaign can be dangerous when transplanted to the seat of power: witness the involvement of Nixon's appointments secretary, Dwight Chapin, in setting up a "dirty tricks" operation directed against Democratic candidates in 1972.

The easy choice may be wrong in another way: the judgment of friends may be skewed by loyalty. It is neither surprising nor exceptional that presidents want to surround themselves with persons who are dedicated to them and who have proved their trustworthiness. As Pierre Salinger said of the Kennedy staff, "What we had in common . . . was our salary . . . and our commitment to the President, which was total. . . . Our faith in him and in what he was trying to do was absolute."[5] The problem is really one of definition: the staff's loyalty must be to more than the person who is president. It also must be to the presidency and to a system of political democracy, civil liberties, and government through the competition of balanced institutions.

"Presidential staff members," wrote Charles M. Hardin, "rarely if ever argue vehemently with [the president] and probably never attack him with scorn and derision, hammering the table and telling him that if he persists in a course of action he is a fool."[6] Edward Weisband and Thomas M. Franck have agreed: "The rule against ruffling Presidential feathers is virtually absolute."[7] Yet the picture of a president surrounded by "yes men" should not be overdrawn. The battles between the Clifford and Steelman forces in the Truman administration, the dissent over Vietnam policy by Moyers and McPherson in the Johnson administration, and the struggle between Moynihan and Burns in the Nixon administration indicate that freedom of thought and speech are not simply abandoned when aides move into the White House. Nor should the absence of resignations in protest be mistaken for the absence of internal dissent.

There is, however, a danger that dissent within the inner circle will grow dimmer the longer a president stays in office, and the president must then make an extra effort to keep in touch with differing opinion. Outside opposition generally forces internal consensus as administration officials begin to huddle together for comfort. And a president, feeling increasingly threatened, turns more and more to those who give the most loyal support. A form of Gresham's law takes over as the loyalists gain ascendancy over those whose loyalty is less single-minded. The "losers" are not disloyal, but they may have other loyalties as well—to certain ideas and principles, to spouse and children. In the end, unless presidents are constantly alert, they may become isolated and overprotected by sycophants. They will no longer have a desirable panoply of judgment on call, and if they are particularly unfortunate, they can be brought down by scandal or bad advice.

Verdicts on the quality of past White House staffs are mixed. George Reedy issued a blanket indictment: they form a "conspiracy of mediocrity—that all too frequently successful collection of the untalented, the unpassionate, and the insincere."[8] But Patrick Anderson concluded that "[f]or the most part, the presidents have brought men of outstanding ability onto their staffs . . . [who often have performed] admirably, even heroically, rendering genuine, little-known services to the country."[9] The truth, as usual, lies somewhere in between. Generally, White House service is the high point of a public career. Although Clark Clifford, Nelson Rockefeller, and James Baker may have gone on to high elective office or a major cabinet post, most presidential assistants have not.[10] And some have used their White House contacts and knowledge later to enrich themselves as lobbyists.

It is hazardous to generalize about the people who have served on White House staffs. They have been notable for diversity. They have come to Washington from all parts of the country, from backgrounds in law, journalism, the military, academics, politics, even theology. Some have been members of the nation's moneyed aristocracy; others have worked their way out of poverty.

They are usually younger than cabinet officers, a trend that has been a by-product of recent activist presidencies and reflects the supposed need for stamina as the White House has become more operations-oriented. Actually, however, the energy of the young aides often draws operational matters into the White House. And the confluence of loyalty and ambition, when unchecked by experience and public scrutiny, has caused egregious conduct in the Watergate and Iran-Contra affairs. Two of the most talented young assistants in the Nixon White House, Egil Krogh and Edward Morgan, went to prison for doing what they thought their president wished to be done. There is no reason to expect the very young to be wise or crafty in the ways of Washington—or even humble in the exercise of the powers they have been given. What is remarkable is that there have been some young presidential assistants who must have been born wise, crafty, and at least outwardly humble, for surely they did not have time to acquire those traits.

Given the real requirements of service in the White House, there is much to recommend having potential presidential aides step down to that service rather than up. For example, Clarence Randall under Eisenhower and Robert Rubin under Clinton, both former chief executives of major corporations, were not overawed in the presence of their president and saw no reason to limit themselves to giving advice that the president might find comforting. But persons with long years of substantial achievement often are made department secretaries rather than presidential assistants. The irony is twofold. The successful executive's experience may have limited applicability and may even prove harmful in running a department. (To paraphrase Charles Wilson: what works for General Motors will not necessarily work at the Department of Defense.) On the other hand, energy-charged young White House aides might be exactly what is needed in the departments to make the lions of bureaucracy do the president's bidding. Stamina gives department executives an important advantage that presidential counselors do not need in the same abundance. Loyalty is necessary in political executives who head departments, where centrifugal forces—often the consumers of the agency's services—work to pull the appointee away from the president. But wisdom is the necessary quality at the White House, where counselors will be the last barrier between a president and a possibly ill-advised decision. Thus, under the present system, presidents often have had the wrong people in the wrong types of jobs at both ends, White House and departments.

Another problem for the president is that of how long to retain the services of a White House aide. As Clark Clifford has pointed out, after a while, either because of their personalities or because of the policies they advocate, aides encounter automatic resistance from certain quarters in the administration. And since the workload in government is so unevenly distributed, principal aides are apt to burn themselves out. The problem, however, often solves itself as the White House aide is attracted to a higher-paying job in the private sector or finds a more prestigious one in a department. (White House staffers in the personnel office are particularly well positioned to find themselves such assignments, a situation that has the added advantage of bringing new recruiters with new networks of contacts into the personnel operation and thus expands the talent available to the president.)

Those who have excelled at the White House, even young staff, have almost always had some previous experience and a feel for Washington and the power equations of government. The obverse also is usually true—the failures often have been newcomers who flouted the conventions of doing business in a complex milieu where the stakes are high and where some journalists make their living by shooting down the mighty. On leaving government after five years in the Nixon administration, Frederic Malek commented, "I used to believe that the highly intelligent, highly capable guy could go in anywhere. You didn't have to worry about his lack of experience. He would adapt. I don't buy that any more. Maybe the guy with the brilliant mind and no experience can do the job, but now I'd say, don't bet on it. I'll take the proven commodity every time, the guy with experience, who has shown he can work in Washington."[11] Firsthand knowledge of how government works can be particularly useful to White House aides who advise presidents on choosing personnel.

Of course, the proven commodity, people with experience, are more likely to have their own agenda. Occasionally a president will choose an assistant whose philosophy differs from his, as when Nixon picked Moynihan as his urban affairs adviser. Such decisions and their potential consequences should be most carefully weighed.[12] Conflict, up to a point, is healthy on a White House staff, and a "multiple advocacy" staff system, exemplified by Moynihan against Arthur Burns in the Nixon White House, promises to produce a well-tested product. But even the leading academic proponent of multiple advocacy, Alexander L. George, noted that "the time required for the give-and-take among advocates may on occasion impose undue delays on decisionmaking."[13] And although adequate representation of alternative proposals helps a president avoid mistakes, a president cannot wait for the perfect proposal. "Presidents definitely want 'good policy,' but they also want immediate results," Paul Light has argued. "Perhaps the only way to be effective is to remove internal conflict."[14] There was, for instance, so much disarray on President Carter's staff that John Kessel concluded that "it would have been very difficult for any combination of issue groups to form a winning coalition." The Reagan staff, on the other hand, was noted for its "similarity of outlook."[15] Undoubtedly these levels of disagreement and like-mindedness contributed to the relative successes of each president during his first year in office. Ultimately presidents must pick aides who reflect their values.

What the better White House aides have *not* had, with some notable exceptions, has been that "passion for anonymity" called for in the Brownlow report. It has been impossible for them to remain anonymous because the media have decreed that their actions and lives are news. Nor should they remain anonymous. Their potential influence is too important to the workings of government for them to stay hidden. This hardly argues for the adoption of White House "sunshine" laws; some confidentiality is vital to the proper functioning of the presidency. Indeed the clash of ideas within the White House—which appears absent only to those who have never been there—would be seriously compromised if internal struggle were constantly exposed to public view. But neither can the principle of executive privilege be used to shield acts of criminality, as Nixon and Clinton attempted to do. Clearly White House aides should have the ability to work gracefully in the limelight, while recognizing always that their powers are derivative.

Although presidents are free to choose their aides, some recent studies have stressed the growing institutional character of the presidency, which can give the impression that presidents are increasingly locked in by form, their sources of advice and their options severely limited by the machinery of the White House. The case histories in chapters 3 through 11, however, indicate that they disregard the system at will. It makes no difference if an office is congressionally mandated or whether it is part of the presidential establishment by tradition. Nixon, for example, abolished the post of science adviser, kept away from the Council on Environmental Quality, listened to one chairman of the Council of Economic Advisers but not to another, and delegated budget responsibility to a subordinate. Presidents also create offices as a way of sloughing off unpleasant duties, a factor in Eisenhower's establishing a congressional relations staff.

The history of the Council of Economic Advisers (CEA), reviewed at length in the previous chapters, illustrates this presidential independence. Congress created the CEA in 1946 to force presidents to accept economic advice in a particular form. Yet they have chosen to use or not use the council, depending on whether they preferred working with an individual council chairman to receiving economic advice from other sources. It has been convenient to have economists close at hand, but the practice has been more the result of the marked increase in the responsibility presidents have had to take for the management of the domestic economy—as, for example, when Clinton created the National Economic Council as his principal advisory system—than because Congress invented an institution whose form was innately correct.

The National Security Council (NSC) is another case in point. The council's membership was legislated by Congress to include those officials it expected presidents to consult. Yet Truman did not regularly meet with the NSC until after the outbreak of the Korean War and did not seek its advice on whether to send troops to Korea. Eisenhower, who placed great emphasis on the NSC, made his decision to send troops to Lebanon outside its chambers. Kennedy dismantled much of the council's machinery and created Ex Comm, supposedly an executive committee of the NSC, to advise him during the Cuban missile crisis. That allowed him to turn to those statutory NSC members who had gained his trust, to exclude others, and to add outsiders to his inner circle. In planning strategy for Vietnam, Johnson narrowed his advisory group to a body of six, two of whom were on the White House staff, and met with them at lunch on Tuesdays, creating—in fact if not in name—a war cabinet. The NSC's greatest value to Nixon was in providing him with a vehicle for building a personal staff to oversee national security matters. At the Reagan White House the NSC staff was used for operational purposes, as seen in the Iran-Contra scandal.

The history of the NSC's operations should give pause to those who wish to impose mandatory sources of advice on presidents. Congress can give the president advisers, but in the words of the congressional committees investigating the Iran-Contra affair, it "cannot legislate good judgment."[16] The NSC often has served the presidency well, particularly by presenting more routine matters in an orderly way. But if Congress had not established it, presidents would still seek advice in some form from the secretaries of State and Defense and other concerned agency heads.

In 1976 Congress also mandated a White House Office of Science and Technology, which forces presidents to have some scientists on their staff. But the office has never become the major policymaking force that Congress intended. The importance of including scientific analysis in making public policy, however, should suggest the need to upgrade the present arrangement into something akin to the Council of Economic Advisers. "Like economics," wrote David Z. Beckler, "the breadth and diversity of science and technology call for a blending of different expertise and viewpoints in coming to policy conclusions. . . . With all council members appointed by the president with Senate confirmation, its consensus on policy conclusions would have political as well as technical standing."[17] Unfortunately, it will be easier for presidents to ignore a science council than to ignore either the CEA or the NSC. Presidents are more apt to see the economy and national security as central to their role. They also are more likely to suspect scientists as special pleaders (after all, the federal government spends billions annually on scientific research and development), and most of the men who have attained the presidency have not been keenly interested in science. Furthermore, White House councils are always of limited value if they deal with matters that are not perceived by presidents as affecting their prospects at the polls.

This lack of immediate applicability would also hamper the effectiveness of a long-range planning office of the sort proposed by Wassily Leontief and others. Two similar planning experiments under Roosevelt and Nixon were disasters. Presidents will continue to think in terms of four-year cycles and will seek professional advice that helps them to meet immediate needs. The success of the CEA has been maintained by the council's recognition that its advice must be useful during the president's time in office. Government does leave too much to chance, but its lack of foresight will continue until long-range planning is built into the regular processes of running the federal government. The failing cannot be corrected by putting another box on the organizational chart of the Executive Office, which presidents can and will ignore with impunity. Advisers in the White House can expect attention only if they operate within the same time frame as the president.

The sum of experience in these matters is that congressional attempts to impose sources of advice on presidents have cluttered the White House without necessarily serving the intended purposes. Presidents, too, have contributed to the clutter by proposing statutory White House offices that are eventually inherited by their successors. Future presidents will continue to ignore unwanted statutory advisers or will distort the mechanisms they have been given to serve other ends. There would be less manipulation and more efficiency in White House operations if presidents had a freer hand in arranging the internal machinery of their office.

Compared with the rest of government, the White House barely qualifies as an organization at all, if the term organization implies the existence of a fixed plan that is likely to look about the same tomorrow as it did yesterday. The very vibrations of the place differ markedly from president to president. The shift is best illustrated when a vice president is thrust into the presidency. For a while at least he will keep many of his predecessor's assistants, yet there will be a perceptible change in atmosphere and results.

Despite repeated reports to the contrary, there have been no Svengalis on the White House staff. Even under the most pyramidal arrangements, those of Eisenhower and Nixon, the men at the top served the purposes of the president. When Sherman Adams and H. R. Haldeman were replaced by men of considerably different mien, the direction of the two presidencies did not measurably change.

There are no immutable designs for organizing the presidency—schemes that usefully transcend a particular administration. For each president has his own way of doing things and is usually too old to change; each has his own objectives and goals that may be better served by one form of organization than by another. Roosevelt would have felt straitjacketed by the orderliness of Eisenhower's system, and Eisenhower would have been disoriented by the chaos of Roosevelt's. Roosevelt's chief objective, coaxing new solutions out of government to respond to the lingering Depression, might not have been realized through Eisenhower's system of noncompetitive jurisdictions. Eisenhower's chief objective, restoring a sense of tranquility to a buffeted nation, might have been more difficult to achieve under Roosevelt's methods of encouraging competition in his administration. Each would have had to find ways to ignore the system of the other if it had been mandated by law.

Ultimately it is the president's style—his work habits, the way he likes to receive information, the people he prefers to have around him, the way he makes up his mind—that will be the key to how the White House is organized. For example, every president gets a daily report on national security intelligence, known as the PDB, or president's daily brief. Clinton liked to get a long written report and often had little use for follow-up oral briefings. George W. Bush likes to receive shorter reports and longer oral briefings. One way is not right and the other wrong.[18]

The Roosevelt and Eisenhower White Houses have come to represent the extremes of presidential organization. Roosevelt's organization has been described as a circle with the president in the middle surrounded by a collection of generalists of no fixed assignment competing for his favor. At its best, such a system allows the president to rub two aides together to light a fire of creativity; at worst, it results in petty quarreling, forcing the president to get rid of one or both combatants. Eisenhower's model has been viewed as pyramidal. In this steeply hierarchical system, each aide, usually a specialist, is given a carefully prescribed duty. At worst, information falls between the boxes on the organization chart or is rendered insipid by the time it reaches the president; at best, information arrives on time and has the support of all parties. The more fluid Rooseveltian organization is likely to produce more policy innovation; the more structured organization of Eisenhower is likely to give more guidance to the permanent government.

The schemas of political scientists, although pedagogically useful, do not truly reflect the world within the White House. But if one were to draw an organizational design, it might most resemble an isosceles trapezoid—a pyramid with its top chopped off. Recent presidents have ultimately relied on a semihierarchical staff system that permits a small group of top aides to have direct access to the oval office. As presidents' needs and perceptions have changed, they have made adjustments. They usually have had to turn to different people for different talents. Both Roosevelt and Nixon found that aides with greater creativity were most needed in the formative period of their administrations. Aides with skills in lobbying Congress and coordinating departments were more necessary after policies were agreed upon. Then, too, the types of people likely to be on the White House staff are highly competitive and inclined to manipulate organizational patterns and job assignments to fit their own talents and ambitions. Louis Koenig noted that successful presidents have always been served "by personal advisers whose talent for the *diabolique* was definitely major league."[19] Moreover, routine systems of decisionmaking have a way of being ignored when presidents are under extreme pressure; elaborate procedures prove to be too slow and are subject to leaks. The more important a decision, the more likely that established channels will break down and be replaced by informal ad hoc arrangements.

The problem of the Nixon White House was not so much that it had a structured staff system, which had served Eisenhower well, but that the system was wrong for Richard Nixon. Eisenhower knew from long experience how to bend such an organizational arrangement to meet his needs; Nixon did not. Of even more importance, a president so given to isolation should have guarded against choosing a system that permitted him to become remote from the people and forces that a president must be in continuous contact with to govern effectively. The greatest danger in organizing the White House can come from a president who chooses to isolate himself.

On assuming office a president usually is prepared to delegate duties to cabinet officers and hold them responsible for performing them. What often happens, however, is that he holds them responsible for functions over which they may have little control or gives them tasks that prove to be impossible to perform because of congressional statutes or civil service regulations. Hiring and firing, for instance, often are assignments that a cabinet officer cannot legally carry out. A proper understanding of those constraints would indicate to presidents that sometimes a cabinet member's best or only available strategy is to make incremental change while continuing to push Congress and the permanent government in the desired direction. The common notion of cabinet officers as "the natural enemies of the President"[20] rarely reflects the true situation, which is that they generally are more willing than able to follow their president's dictates.

Frustrated presidents may quickly assume that they have picked a weak secretary or that the appointee has become a turncoat or a captive of the bureaucracy, Congress, or special interests. Sometimes, of course, presidents do pick the wrong people, and they should promptly fire the ineffective or offending department heads. Not to do so is to invite trouble. Roosevelt compounded confusion by dealing with an assistant secretary rather than removing a secretary of war with whom he had serious policy disagreements. Nixon created additional problems for himself by allowing a secretary of the interior to remain in office after he had lost the president's confidence. Johnson, in retrospect, believed that retaining a cabinet loyal to Kennedy had been a lingering mistake. Only Truman and Ford of the modern presidents have moved expeditiously when they felt that they needed to make changes.

McGeorge Bundy, after serving in the Kennedy and Johnson White Houses, forcefully advocated strengthening cabinet officers' control of their departments as the only means of providing an effective presidential presence within the executive branch. He argued that to do this, presidents must give cabinet officers the right to select their own second- and third-level executives.[21] On the other hand, Martin Anderson contended that one important element of Reagan's first-term success was tight White House control of such appointments. The White House "did not select subcabinet staff without consulting cabinet officers, but it was made clear to the incoming cabinet that they could not freely choose the people who would work for them. All key subcabinet appointments were cleared by Reagan and/or his top personal aides."[22] It is said that while White House control of personnel selection encourages departmental loyalty to the president, allowing department heads to pick their subordinates fosters smooth working relations within the departments. However, the argument over which system is better is somewhat moot. To work well, appointments usually entail something like a double veto, a delicate negotiation between White House personnel officer and cabinet official that leaves neither totally dissatisfied if they cannot agree wholeheartedly. Most important is that all participants understand the rules. New cabinet officers must know how their top aides will be selected. Failing to set things straight at the beginning, a problem in the Carter administration, inevitably leads to friction. But no matter how sophisticated the apparatus, making presidential appointments will always be subject to the intractable tension in the demand for both loyalty and expertise. A new president must somehow balance the deserving claims of campaign and party faithful with the need for quality and experience. Sometimes they happily coincide. Often they do not.

One way of analyzing the qualities desirable in a department secretary is to look at the record of past cabinet members. All department heads are more successful in managing some aspects of their jobs than others, and few people have an opportunity to observe public officials in all facets of their work. Judgments will depend on vantage points and points of view. Most people simply judge cabinet officers by whether they agree with them.[23] Reporters may rate department heads on their openness and the appeal of the image they project; civil servants may judge them first as administrators.

The mix of qualities necessary to perform well will differ somewhat among cabinet jobs, and presidents should be aware of the differences. The secretary of health and human services must work with many more congressional committees than the secretary of defense. The secretary of state spends more time in negotiations than does the secretary of the interior. Some departments resemble integrated enterprises, and others look like holding companies; some deal more with ideas, others more with products. Presidents also should be aware that a department may need different talents at different times. As Joseph Califano pointed out, the primary need in an HEW secretary in 1964 and early 1965, "when the bulk of . . . controversial and far-reaching health and education proposals was working its way through Congress," was a person such as Anthony Celebrezze, who "knew how to lobby." After the legislation was passed, the need was for a secretary such as John Gardner, who could "add a special prestige to service in the department and who could attract . . . brilliant and imaginative talent."[24]

Certain executive talents seem universally self-evident. Executives should keep their word. They should be able to pick talented assistants and draw the most from them. And they should be loyal to their superiors while offering their best independent judgments. Yet seldom recognized, especially when presidents begin to construct their administrations, are the clear differences between the duties of public executives and those of their counterparts in the private sector:

—Cabinet officers probably spend two-thirds of their time dealing with individuals and groups outside their organization. They prepare statements, testify before Congress, and meet with individual legislators. They participate in press conferences, interviews, and television appearances. They maintain relations with the department's constituencies through speeches, travel, and meetings. And they take part in symbolic and political activities, especially if they have elective backgrounds.

—Cabinet officers work in larger and less homogeneous organizations than those likely to be found in the private sector. They must rely on many different kinds of people—whose interests and priorities sometimes clash with their own—for information, ideas, and policy implementation. Federal departments also compensate for the lack of close and long-standing personal relationships by placing heavy emphasis on procedure. The safeguard against dishonesty is red tape.

—Cabinet officers often remain in their positions for only two years. They must learn their jobs faster than in nongovernmental employment, and if they wish to accomplish anything, they must work faster.

—Cabinet officers are employed by the public. The "shareholders" to whom they are ultimately responsible are many, different, and unseen and cannot take their trade elsewhere.

In a further attempt to discover the characteristics that make good department secretaries, I have attempted two cross-sections, one in time, looking collectively at all past secretaries of defense, and the other across an administration, looking collectively at all those who served in Nixon's first-term cabinet.

No cabinet appointments have been as consistently high in quality as those for secretary of defense. Of the twenty men who headed the department from its creation in 1947 until mid-2002, only two or three performed below the level that the public has a right to expect. It should be noted, however, that despite the size and complexity of the department, it is actually easier to achieve success as defense secretary than as the head of some of the domestic agencies. Except for the last years of the Vietnam War, the nation has approved of the department's mission, and the members of Congress to whom the secretary reports, particularly the committee chairmen, have supported that mission to an extent unknown in the legislature's relations with other departments.

Defense secretaries may have been superior to their counterparts in the domestic departments because presidents have selected them more carefully, have been less influenced by demographic or political considerations, and, despite at least two refusals, have probably found it easier to attract talented people to this post than to some other cabinet offices.

In 1957, reviewing the qualities most needed in a defense secretary, Samuel Huntington stated:

> First, he should be a man of experience, possessing some familiarity with the problems with which he will be dealing. . . . Second, the Secretary should be a man of respect, commanding the admiration of informed public opinion. . . . Third, he should be a man of dedication, acting and thinking purely in terms of the needs of the office. . . . Finally, the Secretary must be a man of policy. His greatest needs are breadth, wisdom, insight, and, above all, judgment. He is neither operator, administrator, nor commander. But he is policymaker.[25]

In comparing these expectations with actual Pentagon leadership during the past five decades, it is possible to conclude that while not all secretaries have been household names when appointed, their careers have nevertheless inspired public confidence, because they either had extensive government service or had run large corporations.[26] Their record of familiarity with the problems of their department has surpassed that of other cabinet officers. Eight of them had had previous experience in high-level Pentagon posts, and eight had seen other service related to national security. Only the three corporate presidents—Charles Wilson of General Motors, Neil McElroy of Procter and Gamble, and Robert McNamara of Ford—lacked extensive Washington experience.

They came from various professions or occupations: business, law, academia, politics, and government service. Presidents have varied in their preferences. Truman's secretaries all had Pentagon backgrounds. Eisenhower chose businessmen who were not "men of policy"—indeed Secretary of State John Foster Dulles had more to do with defense policy than did Eisenhower's defense secretaries. Nixon, who chose no businessmen, made sure that the position of deputy secretary was filled by a corporate executive.

What made the defense secretaries unique, and possibly most effective, was the diversity of many of their careers.[27] George Marshall had been secretary of state as well as army chief of staff. Elliot Richardson and Caspar Weinberger had been secretaries of health, education, and welfare; Richardson also had been under secretary of state and Weinberger director of the Office of Management and Budget. James Schlesinger had headed the Atomic Energy Commission and the Central Intelligence Agency; Donald Rumsfeld and Dick Cheney had served in the House of Representatives and as White House chief of staff; Frank Carlucci had been an ambassador and NSC adviser. McNamara, whose career had been almost entirely with the Ford Motor Company, was the remarkable exception.

If consideration of defense secretaries suggests that experience, judgment, and a diverse career make a good cabinet officer, consideration of Nixon's first cabinet suggests additional necessary qualities and some that are not so necessary. Some possibilities for measuring the effectiveness of department heads—as well as the difficulties of constructing a scorecard—were suggested in the results of a September 1971 *Wall Street Journal* poll of how well Washingtonians thought Nixon's cabinet was performing.[28] (At the time, seven of the president's original eleven department heads were in office.)

Cabinet officers were rated most often on their relations with Congress. Those who fared well, such as Rogers Morton and Melvin Laird, had served in Congress or, as in the cases of William Rogers and Elliot Richardson, had had considerable experience in dealing with Congress. Those who did poorly, particularly John Mitchell and Clifford Hardin, were new to Washington.

Cabinet officers' relations with those in their departments and with outside groups also were used as criteria. Department heads with political backgrounds generally did best in working with their agencies' clients. For example, HUD Secretary George Romney was cited for getting along well with mayors. Those who were perceived as being close to the president received the highest marks for improving departmental morale.

Ability as an administrator was mentioned rarely, and there was no comment on how well a department was run day to day or on the quality of a cabinet officer's subordinates. Few officers have concentrated on administering their departments, although presidents often have picked them to do just that. The standard practice is for secretaries to leave administrative detail and internal operations to their deputy secretaries.

Interestingly, five cabinet officers were judged by comparing them with their predecessors. Richardson at HEW and Morton at Interior earned high marks, partly because of the poor records of Robert Finch and Walter Hickel, while James Hodgson at Labor was found wanting as the successor to George Shultz. Fortunate is the person who follows a weak official.

No matter how successful the individual officers, however, collectively the Nixon cabinet had a dysfunctional turnover rate, indicating that the president erred in selecting and using department heads. Public executives must stay in office long enough to learn their jobs and put their knowledge to work. Even the experienced Richardson required two years to plan the reorganization of HEW. This suggests that effective cabinet members should serve at least three years. In that regard, Clinton did exceptionally well, retaining four department heads for his entire two terms. Some people familiar with the high turnover in the upper reaches of government estimate that one-half to two-thirds of all public executives leave because they initially made only a short-term commitment.[29]

Rotating cabinet members, a well-developed technique in Great Britain, can prolong the effectiveness of superior executives in a two-term administration. Nixon made more use of rotation than any of his predecessors but rarely kept his people in place long enough to make the most of their talents. Movement in this case usually solved one problem only to create another.

While the notion of a type appropriate for cabinet service can be overdrawn, my two cross-sections suggest that there are certain qualities that presidents should look for in public executives:

—Persuasiveness. Especially necessary in large, hierarchical organizations where leaders have limited control over personnel and the tug of inertia may be considerable, persuasiveness requires the ability to create excitement about programs and proposals, as well as to argue quietly and effectively with legislators and important client groups.

—Personal stability. Cabinet jobs disrupt family life, require extensive travel, and entail many flattering perquisites. A cabinet member must have stamina, the ability to work under pressure, and a sturdy moral gyroscope. Having a sense of humor also helps, although some have survived without the ability to laugh at themselves.

—Broad intelligence. Cabinet officers need not be intellectuals, but they should be able to see the policy implications and consequences of their actions. They must be adept at juggling projects and move easily from subject to subject. Because they deal mainly with crises and policy changes—always rapidly—they also should be quick studies, able to absorb masses of data in a short period.

—Flexibility. Although they are extensions of the president, often cabinet officers also are answerable to Congress, the bureaucracy, the media, constituent groups, and the public. They may have to change course and must do so without losing sight of the president's ultimate goals. They must recognize an advantageous compromise when they see it. Still, there will be certain basic policies on which they should not give in; then, tenacity can be an advantage.

—A sense of duty. Cabinet officers cannot forget that they are engaged in a public calling. Yet unlike the president and members of Congress, they are not elected. This means, paradoxically, that they must have an even sharper sense of responsibility than an elected official, for they are public officials not directly answerable to the public.

—A thick skin. Cabinet officers should stand between their president and public discontent. If they are doing their jobs properly, they will deflect as much criticism as possible.

—Patience and impatience. Cabinet officers deal with endless procedures, repeated congressional hearings, and careful negotiating, both within government and between government and outside parties—all of which calls for considerable equanimity. Yet at the same time they must prod their subordinates to be more effective and must use their impatience with the status quo as a constructive management technique.

Even a more complete distillation of the qualities necessary for efficient performance would not ensure that qualified cabinet officers could be easily located. The United States has neither a shadow cabinet nor a vocational school for training government officials. Perhaps the closest approach to a shadow cabinet was party chairman Paul Butler's Democratic Advisory Council in the 1950s. Assigning those in the party out of power to track the work of the departments is a constructive enterprise in a democratic society. Undoubtedly it can help develop talent and familiarity with policy. Yet such familiarity is just one element of the department head's job description. As Richard Fenno has pointed out, the personal qualifications most important for successfully managing a department would seem to be "administrative experience in a political environment and some acquaintance with the substantive policy problems of the department involved."[30] The problem, as Marver Bernstein observed, is that "we have developed no theory that explains how professionalized administration is made compatible with the politics of democracy. An agency head is expected to be both political executive and administrative manager; yet the two capacities seldom go together well."[31]

If, as I have assumed here, it is possible for a president to trim the size of the White House staff and to identify and attract good people to government service, there still remains the overarching question of how to fit the pieces together into a functional concept of how the presidency should work. This I discuss in the final chapter.

CHAPTER 13

Toward a More
Functional Presidency

 The Constitution gives and takes away. On the one hand it vests executive power in the president; on the other it assigns numerous administrative powers to Congress. As early as the Treasury Department Act of 1789, Congress created administrative offices with distinct responsibilities. Since then, except in emergency legislation, it has given statutory powers directly to agencies or agency heads instead of to the president. Supreme Court decisions in 1838 and 1935 have upheld this practice.[1] Yet the extent to which a president manages the government has been the key element in the continuing struggle for control between the legislative and executive branches and has been the subject of less passionate battles among scholars.

Writing in 1922, Arthur M. Schlesinger Sr. could distill "the elusive quality of *greatness*" in American presidents without once referring to managerial talents.[2] James Bryce and Harold Laski, the leading British scholars of the presidency, did not make much of the president as manager either.[3] But an early twentieth-century school of public administration, arguing on the basis of "scientific management" rather than constitutional law, made a strong case that the president should be the chief manager. As W. F. Willoughby wrote, "It can be stated without any hesitation that a prime requisite of any proper administrative system is that . . . the chief executive shall be given all the duties and powers of a general manager and be made in fact, as well as in theory, the head of the administration."[4] By 1974 Peter

Drucker would state matter-of-factly, though in sorrow, "The President . . . is first of all a manager."[5]

A president dominant over Congress and fully responsible for the management of the bureaucracy were the major themes of the Brownlow report in 1937. And in his transmittal message President Roosevelt declared that "the Presidency was established [by the Constitution] as a single strong Chief Executive Office in which was vested the entire executive power of the National Government."[6]

Those of a liberal persuasion were comfortable with the theory of a powerful presidential manager until late in the Vietnam War.[7] Conservatives subsequently became comfortable with the managerial presidency concept as it became clear that they were much more likely to control the White House than the Congress. Richard P. Nathan noted that Nixon and Reagan pursued "an administrative strategy" during their presidencies, seeking to carry out important policy objectives by executive action rather than through the enactment of new legislation.[8]

The growth of presidential powers since Franklin Roosevelt's administration has by no means meant that the war between the branches has been resolved in favor of the president. Beneath the surface, Congress—and particularly its committee chairs—has maintained powerful links to the bureaucracy, which still looks to Capitol Hill for its money. The power to legislate, especially to write the fine print, has often been the power to determine the contours of an administration. The power to confirm has reminded appointees that they owe allegiance not just to the president. The power to investigate has been the power to turn a searchlight on the anonymous bureaucracy, as well as the president's political appointees. Moreover, Congress and the president have often seemed to work on a teeter-totter principle with each movement of the board linked to shifts in public opinion so that when presidential esteem has waned, as it did during the Watergate affair, Congress has been able to impose some restrictions on the White House.[9] Then, too, a president's stay in office has been far more limited than that of most members of Congress and the bureaucracy.

The growth of government since the Great Depression in the 1930s has made the managerial function infinitely more difficult. It has not been merely a matter of scale or that the president has lost control of the power to hire and fire. The question has also had to do with what is to be managed. Corporations manage production, and efficiency can be measured in unit costs. But the products, such as justice, equality, and participation, of many of the newer domestic programs have been far less tangible. Other programs—job training for hard-core unemployables, teaching reading skills to those whom conventional methods have failed—have involved ideas and techniques that are frankly experimental, that offer no certifiable answers. Government not only is doing more, it is doing more difficult tasks. What is to be the measure of efficiency? And is efficiency what we should be measuring? Presidents have tried to import such corporate tools of control as planning, programming, and budgeting systems and philosophies such as management by objectives, always with questionable success.

The problem of presidents as managers has been further complicated because, as I have written elsewhere, "Our Presidents, more often than not, have been atrocious administrators. They often come from an occupation (legislator) and a profession (law) that ill-prepares them for management."[10] People rarely think about choosing professional managers for president; they tend to define leadership otherwise. The presidential selection system is designed to screen politicians, and most politicians believe that management questions, except perhaps calls for "economizing," have little political appeal.

What makes this particularly ironic is that the history of the modern presidency has been one of growing presidential involvement in management. Much of the growth in the presidential establishment has been caused by presidents' attempts to take over the operation of high-priority programs (related to poverty and drug abuse, for example) or to exercise greater oversight, and eventually control, over the bureaucracy. It is hardly accidental that the Bureau of the Budget was renamed the Office of Management and Budget. All major study groups since the Brownlow Committee have recommended giving presidents additional tools for management as a means of increasing their control over the executive branch. But one result of making presidents managers is that they spend more and more time doing what they do badly and presumably less time doing what only presidents can handle. In sum, the role of presidents as managers has been distorted in theory and in recent practice, leading them to become involved in tasks that can be performed better by others.

There are various ways out of this dilemma. One solution would be to elect managers to the presidency. If, in fact, the responsibilities of a president are largely managerial, this step would be logical and would only await proper recognition on the part of the electorate. Certainly this is the view of the scientific management school. Yet such a view represents a profound misunderstanding: the primary presidential role is to make choices that are ultimately political. The president is the nation's chief political officer. He tries to control a process that is quintessentially political, and the political process primarily concerns distribution, not production. It decides who gets how much of what is available, not how to make more available at less cost. A political process cannot be managed in the sense that a corporation is managed, for political decisions are judged according to their fairness, both in the way they are made and in their perceived effect.

Assuming that the bigger the government, the more unmanageable it becomes, a second way of relieving presidents of superfluous tasks would be for the federal government to do less, or to turn over more of its collected revenues to states and localities to do things that Americans expect government to do (the principle of revenue sharing) or to contract with private parties to perform services that it has previously delivered (the principle of privatization). The proposition then becomes this: if the president cannot satisfactorily manage the federal establishment, ways must be found to decrease what must be managed rather than to increase the managerial ability of the president. These are political decisions, of course. They could be made if the electorate strongly indicated a desire to move in these directions. They would, however, still leave many activities for the federal government to manage.

A third solution would be to reorganize the executive branch to reflect a more realistic approach to solving problems and delivering services. Most departments represent a collection of past resolutions of yesterday's most important problems, of demands on elected officials by yesterday's most important special interest groups, and of long-forgotten bureaucratic fights over jurisdiction. Given the difficulty of changing existing arrangements, presidents have continued to create new agencies and to pull new problems into the White House, where their authority is greater. The piecemeal history of recent reorganizations has been one of consolidating related activities, of putting all transportation matters in one department, all housing matters in another, and so on. But as housing and transportation, for example, have increasingly seemed interconnected, proposals have been made to create a Department of Community Development and similar functional groupings. Such suggestions would result in fewer and larger departments. From the president's standpoint, the advantage would be in reducing the number of officials he has to track. The "lesser" departments, which are apt to be overlooked by presidents, might be expected to be raised in stature and visibility by consolidation.

But while consolidation can equalize the departments' access to the president, the case has not been firmly made that consolidation could avoid creating bureaucratic monstrosities. If the problems of government are partly the result of bigness, are bigger departments the solution? The histories of the two giants of the federal bureaucracy, HEW (before the E was made into a separate department) and the Defense Department, suggest that there is such a thing as optimum size. Putting together several small agencies may produce greater efficiency; creating agencies that employ 100,000 people may produce greater inefficiency and further loss of presidential control. A lesson of the Pentagon reorganization is that presidents had greater control over spending when each branch of the military service had to compete before them than they have now, when a consolidated department irons out its differences in private and presents the chief executive with a common front.

Whether agencies are big or small, however, organization along functional lines makes sense. Government becomes more understandable—no small consideration in a democratic society—and the prospects of jurisdictional disputes may be lessened. Moreover, functional divisions should increase agency accountability to the president and Congress.

At the same time, when a president accepts advice from those most responsible for carrying out an order, there is a higher probability of achieving results than when policy is imposed by presidential representatives, usually the White House staff, who may be less aware of a department's capabilities and do not have statutory authority to run programs.

Still, the question arises whether reorganizations can long remain in phase with changing priorities, crises, and fads: what might have been established in 1970 as a Department of Environment was ultimately created in 1977 as a Department of Energy. Congress refused to renew the president's reorganization powers in 1981. Should a future president reopen this question, those powers must be flexible enough to allow government to adjust quickly to change. Otherwise government will be constantly drifting into dysfunctionality and presidents will continue to rely on distorted ad hoc arrangements. Yet presidents must be aware that there can be problems of excessive reorganization.[11] "Who is going to be the new Boss? Will she like me? What's the latest rumor?" Constant tinkering takes a toll in the administration of federal programs.

Reorganizing the entire federal government is outside the scope of this study, but it is hardly outside the concern of presidents. The best time to reorganize is as promptly as possible after assuming office (which, of course, is the time presidents are least qualified to act); and changes should be made in such a way that successive presidents can undo them. Whatever format is easiest to change, reverse, or abolish is best in the long run. Changes that can be made informally or by executive order are preferable to those that are formal and statutory, just as changes that can be made by statute are to be preferred to those that require constitutional amendment.

A fourth solution to the problem of management is for presidents to revert to a pre-New Deal level of power. Such proposals have come from Barbara Tuchman and others who, in the wake of Vietnam and Watergate, have feared presidents' initiatives more than they have been troubled by their failing to tame the lions of bureaucracy.[12] The proposals of these scholars would ensure that federal agencies would continue to operate as independent forces, answerable to the president only when they needed presidential support, and that a 535-member legislature would assume a greater role in operational activities. But although life without a president may sometimes have a fantasylike attractiveness, no society as large and complex as the United States could drift for long on the waning momentum of bureaucracy. Autonomous agencies are certainly preferable to presidential corruption; they are not, however, a substitute for enlightened presidential leadership.[13] The American people elect presidents, not civil servants. The problem of how to ensure responsive and humane government performance is real and growing. The question is how it can be achieved within a democratic framework and within the capacities of the types of people most likely to be elected president.

No president sets out to build the largest staff in history, yet the White House has grown in nearly seventy years from a staff of thirty-seven to more than 1,000, with thousands more employed in satellite operations that also serve the presidency.[14] This development corresponds to that of the other parts of the national government. Congress, too, has grown: members' personal staffs totaled 2,030 in 1947 and 11,203 in 2001.[15]

It is not necessary to impute malevolence or a dictatorial impulse to the growth of the White House. Generally it has reflected a greater participation by the United States in world affairs since World War II, a widened concept of what services government should perform, and has filled a vacuum left by the failure of state and local governments to respond to legitimate needs and the transfer of services to the federal level. The growth has also reflected popular support for an increasingly activist concept of the presidency, more complicated interrelationships between government programs, and new offices imposed on the White House by Congress. Then, too, because existing federal agencies have sometimes failed to do an adequate job, presidents have tried to fill the void by creating new White House offices.

White House expansion also mirrors presidents' accedence to demands for group representation on their staffs and to the law of propinquity. Presidents turn to those around them to do what is uppermost on their minds; the harried first-echelon White House aides respond to demand by adding a second echelon to assist them. Expansion follows the bureaucratic imperative as the White House takes on the characteristics of a bureaucracy. Presidents have also been inclined to use the White House as a dumping ground or a face-saving device for high officials who have failed them elsewhere.

These types of White House growth reflect a certain permissiveness on the part of presidents. Faced with difficult choices among programs and personnel, they have followed the course of least political resistance, encouraged by a generation of social scientists nurtured in the glow of the New Deal. Each president lives with the permissiveness of his predecessor. Until recently the consequences of bringing people and programs into the White House have not been spelled out or necessarily recognized as being counterproductive. Possibly it has been made too easy for presidents to solve their problems in this way.

But, above all, the size of the White House staff reflects the failed concept of a managerial presidency. In his meticulously detailed study of federal reorganization planning in the twentieth century, Peri E. Arnold concluded, "The plain fact is that no modern president has fully managed the executive branch. . . . It becomes clear that the managerial conception of the presidency is untenable. It places impossible obligations on presidents. It also raises public expectations about presidential performance that cannot be met. The managerial presidency then becomes a trap, offering increased capacity and influence to presidents but creating even greater expectations about presidential performance."[16] Paradoxically, the centralization of responsibilities in the person of the president has lessened his ability to perform the duties of the office.

It is time to rethink the appropriate role of the president. What follows has been called a minimalist theory of the presidency.[17] Yet it is not meant to minimize the centrality of presidential leadership. Rather it is meant to define the basic functions that presidents perform (generally with the concurrence of Congress).

This job description does not include the president's role as tone setter for the nation ("moral leader" strikes me as too grand for an elected politician). A president should be able to provide effective reassurances and exhortations in difficult periods, give a heightened sense of national purpose, and put before the citizenry a vision of a better society. But such abilities are most affected by the people's trust in a president based on his past record, personal conduct, rhetorical skills, factors such as being in office during a "just" war, and other matters that are not closely correlated with a president's methods of organizing his administration.

Nor does my list include the ceremonial functions of a president. Some have viewed these duties as frivolous, as a waste of valuable presidential time, and have suggested that they be turned over to the vice president or that a separate ceremonial head of state be created.[18] (In fact, many of these duties are currently performed by the president's wife and children.)[19] But ceremonial duties, which can be adjusted to fit the time available, can be useful in keeping a president in touch with the people, in helping create a sense of national unity, and in endorsing worthwhile undertakings.

Much that goes on at the White House is done in the president's name—reports to Congress, greetings and routine letters, proclamations, appointments to honorific positions, and so forth. A book published in 1970 devotes 166 pages to listing just those activities that are a president's legal responsibilities, such as annexing any rock, island, or key not belonging to another government and on which a deposit of guano is found.[20] But most of these duties do not require more of a president's time than the incessant signing of his name, which even under Truman occurred more than 400 times a day. The distinction between responsibilities that need a president's personal attention and those that do not is well illustrated by the experiences of government during the months before Nixon's resignation. The apparent paralysis of the presidency, in fact, affected few of the routine operations of government.

There are, of course, presidential functions that require the active participation of the president:

—Devising policy to ensure the security of the country, with special attention to situations that could involve the nation in war.

—Devising a legislative program that presents recommendations for new initiatives, presumably ranking them in order of importance.

—Preparing the annual budget, which recommends changes in the size of existing programs.

—Sharing responsibility for adjustments of the economy engineered by the government.

—Selecting noncareer government personnel.

—Informing the people and their representatives in Congress of actions taken or proposed and presenting assessments of the state of the nation and of U.S. involvement around the world.

—Resolving conflicts between departments and seeking coordination of departmental policies.

—Overseeing the executive branch with some shared authority for promoting efficient and humane services and for ferreting out corruption.

—Such other duties as the laws require.

Many of the duties of the White House staff do not relate directly to these functions and could be performed by people outside the White House. For example, the types of political operatives who once were employed by a president's national party are now White House staffers. Mitchell E. Daniels Jr., who served as Reagan's assistant for political affairs from 1985 to 1987, has proposed abolishing the office he once headed and instead putting the party's national chairman in the cabinet.[21] Transferring the duties of the political office to the national committee might, at the same time, breathe new life into the party system and increase the president's political outreach. Based on his research in the Nixon archives, John Dillon of the *Christian Science Monitor* has reported that this is what Nixon had in mind when he asked George Bush to be chairman of the Republican National Committee after the 1972 election. "From now on, there would not be a political officer . . . in the White House, Nixon said. Instead, the RNC chairman, Bush, 'will be the President's full-time political adviser.' Bush would be brought into Cabinet and [congressional] leadership meetings, Nixon promised."[22] Because of the Watergate crisis, however, it did not work out this way.

The White House unit whose function is most often questioned is the Office of Public Liaison. While it is true that these assistants represent the president to groups that he needs in order to govern and get reelected, it is often more correct to say that these employees represent certain interests within the White House. Carter's experience with his counselor on aging, Nelson Cruikshank, makes this point. Joseph Califano, who was then secretary of HEW, remembered that on January 24th [1979], Carter called. "Cruikshank is threatening to resign as my Counselor on Aging unless he can speak out publicly against the Social Security reduction proposals."

"I don't see how you can run your government and let a presidential aide attack the President's proposals," I responded.

"Hamilton [Jordan] is concerned that if Cruikshank quits, he will organize all the senior citizens groups against us," Carter said.

"Can't he just stay on and keep quiet? Just not support the proposals actively?" I suggested, seeking to salvage the situation.

"I tried that. But Cruikshank wants to oppose them publicly," Carter said. [Cruikshank stayed on and "delivered a stinging attack" on the social security proposals before the House Committee on Aging.][23]

Congressional lobbying, which even under Truman and Eisenhower was primarily a responsibility of the departments, is increasingly carried out by White House assistants. Some careful observers contend that this growth is justified. Franklin L. Lavin, Reagan's political affairs director in 1988, has said that the Office of Legislative Affairs "can no longer just deal with Congressional leadership on a particular item. Important votes, such as the Bork nomination or Contra aid, involve 'hand-to-hand combat'—working with any number of Members to get their votes."[24] It would be possible, of course, to design a White House office that parallels the congressional whip system, composed of presidential assistants each of whom would be responsible for the care and feeding of legislators from a certain geographic area. Unfortunately, legislators' demands on the president would probably increase faster than the president could add lobbyists.

In some important instances the chief reason presidents have turned to personal assistants is that they have not trusted those who otherwise would have performed these services. Nixon's distrust of the FBI caused him to create the so-called plumber's unit. Thus at its extreme the concentration of responsibilities in the White House reflects the psychological makeup of presidents.

The White House staff is first of all a service unit to assist presidents in their daily routines, to help schedule their time, to aid them in preparing speeches and correspondence, and to assist them with travel plans and relations with the press. But beyond this, presidents have come to rely on their staffs for advice in performing the major tasks of office, and White House aides also have increasingly assumed operational responsibilities for government programs. There have been cases in which a presidential assistant and not the secretary of state has been the chief adviser on foreign policy. The functions assumed by the White House have bloated the presidential system. Staff size merely reflects these changes.

Operating in a much shorter time frame than that of the rest of the executive branch, presidents have viewed the bureaucracy as too slow to respond to their leadership, too unimaginative in proposing changes in policy, too unwilling to accept political direction, too closely allied with special interests. They turn, often in desperation, to those closest at hand. Yet the White House staff is not a sufficient fulcrum to move the weight of the federal establishment. It can never be large enough to do the job.

The presidents' solution so far—salvation by staff—is self-defeating. An enlarged White House staff overprotects presidents in a political environment where their greatest need is the need to know. Sycophancy can replace independent judgment. By extending the chain of command, presidents have built additional delay and distortion into the system. Tensions between White House staff and cabinet officers become inevitable. In the game of "who saw the president last," the department heads are badly positioned, and their exclusion from the inner circle creates a vicious cycle—the loss of power generating the further loss of power. Morale declines in the departments; the careerists who ultimately must implement presidential policy no longer have as much stake in its success. They need only wait long enough and there will be another president.

But presidents cannot wait. Indeed the pressure of time often pushes them to try to overwhelm or circumvent the bureaucracy and Congress. For future presidents, the lesson to be learned from Johnson and Nixon, both of whose careers were cut short, may be in the futility of this approach. But the processes of persuasion and negotiation remain painfully slow, and for these purposes presidents need colleagues. White House aides generally are not colleagues; they are extensions who can be lent presidential powers but who rarely have additional resources to throw into battle on the president's behalf. Among the limited number of people who are in varying degrees beholden to the president, cabinet members are the best bet to extend the reach and effectiveness of presidential leadership. But cabinet members can be a weak reed to rely on unless a president is prepared to hold them personally accountable—in the British sense of the "doctrine of ministerial responsibility"—for the operations of their departments.

Trimming the White House staff is a relatively simple matter for presidents, if there is the will. The political risks are modest. The authority exists. It is a logical place to begin the process of striking a new balance in government. The White House organization and its size will, of course, not remain static. It responds to political, technological, and institutional changes. Still, as a cautionary tale it is useful for a president to start from the position that small is beautiful. Or, in the words of the Tower Commission report, "Predisposition on sizing of the staff should be toward fewer rather than more."[25] Of much greater difficulty will be the effort to create a presidential reliance on the cabinet, to devise mechanisms of support for such an undertaking, and to remove obstacles that historically have worked to create a wedge between presidents and their department heads.

The point is for a president to figure out what a cabinet can and ought to do, what a staff can and ought to do. Chapter 9 reviews the initial success of Reagan's cabinet council system, which had held 112 meetings by the first week of December 1981. There is more to the story:

This meant that on 112 separate occasions a half-dozen or so cabinet members got into their cars and journeyed to the White House. They usually arrived ten or fifteen minutes early and stayed for a while after the meeting. Most of that extra time before and after the meeting was spent in discussion with other cabinet members and senior members of Reagan's White House staff.

Sometimes after a meeting a member or two of the cabinet would join a White House aide in his office for further discussions. These short impromptu discussions among and between the president's policy advisers were probably as important to the advancement and development of his policy as the meetings themselves. Valuable pieces of information were exchanged, disagreements worked out privately, and Reagan's advisers got to know each other personally, intimately. It created, for a while, an unusual degree of harmony between two normally antagonistic groups, the White House staff and the cabinet.[26]

There are guideposts along the path to a more functional presidency. Keep presidents out of matters that are not presidential in nature. Remove the dangers of an overextended White House staff, and guide presidents in the direction of seeking advice from those who will be most responsible for policy implementation. Improve the responsiveness of the bureaucracy to the wishes of the electorate by increasing the leverage of department officials whose fate depends on public mandate. Yet these alone are no guarantee that there will be no Vietnams, no Watergates, no Iran-Contra affairs.

There can be no assurance that presidents will always act wisely, that they will always get good advice, or that they will accept good advice when it is offered. The conclusion reached in chapter 7, which reviewed the wide variety of advice Lyndon Johnson received against escalating the Vietnam war, was that, as Larry O'Brien put it, Johnson "knew the problem. Nonetheless, he went ahead and pursued the war policy that he believed to be the right one."[27] The history of Watergate, reviewed in chapter 8, argues that the cover-up, the act for which Richard Nixon was forced to resign, was a decision made by the president, not the product of a faulty system of advice. Watergate, of course, does reflect on the staff members who assisted Nixon in the cover-up, but in the end it is the president who sets the tone for his administration.

The Reagan history is more confusing, less clearcut. In his first term the president was given credit for having perfect pitch in orchestrating the performance of his administration. On every president's staff, deliberately or inadvertently, initially or eventually, there is a primus inter pares. The PIP is the president's fail-safe mechanism, the last redoubt between him and bad advice. If the PIP does not know the location of all the traps that are set, the president is likely to fall into one. Although the PIP is often thought of as a single person, a Sherman Adams or an H. R. Haldeman, Reagan turned PIP into the acronym of a collective noun. No management expert could have designed the collectivity of James Baker, Edwin Meese, and Michael Deaver, an amalgam of insider and outsider, ideologue and pragmatist. But at the start of his second term Reagan swapped his immensely successful PIP for one that proved to be equally unsuccessful. Was the president merely lucky and then unlucky? Most likely he had not understood the qualities he most needed in organizing his presidency.

Reagan's strange detachment from his own government, the mechanic's conception of leadership held by Jimmy Carter, the moral obtuseness of Richard Nixon, Lyndon Johnson's misplaced machismo, Clinton's raging libido—useful reminders on which to end this study. Organizational design, or lack thereof, will help or hinder a president in reaching his goals, but the decisive element of the American presidency remains the mettle of the president.

Advice for a
President-Elect
1976–1977

I had forgotten how funny I thought it had been until, preparing to revise
this book in 1988, I reread John Osborne's account in the *New Republic* of
December 11, 1976:

> Stephen Hess, a former Nixon assistant and Brookings Institution
> Fellow whose new book, *Organizing the Presidency*, was favorably
> mentioned in this space, learned on Friday, November 19, how per-
> sonally and directly [Jimmy] Carter is involved [in the presidential
> transition]. Hess is a member of the US delegation to the current ses-
> sion of the UN General Assembly. He was in his office at US delega-
> tion headquarters in New York when a secretary told him that a
> Governor Carter was on the telephone. "Governor Carter?" Hess said.
> "What Governor Carter? I don't know any Governor Carter." The
> secretary said it was *the* Governor Carter.[1]

This is the sort of response that must happen all the time when a president-elect who chooses to make his own phone calls decides to call folks
who are not expecting to hear from the president-elect. That call also
began the involvement of this book and its author with the act of organizing a presidency.

On the day after the initial call from Governor Carter, I met in the
White House with President Ford's chief of staff, Dick Cheney, and, based
on the information he gave me, I sent the next president a memorandum on

staffing needs. This was followed by calls from Plains asking for other memos on White House organization.

As a result of my connection with the 1976–77 transition, *Organizing the Presidency* at the time became, in Washington at least, one of those books that people had an opinion about—whether or not they had read it. It was that book about reducing the White House staff and creating "cabinet government." Recalling that time, Carter speechwriter James Fallows wrote, "'Cabinet government' became a good-government rally cry. Carter took up the cry, eagerly accepting a naive book by Stephen Hess. . . ."[2]

During the fall I continued to send memos to the president-elect, sometimes in response to his questions, sometimes on points that I wanted him to be aware of. I also was consulted by members of his transition staff. During one Saturday morning session with the newly appointed cabinet secretary, I drew a diagram of a rectangular table on a blackboard while explaining the seating arrangement at cabinet meetings and how agendas have been prepared in the past. Gradually, however, I eased myself out of the picture as those seeking position and favor in the new administration took aim at each other. (I had early told the president-elect that I did not wish to go back into government.) President Carter and his assistants were unfailingly polite and appreciative of my advice, and since I had been the editor-in-chief of the Republican platform, I was grateful to have had their attention and their goodwill.

My memos of 1976–77 stand as historical curiosities, and therefore may need a few words of annotation. Those that relate to White House trappings (November 30 and December 8) were in response to concerns from Plains, the president-elect being anxious that his administration offer a counterimage to The Imperial Presidency. As a result of one of these memos I stake my claim to a footnote in history. "A President should be able to walk in the woods on a weekend if it helps restore his spirit or rethink his concerns," I wrote to the president-elect. As for Camp David, "Do not dismantle it until you have determined that it does not serve a legitimate need." The advice may have been gratuitous, but I like to think that there could not have been a Camp David accord, the high-water mark of the Carter presidency, had he not followed my advice.

The memos, unlike the book, offered a specific plan for a specific president—a Carter White House design (November 24). As would be expected, it called for a smaller staff, recommending the immediate elimination of seventy-seven jobs (November 22). It accepted that Carter did not want to have a chief of staff, but added: "The key point is that a president need not have a chief of staff—he can divide the duties—but he should not be his own chief of staff. Otherwise he will find that he is spending considerable time on servicing his staff, rather than the other way around." That my plan was not adopted should absolve me of all blame and (worse in Washington) all influence. President Carter, however, did have modest success in reducing the size of the White House office.

As for the second leg of my proposal, the November 24 memo says,

> There are two elements in considering the proper use of the cabinet. The cabinet officers, as heads of the major departments, should have the central role in advising you on the formulation of policy because they are the only ones who can implement policy, and policy formulation cannot be successfully divorced from policy implementation. The cabinet, as the collectivity of your chief advisers, should play a much more useful role than in the past. On the first point, I feel completely confident. The second point may be more of a wish—much of history points the other way. However, my experience as chief of staff to Pat Moynihan on the president's Urban Affairs Council (1969) showed me that the collective cabinet (usually working in subgroups) can be a highly effective policy-proposing body *during the first year of a new administration.* My worry is that the collective cabinet could become less useful after an administration's initial burst of energy and it is this that must be watched carefully.

President Carter's experience with cabinet government, it is agreed, was a disaster. Strangely, instead of reducing the number of cabinet departments, as he had committed himself to do during the campaign, he actually added two, Energy and Education. Again strangely, it was Ronald Reagan, not Carter, who usefully developed subgroups of the cabinet, which he called cabinet councils, as valuable policy-proposing bodies.

The only deletions in the following memos are of addresses, phone numbers, and one personal reference.

November 21, 1976

Based on our Friday telephone conversation, I will be sending you a series of memos on aspects of organizing the presidency. Tomorrow I will write on White House staffing arrangements.

This one deals with a dilemma that is unique to your transition. It concerns the problem of picking cabinet officers for the eleven existing departments while, at the same time, being committed to a government reorganization that is likely to produce fewer than eleven departments, possibly as few as eight. In other words, how do you divide eleven into eight without creating serious personnel problems and adding to the forces that will resist change?

Without meaning to overdramatize: consider that after reorganization, say six months into your administration, you could be faced with the need to fire or reassign several dozen of your own top appointees and that all the top jobs are already filled.

The fact that there were cabinet and subcabinet officers in place adversely affected LBJ's efforts to consolidate the Departments of Commerce and Labor, and later Nixon's efforts to reduce the number of domestic agencies. It would be unusual to expect such officials to be enthusiastic about reorganizing themselves out of their jobs.

Both the Heineman Committee (LBJ, 1967) and the Ash Council (Nixon, 1970) proposed essentially similar plans for functional reorganization of the domestic agencies. The Heineman group suggested domestic departments for (1) Social Services, (2) National Resources and Development, (3) Economic Affairs, and (4) Science and Environmental Preservation (this was before the energy crisis). The Ash Council wanted departments of (1) Natural Resources, (2) Human Resources, (3) Economic Affairs, and (4) Community Development.

Your timetable is particularly important. If you wish to set up a task force and design a reorganization from scratch, the job could take up to a year. This would support picking your cabinet members along traditional lines—since you would not wish to operate for a fourth of your term on the basis of anticipated changes. However, if you wish to accept the basic premises and research of the Heineman and Ash groups, you probably could make the necessary modifications in three months or less. In this case, you might consider a somewhat different type of cabinet.

No matter how you pick your cabinet, there are compelling reasons for building on the Ash Council work: (1) *functional* regroupings make the most sense, which, I believe, was your experience in Georgia; (2) the Ash Council did quality research, which it is not necessary to duplicate; (3) the recommendations provide for a *total* approach, which is superior, in this case, to incremental change; (4) it allows you to move very quickly, when you have the least resistance and the greatest chance of success.

In accord with the Heineman-Ash proposals, the cabinet can be divided into two categories:

The inner cabinet—State, Defense, Treasury, and Justice. These departments remain unchanged, and cabinet members can be selected without regard for future reorganizations. When picking an HEW secretary you could also put the department in this category since it is likely that HEW will be the core of a new department of Human Resources or Social Services, and your HEW secretary would be the presumptive head of the new agency.

The outer cabinet—Commerce, Labor, Agriculture, Transportation, Interior, and HUD. These are the departments (along with HEW) that are likely to form a new configuration through reorganization.

At the very minimum, all these appointees should be fully informed in advance of your dedication to a reorganization, that consolidation might eliminate their departments within months, and you should be satisfied that they are committed to this goal. I should add that on this basis you could have problems getting the people you want for the outer cabinet.

Assuming, however, a rather prompt reorganization, you may wish to try to finesse the problem of redundant cabinet officers by picking (and even announcing that you are picking) persons who will serve only until reorganization, and whose responsibility (besides interim management) will be to evaluate their departments, to help design the reorganization, and to work to bring about the reorganization.

For example, in the three "representational" departments—Commerce, Labor, Agriculture—you might pick distinguished individuals, possibly from the ranks of the three occupations, who would lend their prestige to reorganization, and are "stepping down" (financially) to accept temporary appointment. A prestigious corporate leader, for instance, might take a leave from his company to handle the Commerce portfolio during the reorganization period. On this basis I feel confident you could get anyone you want (assuming possible conflict-of-interest questions were resolved with Congress in advance).

In one or two cases—I particularly have in mind Coleman of Transportation, possibly Usery of Labor—you might consider asking a respected cabinet officer to stay on for several months to run the department until the reorganization.

In short, the problem that faces you in this area is to ensure, in every way possible, that your cabinet officers who are the most affected by reorganization—and potentially have the most to lose—will be working positively to bring about the reorganization that you send to Congress.

November 22, 1976

On Saturday I had a two and one-half hour meeting with Richard Cheney, President Ford's chief of staff. This memo details my impressions of some areas in which the present White House is overstaffed and suggests more appropriate staffing levels.

Legal counsel. This office grew far too big when Nixon needed Watergate defense lawyers, and has not been sufficiently cut back by Ford. There are now fourteen slots, and I seriously doubt that there is enough work to keep them busy. Most of the legal work for the institutional presidency can and should be done by the Office of Legal Counsel at Justice. The legal work involving the personal presidency possibly needs two (three at the most) attorneys.

Note: the title of legal counsel was invented by FDR for Sam Rosenman, who resigned a judgeship to become the president's speechwriter and domestic policy adviser; JFK used the same title for Ted Sorensen. There is no functional reason to go back to this practice. The legal counsel should be the president's personal lawyer.

Office of Public Liaison. This is a euphemism for the "special pleaders." It is the old Chuck Colson operation and includes special assistants to the president for minority affairs (blacks), Hispanic affairs, ethnic affairs, consumer affairs, women, and youth. There are now twenty-three slots. From the standpoint of good government, this operation should be abolished. It will be necessary to do this quickly if it is to be done well. My reasons for opposing this type of White House operation are in my book on pages 9–10 and 127–28. The need here is for one special assistant (not more than three) to serve as a lightning rod for interest groups with a special need to be in direct contact with the White House.

Press relations. There are forty-three slots. This operation now includes the Office of Director of Communications for the Executive Branch, the post that Nixon created for Herb Klein and that became a propaganda mill under Jeb Magruder. At that time it engaged in such activities as organizing letters-to-the-editor campaigns and drafting supportive speeches for members of Congress.

The basic press secretary functions probably need five professionals plus clerical support to service the White House press corps. (This figure does not include the full-time press advance team—now four.) One person probably is needed to deal with the outside-of-Washington press. At one time Nixon had a full-time person (on detail from USIA, I think) to handle the foreign press corps in Washington. I doubt that this is necessary. It seems to me that the foreign reporters can be serviced along with the domestic people, but you should judge this at a later time. There may also be a need for a full-time TV adviser (at least Cheney strongly advises).

The Ford press office, I believe, handles the composition of written presidential statements, such as proclamations and congressional messages. It makes more sense to move this into the speechwriters' department. (My impression is that Ford's arrangement was designed to eliminate a personnel problem.)

While I'm particularly sympathetic to the personnel needs of this office (they are on twenty-four-hour call and receive a heavy volume of phone calls and mail because of the instant prominence of the press secretary), I still recommend starting with the scaled-down model that I indicated above and then reevaluating over time. (This advice, of course, applies to the entire White House staff.)

Domestic Council. There are now forty slots. (There were seventy under Nixon.) This has never been a truly collegial body of cabinet members, but rather an excuse to build a domestic policy staff at the White House. As such, it performs functions similar to the Califano office under LBJ, which had about seven professionals. The Domestic Council was created by statute and has a separate congressional appropriation, so you may wish to leave it in place for the time being.

For the purpose of including possible staffing levels, I think it would be useful to have one professional in the White House for each unit that is likely to be part of whatever domestic department reorganization you are going to propose, such as Natural Resources, Human Resources, Community Development, etc. This gives your department appointees a direct contact at the White House on matters that may be of less than presidential concern. It might also get the cabinet adjusted to operating in the configuration that you will ultimately propose.

National Security Council. About seventy slots. Separate appropriation. Only the assistant to the president for national security affairs is a presidential appointment on the White House payroll.

I have not made inquiries in this area because I have not felt that I had a mandate from you to receive information that may be classified. Therefore, I will limit myself to a few general comments at this time.

The NSC assistant and his staff should be "honest brokers" between the departments; they should not be operational; they should not be out front as spokesmen for the administration. This suggests two comments: picking an NSC assistant who is too prominent will make it more difficult to keep the job in low profile; and a person who is a noted expert in one area of the national security portfolio may have more trouble brokering the full mix of interests (foreign policy, international economics, defense, etc.).

Congressional relations. There are now eighteen slots. Seven are professionals: three handle the House, two the Senate, two have supervisory responsibilities for the entire operation. In addition to lobbying, the office handles a wide variety of services—arranging White House tours, dinner invitations, appointments, congressional mail, etc. Initially, your needs will be different from Ford's. Since he was a product of the Congress, his staff had to find ways to cut down his personal involvements. As an outsider, you will have to build up your links with the Hill. Thus, I do not see cutting the size of this operation; it is probably about right for your immediate needs.

Economics. There are forty on the staff of the Council of Economic Advisers and seven slots on the Economic Policy Board. (Actually, I suspect that there are more people working in this area who are buried elsewhere on the White House manning chart.) My hunch is that the Ford system works as well as it does only because of the personal relationship between the president and Alan Greenspan, and that organizationally there is much room for improvement. I will defer recommendations until I can review a few ideas with Charlie Schultze.

Personal services units. It would be necessary to know a good deal more than I do about your work habits and the people around you to give any useful advice on how to help adjust your campaign staff to the somewhat different demands of the White House. However, I should point out that a chief clerk and a career staff of 235 will be ready to assist you in the White House, handling such matters as correspondence, payroll processing, documents, messengers, etc. These people are among the most dedicated members of the federal civil service and have worked under presidents of both parties. They are also the "historical memory" of the White House Office. They know "how FDR did it"—which is often valuable information. Undoubtedly you will want to make changes, but it is relatively low priority compared with the other matters that now engage you.

President Ford cut the White House Office from about 560 to 485. This has been my first real look at the inside of the Ford White House. (My book stops with Nixon.) And even this surface exercise, as I look back over it, has suggested about 77 staff reductions. You need not be concerned that there is no room for improvement.

November 24, 1976

This White House organizational design attempts to be true to the spirit of the presidency that I expressed in my book. I deliberately did not include a specific plan in the book, and, as you know, I am reluctant to do this now because the major element in any design must be its utility in reflecting the work habits, character, priorities and needs of the president—factors that I am in a poor position to judge.

Important: this design is not meant to restrict access to the president. Access, without regard to boxes on a chart, can only be determined by the President. For example, personnel may come under the Staff Secretariat, but it would be a serious mistake not to give the director of the White House Personnel Office direct access to the president. I would suggest that you consider giving direct access to all staff titles that are underlined [italicized] in this memo.

The plan does not include a chief of staff—a decision you have already made and that I respect—but most of the functions usually given to a chief of staff will still have to be performed, regardless of titles. Many of these duties I am suggesting should go to the cabinet secretary and the staff secretary; other persons, however, can also share the duties. The key point is that a president need not have a chief of staff—he can divide the duties— but he should not be his own chief of staff. Otherwise he will find that he is spending considerable time on servicing his staff, rather than the other way around.

I am not here dealing with numbers. Yesterday's memo indicated to me that it will be easier to scale down the size of the staff than I had imagined. Moreover, the natural forces of putting together an administration in ten weeks works to keep down the initial size of the White House. The problem is to resist the pressures for growth over time.

The main thrust of this design—which distinguishes it from past White House arrangements—is that it is meant to accent that yours will be a cabinet-oriented presidency. The symbolism of this may be more important than the actual design. I am also assuming that under this type of set-up it will be more difficult to exclude the cabinet from a central place in policy deliberations.

There are two elements in considering the proper use of the cabinet. The cabinet officers, as heads of the major departments, should have the central role in advising you on the formulation of policy because they are the only ones who can implement policy, and policy formulation cannot be successfully divorced from policy implementation. The cabinet, as the collectivity of your chief advisers, should play a much more useful role than in the past. On the first point, I feel completely confident. The second point may be more of a wish—much of history points the other way. However, my experience as chief of staff to Pat Moynihan on the president's Urban Affairs Council (1969) showed me that the collective cabinet (usually working in subgroups) can be a highly effective policy-proposing body *during the first year of a new administration*. My worry is that the collective cabinet could become less useful after an administration's initial burst of energy, and it is this that must be watched carefully. At any rate, these two elements are separable; this White House design is meant to be supportive of both.

Cabinet. To include: heads of all departments plus the director of the Office of Management and Budget (OMB) and the chairman of the Council of Economic Advisers (CEA). I would also like to see the majority leaders in the House and the Senate become regular attendees of cabinet meetings. Exclude all secondary and honorific posts, such as U.S. representative to the UN.

The CEA should build in a long-range planning capacity. As the only participant inside the government without vested interests, it should be the convener of all economic advisory groups (eliminating the Economic Policy Board). The three persons on the CEA should have specialized expertise that reflects the three areas of greatest interest to the president, which are probably domestic aggregate forecasting, international economics, and the micro-cum-wage/price area. Charlie Schultze also feels that the CEA should spend less time on drafting the annual economic report, which is of interest mainly in classrooms; perhaps cutting it from 200 pages to 70. My personal impression as a noneconomist (and probably unfair) is that the two member slots on the CEA (not the chairman) have been distributed among the economics fraternity as a high-level sabbatical year, used to explore personal interests rather than the special needs of the president.

Cabinet secretariat. The suggested role of the cabinet secretariat is detailed as items 4 and 6 on pages 213–15 of [the 1976 edition of] my book. In short, it should be the link between the president and the substantive policy areas. I would like to see the National Security Council and the Domestic Council (unless it is abolished) returned to their rightful places as subgroupings of the cabinet. Other ad hoc cabinet task forces should be created from time to time, usually to prepare policy recommendations that cross departmental lines.

The *cabinet secretary* would run the operation, i.e., his job would be that of facilitator, making it as easy as possible for the president to make the maximum use of his cabinet. He would be assisted by the *deputy cabinet secretary-national security* and the *deputy cabinet secretary-domestic* (the closest the White House would come to the jobs once filled by Kissinger and Ehrlichman).

You might also have a *deputy cabinet secretary-science,* which would fold the new Office of Science and Technology into the cabinet arrangement. Since OST is just getting started, it is probably easier to shape it to your needs. The science community fought hard for its establishment, but as the most science-oriented of any recent president you would be in a good position to make a change that might be otherwise viewed with suspicion.

There are two other existing offices that should be considered in this scheme: the Council on Environmental Quality, which could be integrated into a cabinet-oriented White House, and the Office of Telecommunications Policy, which probably should be abolished. The latter must be carefully examined. I have the impression that it is bloated. While it serves a necessary role in the assignment of portions of the radio spectrum reserved for government use and in certain questions of international use of airwaves, I see no reason why this should be done in the Executive Office of the President. OTP played a mischievous role in Nixon's war on the TV networks and thus there would be a certain symbolism attached to your getting it out of your office.

You are probably aware of an interesting proposal made by Senator Mondale to create a Council of Social Advisers, which would prepare an annual social report to the president (similar to the economic report). Because of Senator Mondale's personal interest, you may wish to explore with him the feasibility of having this function performed by the vice president's office. Several attempts have been made to prepare such a document, without notable success, and the advantage of giving this assignment to the vice president is that it could be well tested without becoming institutionalized.

Staff secretariat. While the cabinet secretariat would deal with the *substantive* areas of concern, the staff secretariat would supervise the *personal services* units of the White House.

The *staff secretary* would be responsible for the administrative details of the White House operation, everything from assigning office space to cars, to the White House staff mess, to telephones. This office would oversee the work of the chief clerk, the highest careerist in the White House, whose staff handles such matters as correspondence, payroll processing, documents, and the messengers.

The staff secretary would be the primary person concerned that papers flow to you in an orderly manner, that your time is allocated in a way that best suits your purposes, and that all the proper people have commented on your requests. This office would supervise your scheduling and your daily calendar and would be in charge of your advance men. (The Ford White House uses a system of volunteers around the country, who are paid expenses but do not get salary.) All key members of the staff secretariat should have direct access to you.

The following offices would work through the staff secretariat for administrative purposes, to assure a degree of coordination, and to avoid the chaos of everyone wanting to see you at the same time. But essentially these offices work directly with you on a one-to-one basis. (As such, they could appear separately on an organizational chart if this design appears too structured for your taste.)

Offices of the *Press Secretary, Personnel Director, Legal Counsel, Congressional Relations,* and *Words* (spoken and written). You may also wish to have *special assistant(s)* to represent you to outside groups or to deal with unique problems of high presidential concern, but this is the area where the White House staff tends to grow faster than the need.

I have not included aides who work primarily as political operatives. Nixon had three (Harry Dent, John Sears, Murray Chotiner). I would discourage this arrangement. All your top people should have finely tuned political antennae as part of their mix of skills. However, you will probably have to assign someone on the staff to be your point of contact with the Democratic National Committee. You may wish to choose this person on the basis of his skills without regard to the slot he has in your White House organization.

There are a variety of other offices in the White House that must be looked at, but which do not relate directly to the "business" side of the presidency. These include the chief usher, who manages the residence; the First Lady's staff; and the Office of White House Visitors, which runs the tours. The Office of the Military Aide serves the president as commander-in-chief and as such must be considered by a person you designate to receive the appropriate security clearance. There is also the Office of the President's Physician.

P.S. To keep the record straight, I should add the standard Brookings disclaimer: all my memos to you represent my own views and should not be ascribed to others connected with the Institution.

November 30, 1976

Since many of the presidential "trappings" relate to presidential security, the Ford White House has rightly refused to give me access to this information. However, I would like to make a few general comments because my views may differ from other advice you receive.

Starting with George Reedy's *The Twilight of the Presidency*, the public has been impressed with the argument that trappings have importantly shaped the conduct of presidents. If only the trappings were eliminated, it would seem to follow, all of our problems with recent presidential behavior would also be eliminated. But the behavior of recent presidents was primarily a product of their characters, secondarily of their advisory systems. The question should be considered in the proper perspective.

This is not to argue that the trappings should not be cut down. The primary reasons this should be done are simply that they offend a good many Americans and are symbolically counterproductive to restoring trust in the presidency.

Henry Fairlie (*The New Republic*, November 27) writes: "Surely the Secret Service protection of Presidents—to say nothing of presidential candidates—has gone beyond the stage of mere farce, and become a threat to democracy." Before acting in this area, may I suggest two things that you should do personally.

First, read a random sample of the crank letters you receive. In 1961–62 I had the opportunity to see the threats that were sent to General Eisenhower, who was both in retirement and the most respected man in the nation. There are, unfortunately, unbalanced people whose capacity to injure a president must be taken seriously.

Second, have the head of the White House Secret Service Unit and your military aide discuss with you in detail what they do to try to give adequate protection. Their interests may not be the same as Mr. Fairlie's, but they are not frivolous.

You should not become a captive of your protectors. Yet before determining the degree of protection you require, it is necessary to understand the extent of the problem and the technical details necessary for dedicated professionals to carry out their assignments.

Then, too, some trappings may help a president bear his responsibilities. (Look at a succession of photographs of any president over time and watch the lines become firmly etched in his face.) A president should be able to walk in the woods on a weekend if it helps him restore his spirit or rethink his concerns. Herbert Hoover and John Kennedy were able to buy themselves rustic retreats, but should we have to count on a president being rich? I have never been inside Camp David; judge for yourself whether it is too opulent. Do not dismantle it until you have determined that it does not serve a legitimate need.

What has disturbed me about recent presidents has not been so much the trappings as the lack of *taste*. And by taste I do not mean High Culture; quite the contrary, taste means to me that a president creates an environment that is *natural* to him. The point might be best made by several examples:

—In 1969 a New York society decorator turned the Oval Office into what my children described as "a movie set." They did not mean it as a compliment and they were right. There were presidential seals in gold on all the seat cushions. There were symbols of office—rather than books—in the bookshelves. It all looked too unlived in. No visitor could possibly feel at ease in that office. The office said: I am the President; you are my guest; we are not equal. It was a question of taste, not money.

—All presidents give small gifts to visitors and friends. Kennedy gave PT-boat tie clasps. Johnson and Nixon gave tie clasps and other items emblazoned with the presidential seal. This overuse of the seal along with its use on mundane items was in poor taste, in my opinion. (It strikes me that in the humble peanut you have a possible personal symbol that gives off the right image.)

—Or Nixon's Sunday prayer sessions. Nixon had not been a church-goer; his attempts at religiosity therefore were forced and unnatural. For a different president this might have been tasteful (although it raises questions of separation of church and state), but for Nixon it was out of character and so perceived by many people.

In one area, however, Nixon's symbolic gestures were unerringly correct. I refer to his support of the arts—such as lending his presence to a fundraiser for the Philadelphia Symphony Orchestra, his birthday party for Duke Ellington, and the Andrew Wyeth exhibition at the White House. Presidents should encourage excellence. Your interests and background suggest that you might consider similar gestures in recognition of scientific achievement. For example, you might award the Presidential Medal of Freedom to Norman Borlaug (if it has not already been given to him.)

This award is our highest civilian honor and as close as we come to having a Queen's Honors List. A list of past recipients should be prepared for you. You should make use of the award to help set standards of excellence in our society, but it should not be given so often as to debase the currency.

You have already made two decisions that fit my definition of tasteful symbolism, namely the decision to have a modest inauguration and the decision to send your daughter to a Washington public school.

A president might hold press conferences in open collar (rather than tie and jacket) during the sweltering Washington summers. He might ask the reporters not to stand up when he enters the room. In both cases (and all cases), the question should be: Would these be natural acts that flow from the character of the president?

December 1, 1976

One problem with government organization-structure questions—especially in the White House—is that after the initial effort to straighten out the boxes on the chart, the organizer (president) rarely looks back again. (There are simply too many other matters to engage his attention.)

But the boxes represent people. People change. They get tired. They develop strong or weak relationships with other people. They are replaced by people with different talents. At the same time, new boxes get added and sometimes old boxes are eliminated. The result is that over time the organization that once appeared to work no longer seems to work as well.

The White House organization should be freshly examined periodically—perhaps every six months (certainly once a year).

Who should do the reexamining?

A case can be made for an insider who knows the players, their strong and weak points, the rivalries and the alliances, and, particularly, the president's needs. Such a person might be an elder statesman type without other staff responsibilities. But the tendency would be to pull such a person into the web of government, giving him a personal stake.

I think the stronger case can be made for an outsider, someone with stature, wisdom, government experience, and no ambition to become a permanent part of the enterprise. I have tried to resist making personnel suggestions (except for illustrative purposes), but I do have a candidate for this assignment. He is Don Price, dean of the John F. Kennedy School of Government at Harvard, and a noted authority on government organization (from his days on the Hoover Commission staff). Moreover, as a southerner he might have a special rapport with your presidency. (I have not discussed this idea with him nor do I plan to.)

December 2, 1976

In making your objective for White House reorganization clearly understood, it would be useful if your advisers (and eventually the press) had a visible and easily comprehensible model to refer to.

Schematically, there have been two White House models in the past; I now suggest a third for your administration.

Circle. Used by FDR and JFK. The president at the hub with staff impinging on him from all points along the circumference. The model can work well in running small enterprises (such as the White House during the early New Deal), but tends to create undue chaos and confusion in the modern presidency, especially over time as new people are added to the staff who lack established working relationships with each other and the president.

Pyramid. Used by Eisenhower and Nixon. The president at the apex. Extremely orderly, but may tend to screen out creativity and can lead to excessive secrecy. Only advisable for presidents who have long experience with this model (as did Ike in the military).

Isosceles Trapezoid. (A pyramid with its top sawed off.) The model proposed for Jimmy Carter. Allows wide access to the president in a structured setting. This assumes that you are a highly methodical person who will be ultimately dissatisfied with incomplete staff work or tangled lines of communications, while, at the same time, will wish not to be overly dependent on a small number of aides and as open as possible in your conduct of the presidency.

For shorthand purposes, the new Carter model could be presented as a system of "open efficiency" or "orderly access."

December 7, 1976

You ask about putting the Office of Special Representative for Trade Negotiations in Treasury. The special representative was created by congressional act in 1962; the Office of Special Representative was created in the 1974 act. The function was put in the Executive Office of the President because the fights between Commerce and State and later between Treasury and State were so bitter that it was felt that neutral ground was necessary. While I share the view that as many units as possible should be removed from the Executive Office, I have no feeling that this one has worked badly in its present location (perhaps because so much of the special representative's work and staff is in Geneva). Since an attempt to change the law might lead to a prolonged fight (in the bureaucracy and Congress), I think [you] should seriously consider whether the fight will be worth the effort.

December 8, 1976

I was so anxious to put the question of "trappings" in the proper perspective in an earlier memo that I may have given a false impression that there are no unnecessary perquisites of high office. This memo gives a few examples to suggest otherwise.

The National Park Service maintains houses in resort areas throughout the country that are available to White House staff and ranking department officials at a very nominal cost. For example, there are two in the Virgin Islands. (These houses were not built by the government; they were included in land purchases.) You could instruct Interior to close them if you feel government should get out of this business or you could have them made available to the public on a first-come basis.

The extensive use of an official White House photographer was LBJ's contribution to the Excessive Presidency. Obviously the commercial media provide a full photographic record of a president's days in office. The only thing the White House photographer does that press photographers do not do is to photograph the president with each visitor in the Oval Office. These photographs are autographed and sent to the visitors. While this practice has a political utility, its governmental utility is questionable. Thought should be given to abolishing or greatly contracting the White House photographer's office. (By the way, the White House carpentry shop frames photographs for staff members for free or possibly for a small charge.)

Under Eisenhower the offices of presidential aides were drab and governmental-looking; by the end of the Nixon administration they had become truly elegant with TV sets, rich draperies, well-upholstered sofas and easy chairs. Thought should be given to putting a freeze on redecorating White House staff offices.

Someone should look into the "national health service" that is provided to high officials. They are eligible for executive suites at the Bethesda Naval Hospital, where, I suspect, the cost to them is considerably less than the commercial rates. A legitimate question is whether they should not use the same facilities as other citizens.

There is a very minor service that serves a useful purpose. The national art galleries will loan paintings for White House offices. This is one way to show symbolic support for the arts at no cost. For instance, when I was deputy assistant to the president for urban affairs I filled my office walls with borrowed paintings by black artists. Each artist received a letter of thanks, hoping that they would get satisfaction from knowing that one of their works was being admired and was on display at the White House. I encourage your staff to avail themselves of this opportunity—it may even increase their productivity to be surrounded by beauty!

For the moment I am not going to go into the more obvious trappings (swimming pool, tennis court, movie theatre, bowling alley, White House mess) but I rather doubt that this will be my last word to you on this subject.

December 13, 1976

In discussing the role of vice president in the presidential organization, two points need to be made at the outset.

1. None of these comments are meant to reflect negatively on Senator Mondale. I hope you will share this memo with him.

2. These thoughts are meant to be in keeping with general commitments you made during the campaign. The question is how to make the best use of the vice president.

You have learned the usefulness of Senator Mondale's advice during the transition. While this is a unique period during which his detailed knowledge of Washington must be particularly valuable, there should be ways to continue this close relationship in office. The problem, of course, is that all the experiences of history suggest the difficulty of properly using the vice president. A brief review helps make this point:

—LBJ tried to use Hubert Humphrey's senatorial experience by initially giving him a well-advertised role in congressional lobbying. This led to confusion with the White House Congressional Relations Office as commitments and communications kept getting crossed. Furthermore, some senators resented being lobbied by the body's presiding officer, even one who was as popular as Humphrey.

—Nixon put Agnew in charge of relations with the governors and mayors (again trying to take advantage of a vice president's background). This too was a failure, although it may have been caused by the incompetence of Agnew's Office of Intergovernmental Relations.

—Ford put Rockefeller in charge of the Domestic Council, making him theoretically his chief domestic adviser. This was the worst failure of all. Predictably, Ford could not take all of Rockefeller's advice; the press played up their differences; tensions mushroomed between their staffs; Ford ultimately dropped Rockefeller from the ticket.

—All presidents have created make-work for their vice presidents. Eisenhower put Nixon in charge of a committee on civil rights enforcement in government contracts; Kennedy put Johnson in charge of the Space

Council; Humphrey and Agnew chaired a committee on American Indian Opportunities. These are very peripheral activities; ordinarily they would be handled by a departmental secretary and redelegated to a subcabinet official.

The silliest idea of all—proposed in a *New York Times* op-ed piece last week—is to make the vice president a departmental secretary. The notion of the presiding officer of the Senate also running an executive operating agency is either unconstitutional or very close to it.

How then to take advantage of a vice president's wisdom as an adviser (without creating frictions which come from giving him operational responsibilities) and how to prepare a vice president for possibly assuming the presidency (when the vice president is outside the orbit of responsibilities that draw people into the presidential circle)?

These are some strategies that might help to counter the centrifugal pulls:

—Give the vice president the office space in the White House currently occupied by the chief of staff. (This, obviously, underscores your desire not to have a chief of staff. It also prevents any staff claimant to the office from exercising squatter's rights.) This has the disadvantage of separating the vice president from most of his personal staff and the advantage of making it easier to call the vice president into your office for information sharing.

—Make sure that all staff and department papers that go to you will also go to the vice president. At the least, this would be a valuable part of the vice president's education; at best, it would help make him an automatic fail-safe adviser.

—He should be vice chairman of every cabinet group you chair. As such, he would be invited to all meetings and would chair meetings in your absence.

—Continue two useful practices. Use the vice president as your political party surrogate. When used for campaigning and fund-raising purposes, he relieves some of the strain that comes from a president's having to be a leader of his party and leader of all the people at the same time. Use the vice president for foreign goodwill/fact-finding missions, particularly to countries that you are least likely to visit yourself. This technique could be expanded into the domestic field. By encouraging the vice president to meet with the many groups that deserve high-level attention—especially if you remove the "offices of special pleaders" from the White House—this would be one way to fill a need without concern about presidential staff becoming co-opted. (At the same time, naturally, the vice president should not build a staff for this purpose.)

The most important rule of thumb, in my opinion, is to resist the temptation to give the vice president any assignments that the president would not assume himself if he had the time.

December 23, 1976

In an earlier memo I mentioned that much of the legal work for the president should be performed by the Office of Legal Counsel in the Department of Justice. A short but thorough article on the office has come to my attention and I am attaching three copies. It was written by Frank Wozencraft, who headed the office under President Johnson. I think the article raises serious questions about which (if any) functions could be better performed in the White House proper. This suggests that the most careful attention must be given to a job description before the appointment of a White House Legal Counsel.

Wozencraft details at least five important services that OLC will perform for a president and his staff:

—Legal opinions on all legislative proposals that the administration may wish to send to Congress; legal opinions on proposed executive orders and presidential proclamations.

—Recommendations on whether the president should veto or sign bills passed by Congress.

—Conflict-of-interest questions within the administration.

—All legal research for the White House, including whether the president has constitutional or statutory authority to act.

—Resolution of legal disputes between agencies.

Judge Bell and Mr. Lipshutz may wish to solicit additional information from Mr. Wozencraft.

December 28, 1976

Enclosed is a briefing book on the president's responsibility for the District of Columbia. This was prepared by James Devall, a partner in the Washington law firm of Zuckert, Scoutt & Rasenberger, in consultation with the Executive Committee of Self-Determination for D.C., a national coalition of fifty-three organizations, including the League of Women Voters, NAACP, American Civil Liberties Union, and Common Cause. The president of the coalition is Sterling Tucker, who is also chairman of the D.C. City Council.

I have carefully reviewed this material and find it of a high quality. It could well form the core of a presidential message to Congress. (I should add that the proposal for congressional representation is a plank in the 1976 Democratic platform.) It also graphically illustrates the sort of functions that have unnecessarily involved the president and his staff in recent years. Two examples: the president is now required to review local legislation that has been passed by the city council and vetoed by the mayor; the president appoints local D.C. judges, rather than the mayor with advice and consent of the city council. The briefing book, quite rightly, does not recommend a special assistant at the White House for District affairs.

January 4, 1977

Your transition team's "White House Study Project, Report No. 2" presents you with sensible designs for streamlining the Executive Office of the President (EOP).

I am in agreement with abolishing the following units: Federal Property Council, Energy Resources Council, Council on International Economic Policy, Office of Drug Abuse, and Office of Telecommunication Policy (OTP). The proposal for redistributing the functions of OTP is particularly creative.

One of the two intelligence monitoring units should be eliminated. Before you make a decision, however, it might be useful to have the case presented for retaining the President's Foreign Intelligence Advisory Board (PFIAB) instead of the Intelligence Oversight Board (IOB). This is not an area in which I have any special expertise. Yet my hunch is that the PFIAB offers a stronger base to build on than does the IOB. I am at a loss to suggest who could give you the most dispassionate advice. You will certainly be consulting with Ted Sorensen (who worked closely with the PFIAB during the Kennedy administration) and you may wish to talk with Clark Cifford and Nelson Rockefeller as well.

My own feeling about the work of the Council on Environmental Quality (CEQ) is less generous than that of your transition team. You might consider another option for redistributing CEQ's functions along the lines prescribed for OTP: operational responsibilities to the Environmental Protection Agency (EPA) and advisory responsibilities to the Office of Science and Technology Policy (OSTP). This has the advantage of eliminating one more unit in EOP and strengthening the science adviser's portfolio. A disadvantage would be the further unease of those who are already concerned by your creation of a special assistant for energy. Ultimately, however, the acceptability of this option would depend heavily on how the environmentalists view your appointments to the EPA and OSTP posts. CEQ has now been in business under two presidents and has not met their needs. (This, of course, may say more about the deficiencies of Nixon and Ford than it does about CEQ.) But by making early appointments to CEQ it is probable that you will be locked into retaining it instead of merely "buying time." I would suggest that you ask either OMB or some outsiders (such as Don Price and Dick Neustadt) to study this further.

I agree with your transition team's proposals to retain the office of Special Representative for Trade Negotiations and the Council on Wage and Price Stability (at least until September). Retaining the National Security Council, the Office of Management and Budget, and the Office of Science and Technology Policy are taken as givens.

Whether you prefer option one (abolish Domestic Council, replace with ad hoc meetings) or option two (create Domestic Policy Council as working cabinet committee) may be largely a matter of personal taste. I am not sure that the end would be very different. The keys to success under either arrangement would be the same: a. Unswerving presidential support for working through the cabinet. Will you continue to overlook the serious provocations to operate otherwise? b. The quality of the cabinet. Will your department heads prove to be the people who give the best advice and with whom you have the strongest relations? c. The ability of the White House staff members assigned to facilitating cabinet deliberations. Will they be skillful enough to keep the cabinet system running smoothly and fairly? My own preference is in favor of option two only because its structure may make it more difficult to push the cabinet off the center stage.

The problem of excessive use of a cabinet member's time (an argument for option one) is something of a red herring if one accepts the collegial presidency model since presidential advising, by definition, becomes one of the most important duties of a cabinet member. There are exceptions, of course. It is probable that the secretary of state, for instance, would delegate most of his economic advising responsibilities to the under secretary for economic affairs. But when you choose secretaries of labor and commerce who are respected economists (the first time, I feel sure, that these posts are held simultaneously by professional economists), the premise of collegial government is to make maximum use of their talents beyond their narrow jurisdictions.

Transition Planning
1980

This memorandum was prepared for the Republican presidential nominee in 1980 at the request of Bill Brock, chairman of the Republican National Committee.

May 22, 1980

Between your election on November 4 and your inauguration on January 20, you and your staff will have to turn a campaign into an administration. It's an incredibly difficult task. It always gets done, of course, but there should be ways to lower the risks of mistakes made under pressure and fatigue, and to give you a greater opportunity to take advantage of the national goodwill that exists in the early months of a new presidency.

This memorandum is meant to suggest what transition work should be done before your election, what should not be done, who might do it, who should not do it, and how it could be best done. While it notes activities that have to be undertaken between your election and when you take office, it does not deal with how you may wish to organize this enterprise.

—Pre-election transition work should not propose policy.

—Pre-election transition work should not propose personnel.

These two rules must be inviolate: even the hint that a transition group is "writing policy" or "picking people" will cause a maelstrom of dissension within the campaign organization, sure to be the subject of much divisive speculation.

—Nothing must distract you or your staff from the immediate task at hand, winning the election.

This means that those doing pre-election transition work should be people whom you would not otherwise be using in the campaign.

—Those doing pre-election transition work should make it clear to the public that their mandate formally ends with the submission of the material to the president-elect on the day after the election.

Moreover, if possible, people recruited for pre-election transition work—and especially the chairman of the group—should indicate that they do not plan to hold permanent positions in your government.

In other words, it must be shown in every way that the pre-election working group has been set up to help prepare your staff people, not to supersede them after they have helped you win the election.

(This is the lesson of Carter's 1976 transition planning. It proved almost worthless because of feuds and jockeying for position between the pre-election transition group in Atlanta under Jack Watson and the candidate's personnel staff under Hamilton Jordan.)

—No campaign funds should be diverted to pre-election transition work.

Rather, a ruling should be sought immediately from the Federal Election Commission allowing private money to be raised for the sole purpose of transition planning.

It should be argued that transition work before the election can and will be kept entirely separate from the campaign; none of the transition work will be turned over to the candidate and his staff until after the election. (In 1976 the FEC denied Carter the right to raise money for transition planning because such funds would have constituted illegal campaign gifts. I feel we can make a much more persuasive case for private funding today.)

While it still will be possible to go forward without funds by using volunteers, this would measurably change the nature and utility of the product. Volunteers produce advice (*viz* this memo!); staff produce facts.

Either way, however, a serious attempt should be made to seek cooperation from the president for access to certain nonclassified data. A precedent is in the national security briefings that are offered to the out-party presidential nominee. If pre-election transition work has to be done by volunteers, the availability of government information becomes particularly important. Indeed, if such assistance is not forthcoming, you should consider attacking Carter for playing politics with what is essentially a matter of good government.

—The pre-election transition group should be located in Washington. It should make maximum use of those who have had experience in past Republican administrations as well as Republican congressional staff members.

—There should be a steering committee whose members include heads of organizations with resources that can be made available (office space, secretarial help, researchers).

—Immediately after the national convention, the person you designate to chair this group should sit down with you and your top advisers for an extended discussion of what information, in what form, you wish to have at the minute you become president-elect. Your chairman should not need to contact you again until he presents you with the briefing books (probably election night), but you and your top aides should pass along additional requests for information.

There are various types of information that can be gathered for you while you and your staff are busy campaigning and that will be ready when you are.

Examples:

—Job descriptions for every position to be filled in the Executive Branch at the level of assistant secretary and above.

—A chronological list of the expiration dates of all term appointments, notably at the regulatory agencies.

—Working out a plan(s) for most efficiently and effectively setting up a personnel selection operation after the election—the outline of a process, not a list of names.

—An annotated list of all laws that will be expiring during the first year of your administration.

—Assessments of the most immediate problems in each agency during the first six months of your administration.

—A review of possible reorganization plans.

—Documentation on what will be necessary to translate each of your campaign statements into draft legislation, executive orders, or other forms of implementation.

While all these items and more can be helpful—and should be available to you—they will not provide guidance for what order things should be done in, what must be done at once and what can wait, how long certain decisions can be deferred, and what are the consequences of taking certain actions quickly.

In a sense, you are immediately faced with three-dimensional decision-making: there are people decisions, structure decisions, policy decisions. If you decide first on a person, you may become locked into a structure and/or a policy. Presidents-elect always make people decisions first, then rue many of the consequences.

Would it not be useful to think through what are the fewest people decisions that can be made immediately after the election and still not foreclose any important options? In the first week, need you pick more than your White House chief of staff, press secretary, and personal secretary? What jobs are necessary but might be given on a temporary basis, such as liaison with OMB and NSC?

Assuming that you will want to get on with appointments, as have your predecessors, are there not ways to group together the consideration of certain jobs so as to keep policy and structure in mind at the same time? For example, by concentrating first on the triangle of State-Defense-NSC? This mode of arranging your decisions can help you think about what you want of each agency and what qualities you most desire in a secretary of state, a secretary of defense, and a national security assistant. The same principle would apply to thinking about the key economics positions.

Other factors enter into the appointing process: Do you want to give your cabinet officers the authority to choose their own deputy/under/assistant secretaries? Are there any jobs that can be best filled by setting up search committees? How much conflict/consensus do you wish to build into your advisory system? What sort of commitments do you want to get from your appointees? When you do not have specific people in mind, what are the most useful questions to ask of candidates for each top job? What positions do you wish to abolish? What precedents need be considered, such as a western governor for secretary of the interior? What part do you want Republican members of Congress and the Republican National Committee to play in people decisions? How do you want to go about screening candidates for conflicts of interest and other disqualifying characteristics? There needs to be a strategy for the announcement of appointments. Will you reveal cabinet selections as they are made, in clusters, or all at the same time (à la Nixon in 1968)?

During this period other things are going on: you will have to set up a transition headquarters. Where? (Carter made a mistake in choosing

Plains.) You now will be receiving federal funds for transition purposes, and procedures have to be worked out for budgeting and dispersal. There will have to be a meeting at the White House with the president. What should you ask him for? What might he ask of you? Arrangements will have to be made in case there is a crisis during the interregnum. Other nations—friends and adversaries—will await some sign from you, if only symbolic. Should you send a special emissary abroad as Nixon did in 1968? You will want to take a vacation—even this will require thought and planning, and is subject to misinterpretations in the press. Task forces that you set up during the campaign start reporting in; you may also wish to form other short-term policy advisory groups. Attention will have to be given to how you wish to make use of your vice president. Your campaign staff will have to be phased out and work found for many of them in the transition. But how to fit the skills needed in a campaign organization to the skills needed in a government organization? Special-interest groups will ask to meet with you and will ask for representation on your White House staff or other types of preferment. You will wish to know in advance how different presidents have handled these matters. You will meet with the congressional leadership. Will you want to follow the new executive-congressional practices on the appointment of judges? What should be your posture toward congressional Democrats, especially if they are still in the majority? Arrangements will have to be made for the inauguration. What tone do you want for the ceremonies? An inaugural address must be prepared. Probably the writing of no other speech will take so much of your time. The preparation of Carter's last budget must be monitored and areas where you wish to make changes noted.

Planning must start for a legislative program and possibly early messages to Congress. This will relate to how fast a start you wish to make after January 20. Do you want the equivalent of FDR's 100 days? You may wish to make some overture to the civil service. (Nixon did a swing around the departments: probably not worth the effort.) You may wish to ask certain Carter officials to stay on for a limited period. Which ones? Transition staff and operations must be phased out. There must be careful planning for the first days in the White House. Formal nominations must be sent to Congress, a swearing-in ceremony for cabinet officers, a first cabinet meeting, a first press conference by the new president. How often do you want the cabinet to meet? How often do you wish to hold press conferences? Where do you want to hold your press conferences? East Room of the White

House? Indian Treaty Room of the Executive Office Building? State Department auditorium? What pictures do you want on the walls of the cabinet room? Which past president's desk do you want in the Oval Office? How do you want to allocate office space among your staff? Which aides will be in the east wing, west wing, New Executive Office Building, Old Executive Office Building? There are dozens of minor decisions, yet each one takes on some degree of importance because it is made by you and commented upon by the press, within the government, around the country and the world. The portraits of presidents you choose for the cabinet room are written about as indicating your "role models." Who gets an office in the basement or on the first floor "reflects the White House power structure."

All of these decisions do not have to be made by you, of course. But all of these early actions are viewed as clues as to what kind of president you will be. As such, they will demand more of your personal attention than comparable decisions taken at a later date.

Moreover, sometime during this period there will be a goof-up: a post will be given to someone who turns out to be an embarrassment; some appointee says something that is regrettable; a rumor gets into the press that causes unexpected problems. The more that can be anticipated, the less chance of a goof-up.

The above is not an all-inclusive list of what you will have to do during the transition period. These are illustrations. They are meant to recall the range and types of decisions that have to be made.

They are also meant to suggest that someone or some group should be thinking about these matters from your perspective. There will be briefing papers prepared for you by the federal agencies and outside groups—no shortage of information and proposals. But none of this will be tailored for your special needs.

This memo argues that in addition to the standard technical papers that can be prepared for you, the most useful pre-election transition work should be in the form of *an annotated checklist in time sequence* of everything that must be done by you between November 4 and January 20.

The arrangement of decisions by time blocks—from week 1 through week 11—is critical; it will suggest the interrelationships between the actions that must be taken.

Annotating each action item means that all options and relevant information will be inserted in the checklist at the point a decision is called for.

At a minimum, this exercise should give your staff a starting point and a fresh way of looking at what must be accomplished before taking office; at most, the pre-election transition group could save you the month of November. If it does its job well, you and your staff on election night could be at a point that past presidents-elect have not arrived at until the beginning of December.

Notes

Chapter One

1. William D. Carey, "Presidential Staffing in the Sixties and Seventies," *Public Administration Review*, vol. 39 (September–October 1969), p. 454.

2. Important exceptions, however, discussed in subsequent chapters, include Reagan's creative invention of cabinet councils during his first term; George H.W. Bush's use of his national security adviser, Brent Scowcroft, as an "honest broker" among competing departments; and Clinton's National Economic Council, whose first director, Robert Rubin, successfully blended advice from various government sources.

3. See Bradley H. Patterson Jr., *The White House Staff* (Brookings, 2000), pp. 347–48. Patterson computes the size of the White House Office at 721 (see items 2, 5, 6); the National Security Council staff at 190; and the Office of the Vice President at 144.

4. While this book's narrative reflects the gender of presidents to date, it should be expected that there also will be female presidents in the future.

Chapter Two

1. Of the modern presidents only Franklin Roosevelt and George H. W. Bush had ever served as political executives in Washington.

2. See Richard E. Neustadt, *Presidential Power* (Wiley, 1976), p. 266; and John H. Kessel, *The Domestic Presidency* (Duxbury, 1975), p. 10.

3. Quoted in Arthur M. Schlesinger Jr., *A Thousand Days* (Houghton Mifflin, 1965), p. 127.

4. Consider, for example, Roosevelt's court-packing plan (1937), Kennedy's approval of the Bay of Pigs invasion (1961), and Johnson's decision to escalate the Vietnam War (1965).

5. Ray S. Baker and William F. Dodd, eds., *The Public Papers of Woodrow Wilson*, vol. 1 (Harper, 1926), p. 222.

6. President Reagan was exceptional in that his approval rating was higher at the time of his second inaugural. See Gary King and Lyn Ragsdale, *The Elusive Executive: Discovering Statistical Patterns in the Presidency* (CQ Press, 1988), pp. 305–07.

7. Unidentified adviser quoted in Thomas E. Cronin, *The State of the Presidency* (Little, Brown, 1975), p. 184.

8. The only modern presidents to have their parties gain seats in a midterm election were Franklin Roosevelt in 1934 and Bill Clinton in 1998.

9. Quoted in Harry McPherson, *A Political Education* (Atlantic Monthly Press, 1972), p. 268.

10. Quoted in Theodore C. Sorensen, *Kennedy* (Harper and Row, 1965), p. 509.

11. Quoted in Norman Mailer, *St. George and the Godfather* (New American Library, 1972), p. 120.

12. Quoted in Joseph C. Goulden, *The Superlawyers* (Dell, 1973), pp. 87–88.

13. Milton S. Eisenhower, *The President Is Calling* (Doubleday, 1974), p. 155.

14. *Public Papers of the Presidents, Richard Nixon, 1970* (Government Printing Office, 1971), p. 410.

15. See John H. Kessel, *Presidential Parties* (Dorsey, 1984), pp. 63–65.

16. Quoted in Arthur M. Schlesinger Jr., *The Age of Roosevelt*, vol. 3: *The Politics of Upheaval* (Houghton Mifflin, 1966), p. 513.

17. John Pierson, "Is a Second Term Always Downhill?" *Wall Street Journal*, January 4, 1973, has claimed, however, that Theodore Roosevelt's second term was uphill and that the second terms of Coolidge and Eisenhower were no worse than their first terms.

18. Harold J. Laski, *The American Presidency* (Harper, 1940), p. 65.

19. James David Barber, *The Presidential Character* (Prentice-Hall, 1972), p. 11.

Chapter Three

1. State, War, Treasury, Post Office, Justice, Navy, Interior, Agriculture, Commerce, and Labor. There had been no change in departmental structure since 1913, when Commerce and Labor were divided into separate departments.

2. Raymond Moley, *After Seven Years* (Harper, 1939), p. 128.

3. Anne O'Hare McCormick, "Roosevelt's View of the Big Job," *New York Times Magazine*, September 11, 1932.

4. Moley, *After Seven Years*, p. 110.

5. Samuel I. Rosenman, *Working with Roosevelt* (Harper, 1952), p. 205.

6. Quoted in Louis W. Koenig, *The Invisible Presidency* (Rinehart, 1960), p. 308.

7. Russell Lord, *The Wallaces of Iowa* (Houghton Mifflin, 1947), p. 358.

8. Rexford G. Tugwell, *The Democratic Roosevelt* (Doubleday, 1957), p. 333.

9. Quoted in Arthur M. Schlesinger Jr., *The Coming of the New Deal* (Houghton Mifflin, 1958), p. 515.

10. James MacGregor Burns, *Roosevelt: The Soldier of Freedom* (Harcourt Brace Jovanovich, 1970), p. 60.

11. See Carl Marcy, *Presidential Commissions* (New York: King's Crown, 1945).

12. Quoted in Richard Polenberg, *Reorganizing Roosevelt's Government* (Harvard University Press, 1966), pp. 179–80.

13. Leo C. Rosten, *The Washington Correspondents* (1937; reprint edition, Arno, 1974), p. 348.

14. John Gunther, *Roosevelt in Retrospect* (Harper, 1950), p. 22.

15. Leo C. Rosten, "President Roosevelt and the Washington Correspondents," *Public Opinion Quarterly*, vol. 1 (January 1937), p. 39. See also Edward S. Corwin, *The President: Office and Powers, 1787–1957* (New York University Press, 1957), p. 470.

16. Frank Freidel, *Franklin D. Roosevelt: The Triumph* (Little, Brown, 1956), p. 51.

17. Quoted in Elmer E. Cornwell Jr., *Presidential Leadership of Public Opinion* (Indiana University Press, 1965), p. 261. On the fireside chats, see Arthur M. Schlesinger Jr., *A Thousand Days* (Houghton Mifflin, 1965), p. 715.

18. Robert E. Sherwood, *Roosevelt and Hopkins* (Harper, 1948), p. 214.

19. Rosenman, *Working with Roosevelt*, pp. 333–40.

20. Ickes and Stimson are quoted in Richard F. Fenno Jr., *The President's Cabinet: An Analysis in the Period from Wilson to Eisenhower* (Harvard University Press, 1959), pp. 125, 138.

21. Rosenman, *Working with Roosevelt*, p. 357.

22. Martin Tolchin and Susan Tolchin, *To the Victor . . . Political Patronage from the Clubhouse to the White House* (Random House, 1971), p. 257.

23. President's Committee on Administrative Management, *Administrative Management in the Government of the United States* (Government Printing Office, 1937), pp. 2, 5 (hereafter referred to as Brownlow report). Also see Harvey C. Mansfield, "Federal Executive Reorganization: Thirty Years of Experience," *Public Administration Review*, vol. 29 (July–August 1969), p. 234.

24. George A. Graham, "The Presidency and the Executive Office of the President," *Journal of Politics*, vol. 12 (November 1950), p. 600.

25. Brownlow report, p. 5.

26. See Herbert Emmerich, *Essays on Federal Reorganization* (University of Alabama Press, 1950), pp. 26–27.

27. Executive Order 8248 (September 8, 1939) also included in the president's Executive Office an Office of Government Reports to serve as a clearinghouse for collecting and disseminating information. This was consolidated into the Office of War Information in 1942. Two other short-lived additions to the Executive Office were the Committee for Congested Production Areas (1943–44) and the War Refugees Board (1944–45).

28. Sherwood, *Roosevelt and Hopkins*, p. 741.

29. Edward H. Hobbs, *Behind the President* (Washington: Public Affairs Press, 1954), p. 79.

30. Luther Gulick, "War Organization of the Federal Government," *American Political Science Review*, vol. 38 (December 1944), p. 1174.

31. The authority for creating the OWM was contained in Roosevelt's landmark executive order of September 8, 1939, which stated that "in the event of a national emergency, or threat of a national emergency, such office for emergency management as the President shall determine" was to be set up in the Executive Office.

32. Burns, *Roosevelt: The Soldier of Freedom*, pp. 452–53.

33. Roger Jones, quoted at a Conference on the Institutional Presidency, National Academy of Public Administration, March 1974.

Chapter Four

1. Richard E. Neustadt, *Presidential Power* (Wiley, 1960), pp. 171–79.

2. Richard E. Neustadt, "The Presidency at Mid-Century," *Law and Contemporary Problems*, vol. 21 (Autumn 1956), p. 641.

3. A subsequent national chairman, J. Howard McGrath, was appointed attorney general in 1949, beginning a new tradition that suggested that perhaps a more desirable kind of patronage was available through the Justice Department than through the postal system.

4. See Harold F. Gosnell, *Truman's Crises: A Political Biography of Harry S. Truman* (Westport, Conn.: Greenwood Press, 1980), pp. 228–34, 283–92, 416–21.

5. Harry S. Truman, *Memoirs*, vol. 1: *Years of Decision* (Doubleday, 1955), pp. 12–13, 329, 546.

6. Ibid., pp. 328, 546; and Truman, *Memoirs*, vol. 2: *Years of Trial and Hope* (Doubleday, 1956), pp. 104–05.

7. Quoted in Cabell Phillips, *The Truman Presidency* (Penguin, 1969), p. 133. Also see Gosnell, *Truman's Crises*, pp. 292–95, 421–23.

8. Quoted in Phillips, *Truman Presidency*, pp. 163–64. Also see Robert J. Donovan, *Conflict and Crisis: The Presidency of Harry S. Truman, 1945–48* (Norton, 1977), pp. 271–72.

9. Quoted in Patrick Anderson, *The Presidents' Men* (Doubleday, 1968), p. 115.

10. At a conference of Truman administration officials held in May 1977, several participants took sharp exception with this interpretation. See Francis H. Heller, ed., *The Truman White House: The Administration of the Presidency, 1945–1953* (Lawrence: Regents Press of Kansas, 1980), especially pp. 36–37, 48.

11. Ithiel de Sola Pool, "Inquiries beyond Watergate," *Society*, vol. 10 (September–October 1973), p. 25.

12. See Stanley Kelley Jr., *Professional Public Relations and Political Power* (Johns Hopkins Press, 1956), p. 174; also see Robert J. Donovan, *Tumultuous Years: The Presidency of Harry S. Truman, 1949–53* (Norton, 1982), pp. 114–27.

13. See John Hersey, "Mr. President," *New Yorker* (April 7, 14, 21, 28, and May 5, 1951).

14. See Abraham Holtzman, *Legislative Liaison* (Rand-McNally, 1970), pp. 232–33. Also see Ken Hechler, *Working with Truman: A Personal Memoir of the White House Years* (Putnam's, 1982), pp. 153–56.

15. Quoted in James F. Pollard, *The Presidents and the Press: Truman to Johnson* (Washington: Public Affairs Press, 1964), pp. 43, 48.

16. Truman, *Years of Trial and Hope*, pp. 36–37, 33–34.

17. Richard E. Neustadt, "Presidency and Legislation: The Growth of Central Clearance," *American Political Science Review*, vol. 48 (September 1954), pp. 659, 660, 661. Also see Donovan, *Conflict and Crisis*, p. 269.

18. There were three other additions to the Executive Office during the Truman administration.

The telecommunications adviser to the president was created by Executive Order 10297 (October 9, 1951); its functions were transferred to the Office of Defense Mobilization by Executive Order 10460 (June 16, 1953).

The Office of Defense Mobilization was created by Executive Order 10193 (December 16, 1950) and charged with the direction and coordination of federal agency activities during the Korean War. Its functions were transferred to the new Office of Defense Mobilization by Reorganization Plan 3 of 1953. The ODM, first under the direction of Charles E. Wilson of General Electric, was given broader powers than James Byrnes had had during World War II. Its authority extended to assigning functions, issuing directives, and requiring reports from any agency, including the cabinet departments, on matters of mobilization. John Steelman and an associate later wrote, "Possibly no other legal act of either the Congress or the president ever came so close to the actual creation of an assistant president"; see Steelman and H. Dewayne Kreager, "The Executive Office as Administrative Coordinator," *Law and Contemporary Problems*, vol. 21 (Autumn 1956), p. 704.

The Office of Director for Mutual Security was established by the Mutual Security Act of 1951 and 1952 to furnish military, economic, and technical assistance to other nations. Its functions were transferred to the Foreign Operations Administration on August 1, 1953. The Mutual Security Office was an outgrowth of Truman's appointing Averell Harriman as his senior adviser on foreign and military policy at the beginning of the Korean War. Harriman's office grew so large and became so enmeshed in operations that Congress eventually institutionalized it.

19. E. Ray Canterbery, *Economics on a New Frontier* (Belmont, Calif.: Wadsworth, 1968), p. 130.

20. Rexford G. Tugwell, *The Brains Trust* (Viking, 1968), pp. 525–28.

21. Quoted in Lester G. Seligman, "Presidential Leadership: The Inner Circle and Institutionalization," *Journal of Politics*, vol. 18 (August 1956), p. 419.

22. Edwin G. Nourse, *Economics in the Public Service* (Harcourt, Brace, 1953), p. 380.

23. Quoted in Edward S. Flash Jr., *Economic Advice and Presidential Leadership* (Columbia University Press, 1965), p. 25.

24. Gerhard Colm, "The Executive Office and Fiscal and Economic Policy," *Law and Contemporary Problems*, vol. 21 (Autumn 1956), p. 716.

25. Nourse, *Economics in the Public Service*, p. 378.

26. *The Hoover Commission Report* (McGraw-Hill, n.d.), p. xiii.

27. The first Hoover Commission report recommended that what it called the President's Office should contain six elements: White House Office, Office of the Economic Adviser, Office of Personnel, Office of the Budget, National Security Council, and National Security Resources Board. The Office of the Economic Adviser should replace the CEA and have a single head; the Office of Personnel should be headed by the chairman of the Civil Service Commission; and the membership of the NSC should be determined by the president rather than frozen into law by Congress. See Edward H. Hobbs, "An Historical Review of Plans for Presidential Staffing," *Law and Contemporary Problems*, vol. 21 (Autumn 1956), pp. 683–84.

28. See Herbert Emmerich, *Essays on Federal Reorganization* (University of Alabama Press, 1950), p. 101.

Chapter Five

1. Quoted in Emmet John Hughes, *The Ordeal of Power* (Atheneum, 1963), p. 331.

2. Robert Keith Gray, *Eighteen Acres under Glass* (Doubleday, 1962), pp. 62–63.

3. Sherman Adams, *Firsthand Report* (Harper, 1961), p. 302. Also see Kenneth W. Thompson, ed., *The Eisenhower Presidency* (University Press of America, 1984), pp. 198–99.

4. Dwight D. Eisenhower, *The White House Years: Mandate for Change, 1953–1956* (Doubleday, 1963), p. 197.

5. "Washington Wire," *New Republic* (December 15, 1952), p. 3.

6. Eisenhower, *Mandate for Change*, p. 98. Also see Robert H. Ferrell, *The Eisenhower Diaries* (Norton, 1981), pp. 218–21.

7. Adams, *Firsthand Report*, p. 89.

8. Ibid., p. 304.

9. See Stephen E. Ambrose, *Eisenhower*, vol. 2: *The President* (Simon and Schuster, 1983), p. 467.

10. Ibid., p. 45.

11. Quoted in Arthur M. Schlesinger Jr., *A Thousand Days* (Houghton Mifflin, 1965), p. 136.

12. Fred I. Greenstein prefers the image of lightning rods. See *The Hidden-Hand Presidency: Eisenhower as Leader* (Basic Books, 1982), p. 91.

13. R. Gordon Hoxie, ed., *The White House: Organization and Operations* (New York: Center for the Study of the Presidency, 1971), p. 4.

14. Herbert S. Parmet, *Eisenhower and the American Crusades* (Macmillan, 1972), p. 320.

15. Townsend Hoopes, *The Devil and John Foster Dulles* (Little, Brown, 1973), pp. 500–01.

16. Marquis Childs, *Eisenhower: Captive Hero* (Harcourt, Brace, 1958), p. 292. Richard Neustadt's often-quoted comment that "the Presidency is no place for amateurs" was also directed at Eisenhower. See *Presidential Power* (Wiley, 1960), p. 180.

17. See Greenstein, *Hidden-Hand Presidency,* especially chap. 3.

18. See the comments of William Ewald in Thompson, *Eisenhower Presidency,* p. 24.

19. David E. Lilienthal, *Journals,* vol. 2: *The Atomic Energy Years, 1945–1950* (Harper, 1964), p. 7; and Rexford G. Tugwell, *The Enlargements of the Presidency* (Doubleday, 1960), p. 488.

20. Computations on Eisenhower's staff are based on the *White House Staff Book, 1953–1961,* prepared and privately printed as a sort of college yearbook by two staff members, Frederick Fox and James Lambie, and presented as a farewell gift to all those who had served in the Eisenhower White House.

21. Among the men with business backgrounds on the Eisenhower staff who fit this description were Robert Cutler of Old Colony Trust Co., Clarence Francis of General Foods, Meyer Kestnbaum of Hart, Schaffner & Marx, and Clarence Randall of Inland Steel. Cutler, Francis, and Randall were involved in aspects of foreign policy; Kestnbaum advised on intergovernmental relations.

22. Dwight D. Eisenhower, *The White House Years: Waging Peace, 1956–1961* (Doubleday, 1965), p. 311.

23. See, for example, Robert H. Ferrell, ed., *The Diary of James C. Hagerty: Eisenhower in Mid-Course, 1954–1955* (Indiana University Press, 1983), pp. 52–53.

24. Eisenhower, *Mandate for Change,* p. 300.

25. Ibid., p. 233. Also see Milton Eisenhower's comments in Thompson, *Eisenhower Presidency,* p. 9.

26. Eisenhower's heart attack in 1955 caused a five-month hiatus in press conferences; another two-month break in 1956 resulted from an ileitis operation.

27. Robert Cutler, "The Development of the National Security Council," *Foreign Affairs,* vol. 34 (April 1956), p. 448. The other two men who held the post of special assistant for national security affairs under Eisenhower have also written about the NSC operations: see Dillon Anderson, "The President and National Security," *Atlantic* (January 1956), pp. 42–46; and Gordon Gray, "Role of the National Security Council in the Formulation of National Policy," in Subcommittee on National Policy Machinery of the Senate Committee on Government Operations, *Organizing for National Security: Selected Materials,* 86 Cong. 2 sess. (Government Printing Office, 1960), pp. 62–71. The Cutler and Anderson articles also appear in this document. See also Cutler's *No Time for Rest* (Little, Brown, 1966).

28. Cutler, "Development of the National Security Council," p. 449.

29. Gray, "Role of the National Security Council," pp. 65, 69.

30. The regular invitees were the assistant to the president, the director of the U.S. Information Agency, the under secretary of state, the special assistant to the president for foreign economic policy, the special assistant to the president for

science and technology, the White House staff secretary, the special assistant to the president for national security affairs, the special assistant to the president for security operations coordination, and the executive secretary and deputy executive secretary of the National Security Council.

31. Cutler, "Development of the National Security Council," p. 453.

32. Eisenhower, *Waging Peace*, pp. 634, 712.

33. Douglas Kinnard, *President Eisenhower and Strategy Management* (University Press of Kentucky, 1977), pp. 134–35.

34. James R. Killian Jr., *Sputnik, Scientists, and Eisenhower* (MIT Press, 1977), p. 194.

35. Eisenhower, *Mandate for Change*, p. 114.

36. Eisenhower, *Waging Peace*, p. 224.

37. Adams, *Firsthand Report*, p. 110.

38. Ibid., p. 156.

39. Eisenhower's budget directors were Joseph Dodge (1953–54), chairman, Detroit Bank; Rowland Hughes (1954–56), comptroller, National City Bank of New York; Percival Brundage (1956–58), senior partner, Price Waterhouse, and president, American Institute of Accountants; and Maurice Stans (1958–61), executive partner, Alexander Grant & Co. (certified public accountants).

Chapter Six

1. Theodore C. Sorensen, *Decision-Making in the White House* (Columbia University Press, 1963), p. 58.

2. Roger Hilsman, *To Move a Nation* (Doubleday, 1967), pp. 19–20.

3. Harold Seidman, *Politics, Position, and Power* (Oxford University Press, 1970), p. 92. See also Marver H. Bernstein, "The Presidency and Management Improvement," *Law and Contemporary Problems*, vol. 35 (Summer 1970), p. 512; and Rexford G. Tugwell, "The President and His Helpers," *Political Science Quarterly*, vol. 82 (June 1967), p. 262.

4. Richard E. Neustadt to John F. Kennedy, "Memorandum on Staffing the President-Elect," October 30, 1960 (Kennedy Library).

5. Quoted in Arthur M. Schlesinger Jr., *A Thousand Days* (Houghton Mifflin, 1965), p. 120.

6. Quoted in Jean M. White, "Catching the Flavor of the Way We Were," *Washington Post*, November 25, 1974.

7. George W. Ball, *The Discipline of Power* (Little, Brown, 1968), p. 27.

8. Theodore C. Sorensen, *Kennedy* (Harper and Row, 1968), p. 287.

9. John Kenneth Galbraith, *Ambassador's Journal* (Houghton Mifflin, 1969), p. 7.

10. McGeorge Bundy, *The Strength of Government* (Harvard University Press, 1968), pp. 39–40.

11. David T. Stanley, *Changing Administrations: The 1961 and 1964 Transitions in Six Departments* (Brookings, 1965), p. 21.

12. Schlesinger, *A Thousand Days*, pp. 472, 902.

13. Quoted in Thomas E. Cronin, "'Everybody Believes in Democracy until He Gets to the White House . . .': An Examination of White House-Departmental Relations," *Law and Contemporary Problems*, vol. 35 (Summer 1970), p. 608.

14. Schlesinger, *A Thousand Days*, p. 688. The example was somewhat moot: the post office as a cabinet position was an anachronism and would be converted into an independent agency during the Nixon administration.

15. Sorensen, *Kennedy*, p. 630.

16. See Graham T. Allison, *Essence of Decision* (Little, Brown, 1971), pp. 203–04. Abram Chayes, in *The Cuban Missile Crisis* (Oxford University Press, 1974), pp. 13–14, implied that one reason for restraint in the second Cuban crisis was the number of lawyers offering advice. But since Kennedy rejected the suggestions of lawyers Dean Acheson (a hawk) and Adlai Stevenson (a dove), the proposition is not persuasive. John Franklin Campbell blamed the decision in the first Cuban crisis on the absence of advice from career diplomats, but the successful response to the second crisis cannot be attributed to a State Department presence. See *The Foreign Affairs Fudge Factory* (Basic Books, 1971), p. 51.

17. See Irving L. Janis, *Victims of Groupthink* (Houghton Mifflin, 1972), pp. 14–49, 138–66.

18. See "Pre-Inaugural Task Forces Unprecedented in History," *Congressional Quarterly Weekly Report*, vol. 19 (April 7, 1961), pp. 620–23.

19. Schlesinger, *A Thousand Days*, pp. 680–82.

20. President's Committee on Administrative Management, *Administrative Management in the Government of the United States* (Government Printing Office, 1937), p. 5. See also Louis W. Koenig, *The Chief Executive* (Harcourt, Brace and World, 1968), p. 174.

21. Kennedy's decision to go on live television "changed the presidential press conference more than any other single innovation in the eighty-year history of scheduled meetings between the President and the press," according to Charles Roberts, who covered the Kennedy White House for *Newsweek*. See "Image and Reality," in Kenneth W. Thompson, ed., *The Kennedy Presidency* (University Press of America, 1985), p. 177.

22. See Edward de Grazia, *Congressional Liaison* (American Enterprise Institute, 1965); and G. Russell Pipe, "Congressional Liaison: The Executive Branch Consolidates Its Relations with Congress," *Public Administration Review*, vol. 26 (March 1966), pp. 14–24.

23. Herbert Stein, *The Fiscal Revolution in America* (University of Chicago Press, 1969), p. 379.

24. Walter W. Heller, *New Dimensions of Political Economy* (Harvard University Press, 1966), p. 15.

25. See Robert S. Gilmour, "Central Legislative Clearance: A Revised Perspective," *Public Administration Review*, vol. 31 (March–April 1971), pp. 150–58.

Chapter Seven

1. Eric F. Goldman, *The Tragedy of Lyndon Johnson* (Knopf, 1969), p. 22.

2. On November 11, 1968, President-elect Nixon visited the White House and asked Johnson why he had kept so many Kennedy appointees. "Lyndon answered in a measured, thoughtful tone. 'Well, there are several reasons. One, respect for President Kennedy. He had trusted me, and I tried to put myself in his shoes. How would I have felt if, as soon as I was gone, he had disposed of all my people? I wanted to be loyal to him. Two, I didn't know for a good while whether I had an excellent man or an incompetent. And three, I didn't always have all the troops I needed." Lady Bird Johnson, *A White House Diary* (Dell, 1971), p. 808.

3. Goldman, *Tragedy of Lyndon Johnson*, p. 18. This was not an opinion that Secretary of Agriculture Orville Freeman shared. See "A Cabinet Perspective," in Kenneth W. Thompson, ed., *The Kennedy Presidency* (University Press of America, 1985), p. 167.

4. Lyndon Baines Johnson, *The Vantage Point* (Holt, Rinehart, and Winston, 1971), p. 410.

5. David S. Broder, "Texas, D.C.," *Atlantic* (March 1975), p. 113. Three Texans served in Johnson's cabinet: W. Marvin Watson, postmaster general; C. R. Smith, secretary of commerce; and Ramsey Clark, attorney general.

6. See, however, Emmette S. Redford and Richard T. McCulley, *White House Operations: The Johnson Presidency* (University of Texas Press, 1986), pp. 72–73.

7. "The White House Staff vs. the Cabinet: Hugh Sidey Interviews Bill Moyers," *Washington Monthly* (February 1969), p. 78.

8. Johnson listed former Secretary of State Dean Acheson; former under secretary of state George Ball; General Omar Bradley; McGeorge Bundy (former assistant to the president for national security affairs); Arthur Dean, who had negotiated the Korean War settlement; former Treasury Secretary Douglas Dillon; Ambassador Henry Cabot Lodge; retired diplomat Robert Murphy; General Matthew Ridgway; General Maxwell Taylor; and former deputy secretary of defense Cyrus Vance. See *Vantage Point*, p. 416.

9. "Bill Moyers Talks about LBJ, Power, Poverty, War and the Young," *Atlantic* (July 1968), p. 31.

10. Charles Roberts, *LBJ's Inner Circle* (Delacorte, 1965), pp. 42–43. Also see Redford and McCulley, *White House Operations*, p. 67.

11. Liz Carpenter, *Ruffles and Flourishes* (Doubleday, 1970), p. 253.

12. Goldman, *Tragedy of Lyndon Johnson*, p. 272. However, Redford and McCulley in *White House Operations*, p. 31, contend that there was "very substantial stability in the most important administrative and policy areas."

13. Among those who are known to have declined appointments were Donald C. Cook, American Electric Power Co.; Thomas J. Watson Jr., International Business Machines; Frank Stanton, Columbia Broadcasting System; Abe Fortas; Ben Heineman, Chicago Northwestern Railroad; and Kermit Gordon, who went to the

Brookings Institution in preference to becoming secretary of the treasury. See Lady Bird Johnson, *White House Diary*, pp. 220–21; Lyndon Johnson, *Vantage Point*, p. 545; and Rowland Evans and Robert Novak, *Lyndon B. Johnson: The Exercise of Power* (New American Library, 1966), p. 506.

14. John W. Macy Jr., *Public Service* (Harper and Row, 1971), pp. 227–28.

15. Roberts, *LBJ's Inner Circle*, p. 160.

16. Theodore C. Sorensen, *Watchmen in the Night* (MIT Press, 1973), p. 36.

17. Goldman, *Tragedy of Lyndon Johnson*, p. 275.

18. James Gaither, "Advising the President: A Panel," *Bureaucrat*, vol. 3 (April 1974), p. 25. Also see Redford and McCulley, *White House Operations*, pp. 62–63.

19. George Christian, *The President Steps Down* (Macmillan, 1970), pp. 16–17.

20. Bill Moyers, quoted in Henry F. Graff, *The Tuesday Cabinet* (Prentice-Hall, 1970), p.52.

21. Johnson, *Vantage Point*, p. 328.

22. See Norman C. Thomas and Harold L. Wolman, "The Presidency and Policy Formulation: The Task Force Device," *Public Administration Review*, vol. 29 (September–October 1969), pp. 459–71.

23. Charles Roberts, ed., *Has the President Too Much Power?* (Harper's Magazine Press, 1974), pp. 152–53.

24. Ibid., p. 141.

25. William D. Carey, "Presidential Staffing in the Sixties and Seventies," *Public Administration Review*, vol. 29 (September–October 1969), p. 454.

26. Robert Wood, "When Government Works," *Public Interest*, no. 18 (Winter 1970), p. 42.

27. See Evans and Novak, *Lyndon B. Johnson*, p. 466; and Roberts, *LBJ's Inner Circle*, p. 146.

28. Quoted in Goldman, *Tragedy of Lyndon Johnson*, p. 278. Kennedy had also employed a resident intellectual, Arthur Schlesinger Jr., but Schlesinger had a more political role because of his considerable experience in the liberal wing of the Democratic party, where the president was initially viewed with suspicion. In addition, Kennedy probably retained Schlesinger for the same reason Johnson confided in Doris Kearns, a White House fellow on leave from Harvard—as a hedge against history (or historians). In general, intellectuals have fared poorly on the White House staff unless they have had some reason to be there other than their identification with university life. Goldman finally went back to the campus because Johnson felt uncomfortable in his presence and blamed him for the hostility of intellectuals, just as he seems to have blamed press secretary George Reedy for the hostility of reporters.

29. The so-called Heineman report, available at the Johnson Library in Austin, Texas, states, "The President must inform Cabinet subordinates that he expects them to meet upon the call of the Director; that he expects major matters of interdepartmental program coordination to be settled in the forum provided by the Director; and that, when agency heads remain unable to compose agreement, he expects agreements to emerge and 'to stick' along lines prescribed by the Director."

30. George E. Reedy, *The Twilight of the Presidency* (New American Library, 1970), p. 74.

31. Christian, *President Steps Down*, pp. 235–43. Nevertheless, Johnson "never fired an appointee"; see Richard L. Schott and Dagmar S. Hamilton, *People, Positions, and Power: The Political Appointments of Lyndon Johnson* (University of Chicago Press, 1983), p. 206.

32. Four of the Kennedy cabinet—Dean Rusk, Udall, Wirtz, and Orville Freeman—stayed until the end of the Johnson administration. The others, as had become the practice with holdover appointees, were offered face-saving positions. For instance, HEW Secretary Anthony Celebrezze was made a federal judge and Postmaster General John Gronouski became ambassador to Poland.

33. George E. Reedy, *The Presidency in Flux* (Columbia University Press, 1973), p. 24.

34. Alexander L. George, "The Case for Multiple Advocacy in Making Foreign Policy," *American Political Science Review*, vol. 66 (September 1972), p. 751.

35. Johnson, *Vantage Point*, p. 64.

36. Ibid., p. 147.

37. Ibid., p. 418.

38. James C. Thomson Jr., "How Could Vietnam Happen?" *Atlantic* (April 1968), p. 49.

39. Quoted in Tom Wicker, "The Wrong Rubicon: LBJ and the War," *Atlantic* (May 1968), p. 68.

Chapter Eight

1. *Public Papers of the Presidents, Richard Nixon, 1971* (Government Printing Office, 1972), p. 6; and *Public Papers of the Presidents, John F. Kennedy, 1962* (GPO, 1963), p. 889.

2. Theodore H. White, *Breach of Faith: The Fall of Richard Nixon* (Atheneum and Reader's Digest Press, 1975), p. 62; and John Osborne, *The First Two Years of the Nixon Watch: First Year* (Liveright, 1971), pp. 28, 96.

3. Quoted in Earl Mazo and Stephen Hess, *Nixon: A Political Portrait* (Harper and Row, 1968), pp. 314–15. See also Harold Seidman, *Politics, Position, and Power* (Oxford University Press, 1970), pp. 74–75.

4. William Safire, *Before the Fall* (Doubleday, 1975), p. 116.

5. *Nixon Speaks Out* (Nixon-Agnew Campaign Committee, 1968), pp. 242–43.

6. *Nixon on the Issues* (Nixon-Agnew Campaign Committee, 1968), p. 76.

7. Rowland Evans Jr. and Robert D. Novak, *Nixon in the White House* (Random House, 1971), p. 10.

8. Arthur Schlesinger Jr., "Presidential War," *New York Times Magazine* (January 7, 1974), p. 28.

9. Kevin P. Phillips, *Mediacracy* (Doubleday, 1975), pp. 179–80. In addition to Laird, Nixon subsequently chose three more members of Congress: Rogers Morton of Maryland, secretary of the interior; George Bush of Texas, U.S. repre-

sentative to the United Nations; and Senator William Saxbe of Ohio, attorney general.

10. Secretary of Agriculture Hardin had been chancellor of the University of Nebraska; Secretary of Labor Shultz had been dean of the Graduate School of Business, University of Chicago. Two later department heads, Henry Kissinger of Harvard (State) and James R. Schlesinger, formerly of the University of Virginia (Defense), were also academics. White pointed out that in Nixon's second term his cabinet and staff "were more heavily dominated by Harvard men than those of any of the six Harvard men who had been Presidents of the United States." *Breach of Faith*, p. 252.

11. Secretary of State Rogers had been attorney general; Commerce Secretary Stans had been Eisenhower's last budget director; and Transportation Secretary Volpe had served as federal highway administrator. Elliot Richardson, who later held three cabinet appointments in the Nixon administration, had been an assistant secretary of HEW under Eisenhower.

12. Besides Henry Jackson (Defense), Nixon is known to have been rejected by Hubert Humphrey and Edward Brooke, both of whom were offered the post of U.S. representative to the UN.

13. See Henry A. Kissinger, *White House Years* (Little, Brown, 1979), p. 11; and Leonard Garment, "Objectives and People," in Kenneth W. Thompson, ed., *The Nixon Presidency* (University Press of America, 1987), p. 102.

14. Tom Wicker, "Introduction," in Osborne, *First Two Years of the Nixon Watch: First Year*, p. vii.

15. Jeb Stuart Magruder, *An American Life: One Man's Road to Watergate* (Atheneum, 1974), p. 93.

16. *Presidential Campaign Activities of 1972, Senate Resolution 60*, Hearings before the Senate Select Committee on Presidential Campaign Activities, 93 Cong. 1 sess. (GPO, 1973), bk. 2, pp. 648–49 (hereinafter referred to as Ervin Committee.) Also see Herbert G. Klein, *Making It Perfectly Clear* (Doubleday, 1980), p. 322; and Raymond Price, *With Nixon* (Viking, 1977), p. 31.

17. See Elmer E. Cornwell Jr., *Presidential Leadership of Public Opinion* (Indiana University Press, 1965), p. 222.

18. Safire, *Before the Fall*, p. 100. Also see Klein, *Making It Perfectly Clear*, p. 322.

19. Kenneth P. O'Donnell and David F. Powers, *Johnny, We Hardly Knew Ye* (Little, Brown, 1972), p. 255.

20. Ervin Committee, bk. 21, pp. 9687, 9713.

21. *Public Papers, 1970*, pp. 470–71.

22. See John Ehrlichman, *Witness to Power* (Simon and Schuster, 1982), p. 245.

23. *Public Papers, 1969*, p. 12.

24. Nixon contends otherwise, however. See *RN: The Memoirs of Richard Nixon* (Grosset and Dunlap, 1978), p. 342.

25. For Moynihan's description of the Council for Urban Affairs, see *The Politics of a Guaranteed Income* (Random House, 1973), pp. 73–75.

26. *Public Papers, 1969*, p. 645.

27. See John Ehrlichman, "The White House and Policy-Making," in Thompson, *Nixon Presidency*, pp. 130–33.

28. *Public Papers, 1969*, p. 511.

29. Theodore C. Sorensen, *Decision-Making in the White House* (Columbia University Press, 1963), p. 38.

30. Theodore H. White, *The Making of the President 1972* (Atheneum, 1973), p. 355.

31. Richard M. Nixon, *Six Crises* (Doubleday, 1962), pp. 1, 73, 131, 183.

32. For example, note how some staff members point to Charles Colson as "reflective of Nixon's darker side." See Price, *With Nixon*, p. 30; and Klein, *Making It Perfectly Clear*, p. 335.

33. See John Whitaker in Allen Drury, *Courage and Hesitation* (Doubleday, 1971), p. 122.

34. Safire, *Before the Fall*, p. 288. Haldeman obviously disagrees with this interpretation; see *The Ends of Power* (Times Books, 1978), pp. 58–59.

35. Testimony of William H. Marumoto, presidential assistant for coordinating administration efforts on behalf of Spanish-speaking Americans, Ervin Committee, bk. 13, p. 5279.

36. Magruder, *An American Life*, pp. 55–60, 112. Also see Bryce Harlow, "The Man and the Political Leader," in Thompson, *Nixon Presidency*, p. 15.

37. John Osborne, *The Third Year of the Nixon Watch* (Liveright, 1972), p. 134.

38. Lewis W. Wolfson and James McCartney, *The Press Covers Government: The Nixon Years from 1969 to Watergate* (Washington, D.C.: National Press Club, 1973), p. 6.

39. Joel D. Aberbach and Bert A. Rockman, "Clashing Beliefs within the Executive Branch: The Nixon Administration Bureaucracy," *American Political Science Review*, vol. 70 (June 1976), pp. 466–67.

40. George Christian, *The President Steps Down* (Macmillan, 1970), p. 258.

41. Aberbach and Rockman, "Clashing Beliefs," p. 467.

42. James Keogh, *President Nixon and the Press* (Funk and Wagnall's, 1972), p. 39. Also see Ehrlichman, *Witness to Power*, p. 265; and Nixon, *Memoirs*, p. 354.

43. See Samuel Kernell, *Going Public* (CQ Press, 1986), p. 91.

44. Magruder, *An American Life*, p. 95.

45. Richard P. Nathan, *The Plot That Failed: Nixon and the Administrative Presidency* (Wiley, 1975), p. 49. Nathan expands his discussion of Nixon's strategy in *The Administrative Presidency* (Wiley, 1983).

46. For a detailed study of the Ash Council's work, see Peri E. Arnold, *Making the Managerial Presidency* (Princeton University Press, 1986), pp. 277–97.

47. *Public Papers, 1970*, p. 259.

48. See Hugh Heclo, "OMB and the Presidency—The Problem of 'Neutral Competence,'" *Public Interest*, no. 38 (Winter 1975); and Larry Berman, *The Office of Management and Budget and the Presidency, 1921–1979* (Princeton University Press, 1979), especially chap. 5.

49. John H. Kessel, *The Domestic Presidency* (North Scituate, Mass.: Duxbury, 1975), p. 29.

50. See Edwin Harper, "Advising the President: A Panel," *Bureaucrat*, vol. 3 (April 1974), p. 24.

51. Nathan, *The Plot That Failed*, p. 47.

52. Chester E. Finn Jr., "Staffing the Subcommittee on Education of the Council for Urban Affairs" (Ph.D. dissertation, Harvard, 1970), pp. 59, 92 of "Final Report Abstract." In a different form the study became *Education and the Presidency* (Lexington Books, 1977), pp. 34–35.

53. Kessel, *Domestic Presidency*, pp. 101–02.

54. The creation of the U.S. Postal Service was recommended to President Johnson by the Commission on Postal Organization in June 1968. Nixon proposed it in a special message to the Congress, April 16, 1970, and signed it into law on August 12, 1970. See *Public Papers, 1970*, pp. 359–64, 666–68.

55. *Public Papers, 1972*, pp. 1148–50.

56. John Herling, "Peter Brennan: Joining the Ambassadorial Ranks?" *Washington Post*, January 29, 1975.

57. Safire, *Before the Fall*, p. 406.

58. Osborne, *Third Year of the Nixon Watch*, pp. 48–49.

59. See I. M. Destler, "The Nixon System, A Further Look," *Foreign Service Journal* (February 1974), pp. 9–14, 28–29.

60. Henry A. Kissinger, *A World Restored: Metternich, Castlereagh, and the Problems of Peace, 1812–22* (Houghton Mifflin, 1973), pp. 326–27.

61. Quoted in Marvin Kalb and Bernard Kalb, *Kissinger* (Little, Brown, 1974), p. 447.

62. "Bentsen Bill Would Split Kissinger's Two Key Jobs," *New York Times*, May 7, 1975.

63. See John Herbers, "President's Grip Found Looser on Bureaucracy," *New York Times*, June 7, 1974.

64. White, *Breach of Faith*, p. 325. A similar observation was made by a former Nixon speechwriter: "Nixon became the victim of his own system. . . . And part of it, of course, was the men he chose to guard that wall"; John R. Coyne Jr., "Quit Does: The Story of 'P,'" *National Review* (April 25, 1975), p. 466.

65. Joseph Kraft, "Government by Professor," *Washington Post*, February 7, 1974.

66. Quoted in *Newsweek* (March 19, 1973), p. 24.

67. Safire, *Before the Fall*, p. 603.

68. John Osborne, *The Last Nixon Watch* (New Republic, 1975), p. 117.

69. Nixon, *Memoirs*, p. 925.

70. *Presidency 1974* (Congressional Quarterly, 1975), p. 89.

71. Gerald R. Ford, *A Time to Heal* (Harper and Row, 1979), p. 126.

72. Ibid., p. 38.

73. Quoted in Samuel Kernell and Samuel L. Popkin, eds., *Chief of Staff* (University of California Press, 1986), p. 73.

74. Ford's first press secretary, Jerald F. terHorst, served for thirty days, resigning because he could not support the decision to pardon Nixon. See his *Gerald Ford and the Future of the Presidency* (New York: Third Press, 1974), pp. 225–40.

75. Ford, *Time to Heal*, p. 186.

76. John Casserly, *The Ford White House: The Diary of a Speechwriter* (Boulder, Colo.: Associated University Press, 1977), p. 267.

77. Robert T. Hartmann, *Palace Politics* (McGraw-Hill, 1980), pp. 165, 167, 282.

78. Ford, *Time to Heal*, p. 148.

79. Hedley Donovan, *Roosevelt to Reagan* (Harper and Row, 1985), p. 139.

80. Kernell and Popkin, *Chief of Staff*, p. 174.

81. Roger B. Porter, *Presidential Decision Making: The Economic Policy Board* (Cambridge University Press, 1980), pp. 99–100; also see pp. 3, 43, 48, 54, 57.

82. John Osborne, *White House Watch: The Ford Years* (New Republic Books, 1977), p. 199.

83. Kernell and Popkin, *Chief of Staff*, p. 73.

84. Ford, *Time to Heal*, p. 129.

85. Michael Medved, *The Shadow Presidents* (New York Times Books, 1979), p. 338.

86. Osborne, *White House Watch*, p. 217.

87. Paul Charles Light, *The President's Agenda* (Johns Hopkins University Press, 1982), pp. 36–37.

88. Frederic V. Malek, *Washington's Hidden Tragedy: The Failure to Make Government Work* (Free Press, 1978), pp. 18–19.

89. Letter to the author, February 1, 1988.

Chapter Nine

1. Quoted in James Fallows, "The Passionless Presidency," *Atlantic* (May 1979), p. 46.

2. Jack Knott and Aaron Wildavsky, "Jimmy Carter's Theory of Governing," *Wilson Quarterly*, vol. 1 (Winter 1977), pp. 49–65.

3. Martin Anderson, *Revolution* (Harcourt Brace Jovanovich, 1988), pp. 230–31.

4. Jimmy Carter, *Keeping Faith: Memoirs of a President* (Bantam Books, 1982), p. 57.

5. Griffin Bell, *Taking Care of the Law* (Morrow, 1982), pp. 46–47.

6. Joseph A. Califano Jr., *Governing America: An Insider's Report from the White House and the Cabinet* (Simon and Schuster, 1981), p. 403.

7. Zbigniew Brzezinski, *Power and Principle: Memoirs of the National Security Adviser 1977–1981* (Farrar, Straus, Giroux, 1983), p. 71.

8. See Dom Bonafede, "How the White House Helps Carter Make Up His Mind," *National Journal* (April 15, 1978), p. 584.

9. Quoted in Walter Shapiro, "During His First 100 Days . . ." *Time* (May 2, 1988), p. 29.

10. Erwin C. Hargrove, "Jimmy Carter: The Politics of Public Goods," in Fred I. Greenstein, ed., *Leadership in the Modern Presidency* (Harvard University Press, 1988), p. 233.

11. Bert A. Rockman, "An Imprint but Not a Revolution," in B. B. Kymlicka and Jean V. Matthews, eds., *The Reagan Revolution?* (Homewood, Ill.: Dorsey Press, 1988), p. 203.

12. Terrel H. Bell, *The Thirteenth Man: A Reagan Cabinet Memoir* (Free Press, 1988), p. 32.

13. Ann Reilly Dowd, "What Managers Can Learn from Manager Reagan," *Fortune* (September 15, 1986), p. 36.

14. Donald T. Regan, *For the Record: From Wall Street to Washington* (Harcourt Brace Jovanovich, 1988), p. 142.

15. Ibid., p. 143.

16. Quoted in Dowd, "What Managers Can Learn From Manager Reagan," p. 41.

17. David A. Stockman, *The Triumph of Politics: How the Reagan Revolution Failed* (Harper and Row, 1986), p. 90.

18. Anderson, *Revolution*, p. 290.

19. Regan, *For the Record*, pp. 267–68.

20. Hedley Donovan, *Roosevelt to Reagan: A Reporter's Encounters with Nine Presidents* (Harper and Row, 1985), p. 215.

21. Quoted in Michael Medved, *The Shadow Presidents* (New York Times Books, 1979), p. 351.

22. Fallows, "Passionless Presidency," p. 39.

23. John H. Kessel, "The Structures of the Carter White House," *American Journal of Political Science*, vol. 27 (August 1982), p. 461.

24. Joel Havemann, "The Cabinet Band—Trying to Follow Carter's Baton," *National Journal* (July 16, 1977), p. 1107.

25. Fallows, "Passionless Presidency," p. 42.

26. Kessel, "Structures of the Carter White House," pp. 433–39.

27. Michael K. Deaver, *Behind the Scenes* (Morrow, 1987), p. 128.

28. Larry Speakes, *Speaking Out: The Reagan Presidency from Inside the White House* (Scribner's, 1988), p. 112.

29. Regan, *For the Record*, pp. 253–55.

30. Quoted in Colin Campbell, *Managing the Presidency: Carter, Reagan, and the Search for Executive Harmony* (University of Pittsburgh Press, 1986), p. 104.

31. Speakes, *Speaking Out*, p. 70.

32. Regan had attained that position in an extraordinary fashion. Baker complained to the treasury secretary that he was tired of running the White House. Half joking, Regan suggested they swap jobs, and to his surprise Baker agreed. Incredibly, President Reagan expressed only mild interest when the switch was proposed, even though it meant replacing the proven, politically masterful Baker with a man who even after four years Reagan barely knew, particularly at a time when a second trusted adviser, Meese, would be leaving the White House to

become attorney general. Regan himself was astounded at the president's attitude. "He seemed to be absorbing a *fait accompli* rather than making a decision. One might have thought that the matter had already been settled by some absent party." See *For the Record*, p. 229.

33. Bert A. Rockman, "The Style and Organization of the Reagan Presidency," in Charles O. Jones, ed., *The Reagan Legacy: Promise and Performance* (Chatham House, 1988), p. 25.

34. Quoted in Dick Kirschten, "As Events Enable Regan to be Regan . . ." *National Journal* (July 27, 1985), p. 1751.

35. Quoted in Dick Kirschten, "Around the White House Bunker . . ." *National Journal* (December 6, 1986), p. 2950.

36. Lou Cannon, "Baker, Man for the Moment," *Washington Post*, July 4, 1988.

37. Bradley H. Patterson Jr., *The Ring of Power: The White House Staff and Its Expanding Role in Government* (Basic Books, 1988), pp. 209–11.

38. Fallows, "Passionless Presidency," p. 41.

39. Charles O. Jones, *The Trusteeship Presidency: Jimmy Carter and the United States Congress* (Louisiana State University Press, 1988), p. 6.

40. Samuel Kernell, *Going Public: New Strategies of Presidential Leadership* (CQ Press, 1986), p. 37.

41. Quoted in John Tebbel and Sarah Watts, *The Press and the Presidency: From George Washington to Ronald Reagan* (Oxford University Press, 1985), p. 531.

42. See Michael Baruch Grossman and Martha Joynt Kumar, *Portraying the President: The White House and the News Media* (Johns Hopkins University Press, 1981), pp. 99–100.

43. Tebbel and Watts, *Press and the Presidency*, p. 531.

44. Bill Plante, "Why We Were Shouting at the President," *Washington Post*, October 11, 1987.

45. Sam Donaldson, *Hold On, Mr. President!* (Random House, 1987), p. 123.

46. John H. Kessel, "The Structures of the Reagan White House," *American Political Science*, vol. 28 (May 1984), p. 235.

47. Terry Moe, "The Politicized Presidency," in John E. Chubb and Paul E. Peterson, eds., *The New Direction in American Politics* (Brookings, 1985), p. 260.

48. Bell, *Thirteenth Man*, p. 39.

49. Quoted in Martin Anderson, *Revolution*, p. 285.

50. Dom Bonafede, "Carter Sounds Retreat from 'Cabinet Government,'" *National Journal* (November 18, 1978), p. 1856.

51. Dom Bonafede, "White House Reorganization—Separating Smoke from Substance," *National Journal* (August 20, 1977), p. 1307.

52. See Patterson, *Ring of Power*, p. 339.

53. Laurence I. Barrett, *Gambling with History: Ronald Reagan in the White House* (Doubleday, 1983), p. 71. Of Reagan's original thirteen cabinet secretaries, only five remained at the start of his second term. James Baker succeeded Regan at Treasury, Meese moved into Smith's spot at Justice, and George Shultz, who had the Labor and Treasury portfolios in Nixon's cabinet, became secretary of state.

Interior Secretary James Watt was first replaced by William Clark, a close friend of the president's, and then by under secretary Donald Hodel. Elizabeth Dole went from the White House to Transportation. William Bennett, chair of the National Endowment for the Humanities, was Reagan's second education secretary. John Herrington, a presidential assistant, became secretary of energy. Former Massachusetts congresswoman Margaret Heckler replaced Schweiker at HHS, and was then replaced with Otis Bowen, a former governor of Indiana. Energy Secretary Edwards and Education Secretary Bell were uncomfortable in their jobs, but left of their own free will; Watt, Haig, and Heckler were pushed out.

54. Bell, *Taking Care of the Law*, p. 22.

55. Bruce Adams and Kathryn Kavanagh-Baran, *Promise and Performance: Carter Builds a New Administration* (Lexington Books, 1979), p. 60.

56. Cyrus Vance, *Hard Choices: Critical Years in America's Foreign Policy* (Simon and Schuster, 1983), p. 35.

57. Bell, *Taking Care of the Law*, p. 45.

58. Carl M. Brauer, *Presidential Transitions: Eisenhower through Reagan* (Oxford University Press, 1986), p. 192.

59. Quoted in Califano, *Governing America*, p. 411.

60. HUD Secretary Patricia Harris went to HEW, Federal Reserve chairman William Miller to Treasury, and deputy defense secretary Charles Duncan took over the Energy Department. Deputy attorney general Benjamin Civiletti moved up to attorney general, Neil Goldschmidt, mayor of Portland, Oregon, was appointed transportation secretary, and New Orleans mayor Moon Landrieu filled the vacancy left by Harris at HUD.

61. Quoted in Rochelle L. Stanfield, "What to Expect from Carter's New Cabinet," *National Journal* (July 28, 1979), p. 1241.

62. Moe, "Politicized Presidency," p. 260.

63. Quoted in Dick Kirschten, "Decision Making in the White House: How Well Does It Serve the President?" *National Journal* (April 3, 1982), p. 588.

64. The other five cabinet councils were Commerce and Trade (chaired by Commerce and meeting 91 times), Natural Resources and Environment (Interior, 66 times), Human Resources (Health and Human Services, 35 times), Food and Agriculture (Agriculture, 24 times), and Legal Policy (Justice, 16 times). Alexander Haig complained: "In practice, the chairmanship went to the Cabinet officer with the strongest vested interest in the subject at hand, an efficient method for setting the fox among the chickens and producing solutions that were politically loaded in favor of the major domestic vested interest concerned." See his *Caveat: Realism, Reagan, and Foreign Policy* (Macmillan, 1984), p. 82.

65. Anderson, *Revolution*, p. 228.

66. Regan, *For the Record*, pp. 153, 154.

67. Anderson, *Revolution*, p. 249.

68. The Ford presidency, however, tried to remove "the taint of politicization." See Larry Berman, *The Office of Management and Budget and the Presidency, 1921–1979* (Princeton University Press, 1979), pp. 127–28.

69. See Jonathan Rauch, "Stockman's Quiet Revolution at OMB May Leave Indelible Mark on Agency," *National Journal* (May 25, 1985), pp. 1212–17.

70. Brzezinski, *Power and Principle*, p. 34.

71. Bell, *Taking Care of the Law*, p. 24.

72. Donovan, *Roosevelt to Reagan*, p. 161.

73. Carter, *Keeping Faith*, p. 52.

74. Vance, *Hard Choices*, p. 36.

75. Haig, *Caveat*, p. 356.

76. Ibid., p. 306.

77. Speakes, *Speaking Out*, p. 265.

78. Regan, *For the Record*, p. 144.

79. Stockman, *Triumph of Politics*, p. 76.

80. Fred Barnes, "Powell in Command," *New Republic* (May 30, 1988), p. 14.

81. Jeremiah O'Leary, "From Yet Another Insider," *Washington Times*, June 2, 1988.

Chapter Ten

1. For an analysis of the causes and effects of the turn-of-the-century polarization of Congress, see James P. Pfiffner, "The President and Congress at the Turn of the Century: Structural Sources of Conflict," in James A. Thurber, ed., *Rivals for Power*, 2d ed. (Rowman and Littlefield, 2002), pp. 27–48.

2. For an analysis of these developments, see James P. Pfiffner, *The Modern Presidency*, 3d ed. (Bedford-St. Martin's, 2000).

3. David Gergen, "Bush's Start: A Presidency 'On the Edge of a Cliff,'" *Washington Post*, March 5, 1989.

4. David Hoffman, "Watkins, Bennett Named to Cabinet; Bush Orders New Team to Think Big, Avoid Kiss-and-Tell Books," *Washington Post*, January 13, 1989.

5. For examples of initiatives taken without full White House clearance, see John Burke, *Presidential Transitions* (Lynn Rienner Publishers, 2000), pp. 238–39.

6. Quoted in Burt Solomon, "When the Bush Cabinet Convenes . . . It's a Gathering of Presidential Pals," *National Journal* (July 1, 1989), p. 1704.

7. For analyses of the Bush White House–cabinet interaction see Shirley Anne Warshaw, *The Domestic Presidency: Policy Making in the White House* (Allyn and Bacon, 1997), pp. 145–78; and David Mervin, *George Bush and the Guardianship Presidency* (Macmillan, 1996), pp. 58–85.

8. For a full account of the Clinton transition, see James P. Pfiffner, *The Strategic Presidency: Hitting the Ground Running*, 2d ed. (University Press of Kansas, 1996).

9. See Burke, *Presidential Transitions* , p. 311.

10. They hired the couple from Peru to care for their children, and their lawyer had mistakenly advised them that they did not have to pay Social Security taxes until the couple received a Social Security number, which they were helping the

couple obtain. See John Anthony Maltese, *The Selling of Supreme Court Nominees* (Johns Hopkins University Press, 1995), p. 145.

11. See Elizabeth Drew, *On the Edge* (Simon and Schuster, 1994), p. 53.

12. Ibid., p. 34.

13. *United States Government Manual 1996–1997* (Government Printing Office, 1997), p. 89. The positions included chief of staff, CIA director, OMB director, CEA chair, EPA director, U.S. trade representative, "drug czar," FEMA director, SBA director, UN representative, and counselor to the president.

14. Quoted by Bernard Weinraub, "Unlikely Alliance atop Bush's Staff," *New York Times*, June 19, 1989.

15. David Gergen, "George Bush's Balky Start," *U.S. News and World Report* (January 30, 1989), p. 34.

16. Quoted by Warshaw, *The Domestic Presidency*, p. 167.

17. James P. Pfiffner, "Presidential Policy Making and the Gulf War," in Marcia Lynn Whicker, James P. Pfiffner, and Raymond A. Moore, eds., *The Presidency and the Persian Gulf War* (Praeger, 1993), pp. 2–23.

18. There have been four domineering chiefs of staff in the modern White House: Sherman Adams for Eisenhower, H. R. Haldeman for Nixon, Donald Regan for Reagan, and John Sununu for George Bush. Each resigned in disgrace. For an argument that the chief of staff's job can be done effectively without adopting a domineering approach, see James P. Pfiffner, "The President's Chief of Staff: Lessons Learned," *Presidential Studies Quarterly* (Winter 1993), pp. 77–102.

19. See Burt Solomon, "No-Nonsense Sununu," *National Journal* (September 16, 1989), p. 2251.

20. *Time* (September 30, 1991), p. 19; *Newsweek* (December 30, 1991), p. 4. The existence of this avenue of communication was publicly confirmed by HHS secretary Louis Sullivan, who admitted on television that he used the channel to communicate advice to the president. For Sullivan's comments, see "This Week with David Brinkley," ABC News, transcript of program of February 2, 1992, p. 13.

21. Bob Woodward, "The President's Key Men," *Washington Post*, October 7, 1992.

22. Sidney Blumenthal, "So Long, Sununu," *Vanity Fair* (February 1992), p. 168.

23. Charles Babcock and Ann Devroy, "Sununu Deems Only 4 Plane Trips 'Personal,'" *Washington Post*, April 24, 1991. See also Maureen Dowd, "Sununu: A Case Study in Flouting the Rules," *New York Times*, May 5, 1991.

24. Dan Goodgame, "Fly Free or Die," *Time* (May 13, 199), p. 18.

25. Andrew Rosenthal, "Sununu Says Bush 'Ad-Libbed' Comment on Credit Card Rates," *New York Times*, November 23, 1991.

26. Fiona Houston, "Youth Actively Served by Junior Clinton Aides," *New York Times*, March 28, 1993.

27. See Kathryn Dunn Tenpas and Stephen Hess, "The Bush White House: First Appraisals," Brookings working paper, January 30, 2002, p. 10.

28. For Gergen's account of his experience, see David Gergen, *Eyewitness to Power* (Simon and Schuster, 2000), pp. 249–342.

29. Quoted in Michael Duffy, "The State of Bill Clinton," *Time* (February 7, 1994), p. 26.

30. Gergen, *Eyewitness to Power*, p. 292.

31. Robert Reich, *Locked in the Cabinet* (Knopf, 1997), pp. 171, 180.

32. Ibid., p. 180. Italics in original.

33. Quoted by Jonathan Orszag, Peter Orszag, and Laura Tyson, "The Process of Economic Policy-Making during the Clinton Administration," in Jeffrey Frankel and Peter Orszag, eds., *American Economic Policy in the 1990s* (MIT Press, 2002), p.1020. For an account of the passage of President Clinton's first budget, see James P. Pfiffner, "President Clinton and the 103rd Congress: Winning Battles and Losing Wars," in James A. Thurber, ed., *Rivals for Power* (CQ Press, 1996), pp. 170–90.

34. Mary Anne Borrelli, Karen Hult, and Nancy Kassop, "The White House Counsel's Office," *Presidential Studies Quarterly*, vol. 31, no. 4 (December 2001), p. 576. See also Bradley Patterson, *The White House Staff* (Brookings, 2000), pp. 96–113.

35. For an analysis of the role of the Office of Communications and different strategies of recent administrations, see Martha Joynt Kumar, "The Office of Communication," *Presidential Studies Quarterly*, vol. 31, no. 4 (December 2001), pp. 609–34.

36. Quoted by Mark Rozell, "The Press and the Presidency," in James P. Pfiffner and Roger H. Davidson, *Understanding the Presidency*, 3d ed. (Longman, 2003), p. 142.

37. *U.S. News and World Report* (April 17, 1989), p. 22; *Newsweek* (April 17, 1989), p. 21.

38. See Stephen Hess, "President Clinton and the White House Press Corps—Year One," *Media Studies Journal* (Spring 1994), p. 4.

39. Joe Klein, *The Natural* (Doubleday, 2002), pp. 137, 165, 174.

40. See Kathryn Dunn Tenpas, "The American Presidency: Surviving and Thriving amidst the Permanent Campaign," in Norman Ornstein and Thomas Mann, eds., *The Permanent Campaign and Its Future* (American Enterprise Institute and Brookings Institution, 2000), pp. 123–24.

Chapter Eleven

1. "Transcript of President-elect Bush's News Conference," December 28, 2000. Transcribed by eMediaMillWorks for www.washingtonpost.com/onpolitics (January 30, 2001).

2. Quoted in John P. Burke, "The Bush Transition in Historical Context," *PS* (March 2002), p. 24.

3. Dana Milbank, "White House Distaff Staff Make Family a Priority," *Washington Post*, February 15, 2001. Milbank notes that in 1998 six of the twenty-nine top Clinton staffers were women.

4. "Transcript of President-elect Bush's News Conference," December 28, 2000.

5. "Bush Introduction of Elaine Chao for Labor, Robert Zoellick as U.S. Trade Rep," January 11, 2001. Transcribed by eMediaMillWorks for www.washingtonpost.com/onpolitics (January 30, 2001).

6. Ibid.

7. Dana Milbank and Thomas D. Edsall, "Chavez Pulls Out as Labor Nominee; Bush Pick Acknowledges She 'Wasn't Forthcoming' on Illegal Immigrant Issue," *Washington Post*, January 10, 2001.

8. David S. Broder, "Who Is Ashcroft?" *Washington Post*, January 23, 2001.

9. "Excerpts from Remarks in the Senate Debate on the Ashcroft Nomination," *New York Times*, February 2, 2001.

10. Rebecca Adams, "Norton Outmaneuvers Critics," *Congressional Quarterly Weekly* (January 27, 2001), p. 230.

11. "President-elect Bush Names Staff Members," December 17, 2000. Transcribed by eMediaMillWorks for www.washingtonpost.com/onpolitics (January 30, 2001).

12. "Bush Announces Three Cabinet Nominees," January 2, 2001. Transcribed by eMediaMillWorks for www.washingtonpost.com/onpolitics (January 30, 2001).

13. Milbank and Edsall, "Chavez Pulls Out as Labor Nominee."

14. "Top Government Posts Remain Vacant," press release, Brookings, March 1, 2002.

15. See Ellen Nakashima and Dana Milbank, "Bush Cabinet Takes Back Seat in Driving Policy," *Washington Post*, September 5, 2001.

16. Dana Milbank, "Serious 'Strategery'; As Rove Launches Elaborate Political Effort, Some See a Nascent Clintonian 'War Room,'" *Washington Post*, April 22, 2001.

17. Dana Milbank and Bradley Graham, "With Crisis, White House Style Is Now More Fluid," *Washington Post*, October 10, 2001.

18. Information obtained from Bradley Patterson, July 2001.

19. James A. Barnes, "The Imperial Vice Presidency," *National Journal* (March 17, 2001), p. 814.

20. Joseph Kahn, "Bush's Selections Signal a Widening of Cabinet's Role," *New York Times*, December 31, 2000.

21. Notable cases involved the drafting of education legislation and the anthrax scare. See Martha Joynt Kumar, "Recruiting and Organizing the White House Staff," *PS* (March 2002), p. 36.

22. See chapter 7, "Organizing for Success," in Michael E. O'Hanlon and others, *Protecting the American Homeland: A Preliminary Analysis* (Brookings, 2002), pp. 99–124.

23. For an account of the strained relations between Ridge and Congress during this period, see Adriel Bettelheim, "Turf Wars Take Toll on Ridge," *CQ Weekly*, April 27, 2002, pp. 1071–72.

24. See David Von Drehle and Mike Allen, "Bush Plan's Underground Architects," *Washington Post*, June 9, 2002.

25. See "Special Report: Homeland Security," *CQ Weekly*, June 8, 2002, pp. 1498-1508.

26. See Dana Milbank, "White House Staff Switches Gears," *Washington Post*, September 17, 2001.

27. Walter Pincus and Karen DeYoung, "U.S. Says New Tape Points to Bin Laden," *Washington Post*, December 9, 2001.

Chapter Twelve

1. Ben W. Heineman Jr. and Curtis A. Hessler, *Memorandum for the President: A Strategic Approach to Domestic Affairs in the 1980s* (Random House, 1980), p. 189; also see "Where We Succeeded, Where We Failed: Lessons from Reagan Officials for the Next Conservative Presidency," *Policy Review* (Winter 1988), especially Linda Chavez (p. 47), Donald J. Devine (p. 49), Charles Heatherly (p. 50), and John A. Svahn (p. 55).

2. Roger Hilsman, "Improving Foreign Policy 'Machinery,'" in Thomas E. Cronin and Sanford D. Greenberg, eds., *The Presidential Advisory System* (Harper and Row, 1969), p. 278. Also see Joseph A. Califano Jr., *Governing America: An Insider's Report from the White House and the Cabinet* (Simon and Schuster, 1981), pp. 396–97, for the problems that Carter had with his counselor on aging.

3. Letter to author, March 15, 1988.

4. Theodore Lowi, *The End of Liberalism* (Norton, 1969).

5. Pierre Salinger, *With Kennedy* (Doubleday, 1966), p. 63.

6. Charles M. Hardin, *Presidential Power and Accountability* (University of Chicago Press, 1974), p. 25.

7. Edward Weisband and Thomas M. Franck, *Resignation in Protest* (Grossman, 1975), p. 137.

8. George E. Reedy, *The Twilight of the Presidency* (World Publishing, 1970), p. xiv.

9. Patrick Anderson, *The President's Men* (Doubleday, 1968), p. 398.

10. Reagan was unique in promoting so many White House aides to his cabinet: James Baker (Treasury), Edwin Meese (attorney general), Frank Carlucci (Defense), William Clark (Interior), Elizabeth Dole (Transportation), and John Herrington (Energy).

11. Quoted in Alan L. Otten, "Politics and People," *Wall Street Journal*, September 5, 1974.

12. Patrick J. Buchanan recounts how "the newly installed president was not an inattentive student to the engaging Dr. Moynihan. . . . And so, the president made a conscious decision to shift leftward on domestic and social policy." See *Conservative Voters, Liberal Victories* (Quadrangle, 1975), p. 17.

13. Alexander L. George, *Presidential Decisionmaking in Foreign Policy: The Effective Use of Information and Advice* (Westview Press, 1980), p. 205.

14. Paul Charles Light, *The President's Agenda* (Johns Hopkins University Press, 1982), p. 200.

15. John H. Kessel, *Presidential Parties* (Dorsey Press, 1984), pp. 81, 84, 88. Kessel noted of the Carter White House that "if one had selected a staff randomly from all campaign activists, the same level of agreement should have existed."

16. *Report of the Congressional Committees Investigating the Iran-Contra Affair,* S. Rept. No. 100–216 and H. Rept. No. 100–433, 100 Cong. 1 sess., 1987, p. 423.

17. David Z. Beckler, "Science and Technology in Presidential Policy-Making: A New Dimension and Structure," in William T. Golden, ed., *Science and Technology Advice to the President, Congress, and Judiciary* (Pergamon Press, 1988), p. 37.

18. See Walter Pincus, "Under Bush, the Briefing Gets Briefer," *Washington Post,* May 24, 2002, A33.

19. Louis W. Koenig, *The Invisible Presidency* (Rinehart, 1960), p. 24.

20. Charles G. Dawes, quoted in Harold Seidman, *Politics, Position, and Power* (Oxford University Press, 1970), p. 72.

21. See McGeorge Bundy, *The Strength of Government* (Harvard University Press, 1968), pp. 39–40.

22. Martin Anderson, *Revolution* (Harcourt Brace Jovanovich, 1988), p. 199.

23. See, for example, "Who Should've Been This President's Men?" *Wall Street Journal,* April 6, 1988, in which prominent people list the best and worst of Reagan's appointees. Attorney General Edwin Meese was voted best by Edwin Feulner, president of the conservative Heritage Foundation, and worst by liberal columnist Hodding Carter. Others who were both best and worst included George Shultz, Donald Regan, Frank Carlucci, and David Stockman.

24. Joseph A. Califano Jr., *A Presidential Nation* (Norton, 1975), pp. 195–96.

25. Samuel P. Huntington, *The Soldier and the State* (Harvard University Press, 1957), pp. 453–55.

26. Secretaries of defense (and the year of their appointment) are James V. Forrestal (1947), Louis A. Johnson (1949), George C. Marshall (1950), Robert A. Lovett (1951), Charles E. Wilson (1953), Neil H. McElroy (1957), Thomas S. Gates (1959), Robert S. McNamara (1961), Clark M. Clifford (1968), Melvin R. Laird (1969), Elliot L. Richardson (1973), James R. Schlesinger (1973), Donald H. Rumsfeld (1975), Harold Brown (1977), Caspar W. Weinberger (1981), Frank C. Carlucci (1987), Richard Cheney (1989), Les Aspin (1993), William Perry (1994), William Cohen (1997), Donald Rumsfeld (2001).

27. For an opposing view, see Douglas Hallett, "The President's Men: Mistaken Identities," *Washington Post,* June 23, 1974, who felt that high mobility is not desirable in public executives. Citing one White House aide who subsequently went to prison for his part in Watergate, Hallett wrote, "He made it as far as the White House precisely because the one special quality he did have was a willingness at each stage to leave behind his past, to abandon his home and friends, and reach for the next brass ring."

28. See Alan L. Otten, "The Scorecard: President's Cabinet Gets Mixed Reviews for Efforts to Date," *Wall Street Journal,* September 8, 1971.

29. See Marver H. Bernstein, *The Job of the Federal Executive* (Brookings, 1958), p. 162.

30. Richard F. Fenno Jr., *The President's Cabinet* (Harvard University Press, 1959), p. 224.

31. Marver H. Bernstein, "The Presidency and Management Improvement," *Law and Contemporary Problems*, vol. 35 (Summer 1970), pp. 517–18.

Chapter Thirteen

1. The decisions are *Kendall* v. *U.S.* (1838) and *Humphrey's Executor* v. *U.S.* (1935). See Frederick C. Mosher and others, *Watergate: Implications for Responsible Government* (Basic Books, 1974), pp. 44–45.

2. Arthur Meier Schlesinger, *New Viewpoints in American History* (Macmillan, 1922), pp. 123–24.

3. In *The American Commonwealth*, vol. 1 (Macmillan, 1922), p. 54, James Bryce stated, "The direct domestic authority of the President is in time of peace small, because the larger part of law and administration belongs to the State governments, and because Federal administration is regulated by statutes which leave little discretion to the executive." In *The American Presidency* (Harper, 1940), pp. 28–30, Harold J. Laski listed fifteen presidential qualities, of which only three could be considered executive.

4. W. F. Willoughby, *Principles of Public Administration* (Johns Hopkins University Press, 1927), p. 36. As rationale for this arrangement, Willoughby wrote, "Fundamentally these advantages consist in making the administrative branch, both as regards its organization and its practical operations, a single, integrated piece of administrative machinery, one in which its several parts, instead of being disjointed and unrelated, will be brought into adjustment with each other and together make a harmonious whole; one that possesses the capacity of formulating a general program and of subsequently seeing that such program as is formulated is properly carried out; one in which means are provided by which duplication of organization, plant, personnel, or operations may be eliminated, conflicts of jurisdiction avoided or promptly settled, and standardization of methods of procedure secured; and finally, one in which responsibility is definitely located and means for enforcing this responsibility provided" (p. 51).

5. Peter F. Drucker, "How to Make the Presidency Manageable," *Fortune* (November 1974), p. 146. Drucker, however, is not associated with the scientific management school, which stresses efficiency. Rather, the emphasis of his work has been on organizational effectiveness. Also see *The Age of Discontinuity* (Harper, 1969).

6. President's Committee on Administrative Management, *Administrative Management in the Government of the United States* (Government Printing Office, 1937), p. v. A few scholars, either strict constitutional constructionists or political conservatives, demurred. See Edward S. Corwin, *The President: Office and Powers, 1787–1957* (New York University Press, 1957), p. 98: "Certainly, to conceive of the President as a potential 'boss of the works' save in situations raising broad issues of policy would be both absurd and calamitous." Also see Alfred de Grazia, "The

Myth of the President," in Aaron Wildavsky, ed., *The Presidency* (Little, Brown, 1960), pp. 49–73.

7. Not all liberal scholars, however, theorized to fit their political convictions. Richard E. Neustadt, who had served on Truman's staff and was highly critical of Eisenhower, saw the presidency not as having inherent powers over the executive branch but as an office hemmed in by competing powers in which a president's success largely depended on his skill at persuasion. See his *Presidential Power* (Wiley, 1960), especially chap. 3.

8. Richard P. Nathan, *The Administrative Presidency* (Wiley, 1983), p. 7.

9. Congressional assertiveness in the aftermath of Watergate included making future appointments of the director and deputy director of the Office of Management and the Budget subject to senatorial confirmation, passing the War Powers Act requiring congressional approval for any new commitment of U.S. troops abroad for more than sixty days, creating the Congressional Budget Office, and levying prohibitions on presidential impoundment. Claims of executive privilege also became subject to court adjudication. See Judith H. Parris, "Congress in the American System," *Current History* (June 1974), pp. 262–63.

10. Stephen Hess, *The Presidential Campaign*, 3d ed. (Brookings, 1988), p. 53.

11. See Martha Derthick, *Uncontrollable Spending for Social Services Grants* (Brookings, 1975), p. 113.

12. See Barbara W. Tuchman, "Should We Abolish the Presidency?" *New York Times*, February 13, 1973.

13. For proposals on the establishment of an independent Justice Department, for example, see *Removing Politics from the Administration of Justice*, Hearings before the Subcommittee on Separation of Powers of the Senate Judiciary Committee, 93 Cong. 2 sess. (GPO, 1974).

14. See Bradley H. Patterson Jr., *The White House Staff* (Brookings, 2000), pp. 347–48, items 1–6, for a "basic" White House staff size.

15. See Norman J. Ornstein, Thomas E. Mann, and Michael J. Malbin, *Vital Statistics on Congress, 2001–2002* (AEI Press, 2002), p. 126.

16. Peri E. Arnold, *Making the Managerial Presidency* (Princeton University Press, 1986), pp. 361–62.

17. Bruce Buchanan, *The Citizen's Presidency: Standards of Choice and Judgment* (CQ Press, 1987), p. 125.

18. See Michael Novak, *Choosing Our King* (Macmillan, 1974), pp. 262–64.

19. For interesting accounts of the degree to which the First Lady has become the ceremonial head of state, see Lady Bird Johnson, *A White House Diary* (Holt, Rinehart, and Winston, 1970); Betty Ford, *The Times of My Life* (Harper and Row, 1978); Rosalynn Carter, *First Lady from Plains* (Houghton Mifflin, 1984); Nancy Reagan, *My Turn* (Random House, 1989); and Barbara Bush, *A Memoir* (Scribner's, 1994).

20. See Aspen Systems Corporation, *The Powers and Responsibilities of the President* (Pittsburgh, 1970).

21. Letter to the author, January 6, 1988.

22. John Dillon, "Bush's Vita: Nixon Threw Him into the Breach during Crisis," *Christian Science Monitor,* May 9, 1988.

23. Joseph A. Califano Jr., *Governing America: An Insider's Report from the White House and the Cabinet* (Simon and Schuster, 1981), pp. 396–97.

24. Letter to the author, February 3, 1988.

25. *Report of the President's Special Review Board* (February 26, 1987), p. V-4.

26. Martin Anderson, *Revolution* (Harcourt Brace Jovanovich, 1988), pp. 225–26.

27. Lawrence F. O'Brien, *No Final Victories* (Doubleday, 1974), p. 190.

Appendix A

1. John Osborne's columns have been gathered in book form. This one can be found in *White House Watch: The Ford Years* (New Republic Books, 1977), pp. 446–50.

2. James Fallows, "The Passionless Presidency," *Atlantic* (March 1979), p. 39.

Index

Reedy, George E., 82, 83, 87, 182, 253, 254, 266
Regan, Donald T., 125, 126, 130–31, 136, 140, 144, 259, 263
Reich, Robert, 158, 264
Reno, Janet, 152
Reorganization Act (*1939*), 30–31, 34
Ribicoff, Abraham, 67–68
Rice, Condoleezza, 165, 168
Richardson, Elliot L., 111, 120, 194, 195, 255, 267
Richberg, Donald, 26, 28, 30
Ridge, Tom, 172, 265
Riley, Richard, 151
Rockefeller, Nelson, 62, 63, 114, 117, 121, 182, 229, 232
Rockman, Bert A., 106, 124–25, 256, 259, 260
Roe v. Wade, 167
Rogers, William P., 94, 95–96, 101, 111–12, 142, 194, 255
Rollins, Edward, 130
Romney, George W., 94, 95, 194
Roosevelt, Eleanor, 25, 27
Roosevelt, Franklin D.: administration, 1–2, 4, 21–35, 161, 199; administrative style, 22, 24, 25–26, 28–30, 34–35, 40–41, 44, 49, 65–66, 81, 83–84, 99, 101, 116, 188–89, 226; agencies created by, 2, 29–30, 33–34, 35, 73; appointees, 22–26, 33–34, 36–37, 66–67, 76; background, 26; cabinet, 2, 21, 23–26, 29, 35–38, 41, 94, 95, 190; concept of presidency, 1, 2, 4, 6, 22, 48, 74, 76, 83, 199; Congress and, 2, 26–27, 31, 33; executive agencies reorganization, 2, 30–31; and government bureaucracy, 13, 21; government restructuring, 14–15, 35; long-range planning, 187; and Johnson, 4, 83; objective, 188; organization of presidency, 47; personality, 20, 27–28, 83; press conferences, 26, 27–28, 42, 59;

reelection strategies, 18; schedule, 26; second term, 18, 19, 28; speeches, 25, 26, 28, 34, 74, 216; Supreme Court and, 19, 30, 72; third term, 2; White House staff, 1–2, 5, 18, 21, 24–26, 31, 34–35, 41, 56, 83–84, 216
Roosevelt, Theodore, 1, 146
Roper, Daniel, 22, 23
Rosenman, Samuel I., 18, 22, 23, 24, 25, 28, 29, 32–33, 35, 38, 41, 74, 216, 244, 245
Rosten, Leo C., 27, 245
Rostow, Walt W., 88
Rove, Karl, 165, 170, 173
Rowe, James, 30, 31
Rozell, Mark, 264
Rubin, Robert, 159, 183, 243
Rumsfeld, Donald H., 115–16, 117, 118–20, 165, 169, 172, 194, 267
Rusk, Dean, 68–69, 71, 79, 88, 254

Safire, William, 93, 98, 111, 114, 255, 256, 257
Salinger, Pierre, 73, 74, 76, 97, 181, 266
Sanders, H. Barefoot, 79
Santarelli, Donald, 113
Saxbe, William, 117, 255
Schlesinger, Arthur M., Jr., 67, 70, 71, 73, 94, 243, 244, 245, 248, 250, 253, 254
Schlesinger, Arthur M., Sr., 200, 268
Schlesinger, James R., 113, 119–20, 135, 139, 194, 255, 267
Schoeneman, George, 41
Schultze, Charles, 86, 126, 218, 220–21
Schumer, Charles E., 167
Schweiker, Richard, 136
Schwellenbach, Lewis, 38
Scowcroft, Brent, 120, 150, 153, 243
Sears, John, 96, 223
Seaton, Fred, 52